Physical Science

Physical Science

by

Robert H. Marshall

Donald H. Jacobs

AGS®

American Guidance Service, Inc.
Circle Pines, Minnesota 55014-1796
1-800-328-2560

About the Authors

Robert Marshall, M.Ed., teaches high school physics and algebra for the Baltimore City Public Schools.

Donald H. Jacobs, M.Ed., teaches high school mathematics for the Baltimore City Public Schools. He has also been the coordinator of computer programming at the Talmudical Academy of Baltimore. Mr. Jacobs is the co-author of Basic Math Skills and Life Skills Math, both published by AGS.

Consultants

Bonnie Buratti
Research Astronomer
Jet Propulsion Laboratory
California Institute of Technology

Norman Gelfand
Physicist
Fermi National Accelerator Laboratory (Fermilab)

Lorraine S. Taylor, Ph.D.
Professor of Special Education
State University of New York at Newpaltz

Editorial and production services provided by Navta Associates, Inc.

Photo Credits: p. 2—Steven Peters/Tony Stone Images; p. 26—Nancy Simmerman/Tony Stone Images; pp. 28, 29, 33—First Image West; p. 50—Scala/Art Resource; p. 53—Mark E. Gibson/Visuals Unlimited; p. 54—James Randklev/Tony Stone Images; p. 78—Rich Treptow/Visuals Unlimited; p. 96—Donovan Reese/Tony Stone Images; p. 102—Ed Pritchard/Tony Stone Images; p. 122—Kevin Miller/Tony Stone Images; p. 130—Guy Rolland/First Image West; p. 132—Fisher Scientific; p. 141 (upper left, lower middle, lower right), 167, 210, 304—Tony Freeman/PhotoEdit; p. 141 (lower left), 143, 151—Stephen Frisch; p. 152—Chuck Pelley/Tony Stone Images; p. 180—Warren Faubel/Tony Stone Worldwide, LTD; p. 189—José Carrillo/Photo Edit; p. 238—Superstock; p. 251—Tony Stone Images; p. 255—Don Bensey/Tony Stone Images; p. 270—Michael Orton/Tony Stone Images; p. 316—Peter Pearson/Tony Stone Images; p. 320—Corbis-Bettmann

Printed in the United States of America
ISBN 0-7854-1017-1 (hardcover)
ISBN 0-7854-1181-X (softcover)
Product Number 90290 (hardcover)
Product Number 90297 (softcover)
A 0 9 8 7 6 5

Contents

The Metric System

Meters. Grams. Liters. Do any of these words sound familiar to you? They are part of a measurement system that scientists use, which is called the metric system. Many countries around the world use metric measurements, too. As you will learn in this chapter, the metric system is easy to use. In no time at all, you'll be "thinking metric"—just like a scientist!

ORGANIZE YOUR THOUGHTS

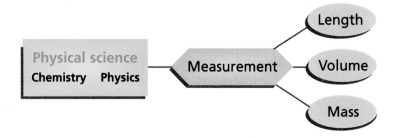

Physical science
Chemistry   Physics

Measurement

Length

Volume

Mass

Goals for Learning

▶ To explain what matter and energy are

▶ To explain why measurement is important

▶ To use the basic metric units of length, volume, and mass

▶ To explain the meaning of prefixes used with metric units of measurements

▶ To calculate area and volume, using metric units

▶ To convert metric units

Have you ever wondered how a camera or a computer works? Do you listen to music on the radio or a boombox? Do you know how the sound is produced by these machines? Have you ever noticed that your body seems to weigh less in water? Do you know why?

All of these questions—and many more—can be answered by studying **physical science.** Physical science is the study of the things around you. It deals with **matter** and energy.

The Study of Matter and Energy

Look around you. What do you have in common with all the objects you see—your desk, the floor, the air? At first, you might think you have very little in common with these objects. But, in fact, all of them—including you—are made of matter. Matter is anything that takes up space. You can see other examples of matter in the picturebelow.

What do all these objects have in common?

Physical science

The study of things around you.

Matter

Anything that has mass and takes up space.

Mass

The amount of material an object has.

All matter has **mass.** Mass is the amount of material that an object has. All of the objects in the picture above have mass. The potted plant has more mass than the baseball.

Energy is different from matter. You cannot hold energy or measure it with a ruler. But you are familiar with energy. Energy is needed to make things move. You use it to move your body. A car uses energy to move, too. You will learn more about energy in Chapter 8.

Two Areas of Physical Science

Physical scientists study many different things. Physical science can be divided into two areas. One area is **chemistry.** Chemistry is the study of matter and how it changes. Chemistry can explain how a cake rises or how acid rain forms. Chemistry is also the study of how matter can be made into new materials. By studying chemistry, scientists have made new medicines, food, clothing, fragrances, and soaps. They have even made artificial skin and bones for people.

Chemistry

The study of matter and how it changes.

A second area of physical science is **physics.** Physics is the study of energy and how it acts with matter. Physics can explain how helium balloons rise or how lasers work. Scientists studying physics have developed television, cellular phones, stereo systems, computers, space satellites, microwave ovens, and jet airplanes.

Physics

The study of how energy acts with matter.

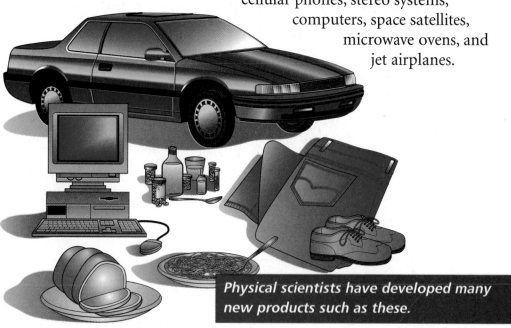

Physical scientists have developed many new products such as these.

The Tools of Physical Scientists

Physical scientists—and all scientists—need many different skills. Scientists need curiosity to ask questions such as "Why does sugar dissolve in water when sand does not?" Scientists want to know how and why things are the way they are.

Scientists answer their questions by doing experiments. You will also do experiments to answer questions. In this book, these experiments are called Investigations.

Scientists have to know how to use scientific tools. In the illustration below, you can see some of the tools scientists use. You will use many of these tools as you do Investigations.

Scientists also need to know how to make measurements. Measurements are an important part of the information scientists gather. In the following lessons, you will learn how to measure like a scientist.

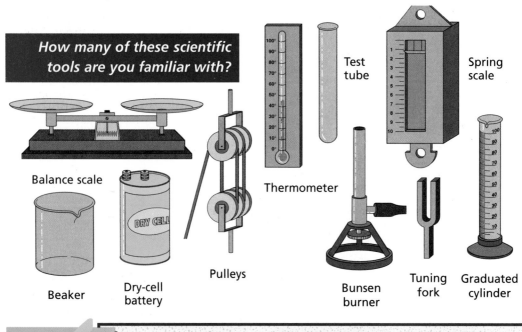

How many of these scientific tools are you familiar with?

Balance scale

Beaker

Dry-cell battery

Pulleys

Thermometer

Test tube

Bunsen burner

Tuning fork

Spring scale

Graduated cylinder

Self-Check

1. What is physical science?
2. What are two examples of matter?
3. What are two areas of physical science? What kinds of things do scientists in each area study?

Look at the poles in the picture below. Which one do you think is tallest? Use a ruler to measure each one.

Which pole is tallest?

Are you surprised to learn that the poles are all the same height? Measurements are important because we cannot always trust observations made with our eyes. Measurements help us gather exact information. Exact measurements are especially important to a scientist.

Units of Measurement

When you measured the poles in the figure above, you probably measured with a ruler marked in inches. You compared the length of the pole to a known measurement, the inch. A known amount in measurement, such as the inch, is called a **unit.** Other units you might be familiar with are the yard, mile, minute, and day.

If you had lived thousands of years ago, you most likely would have used units of measurement that were based on the length of certain parts of your body. For example,

Unit

A known amount used for measuring.

Egyptians used the cubit to measure length. A cubit was the distance from the elbow to the tip of the middle finger. The Romans used the width of their thumb to measure length. This unit of measurement was called an uncia.

Compare the widths of the thumbs of each person in your classroom. Do you think they are all the same? Probably not. So you can see why using units of measurement based on body parts does not work very well. The exact length of an uncia or a cubit could vary from person to person.

In order for a unit of measurement to be useful, it has to be the same for everybody. When one scientist tells another scientist that something is a certain length, that measurement should mean the same thing to both of them.

Systems of Measurement

English system

System of measurement that uses inches, feet, and yards.

You probably measure in units based on the **English system.** Some English units you probably are familiar with for measuring length are the inch, foot, yard, and mile. English units also can be used to measure time, weight, and other amounts.

Metric system

System of measurement used by scientists.

Scientists and most other people throughout the world use a different system of measurement. They use the **metric system**. Metric units are the most common units of measurement in the world. The metric system is simpler to use and easier to remember than the English system. You will use the metric system in this book.

Self-Check

1. Why are measurements important?
2. Why is it important to use units of measurement that are the same for everyone?
3. What are some common units in the English system of measurement?
4. What is the name of the system of measurement that scientists use?

How Can You Use Metric Units to Measure Length?

Objectives

After reading this lesson, you should be able to

▶ identify and explain some common metric units of length.

▶ explain the meaning of prefixes used with metric units of measurement.

The metric system is similar to the money system used in the United States. As the illustration below shows, there are 10 pennies in a dime, 10 dimes in a dollar, and 10 dollars in a 10-dollar bill. You can say that the money system is based on a system of tens. Likewise, you will see that the metric system is based on a system of tens.

This money system is based on tens.

Meter

The basic unit of length in the metric system (about 39 inches).

Using Meters

In the metric system, you measure length in **meters** or parts of a meter. A meter is a little more than 39 inches, or a bit longer than a yard. The length of an adult man's arm is about one meter. A football field is just over 90 meters long. The abbreviation for meter is *m*. A period is not used with abbreviations for metric units.

1 meter

A meter is a little longer than a man's arm.

The common tool for measuring length in the metric system is the **meter stick.** It is one meter long.

The illustration below shows part of a meter stick. Notice that it is divided into equal units. Each of these units is a centimeter. A centimeter is 1/100 of a meter. You can use centimeters when the meter is too long a unit. For example, it might be difficult to measure the width of your book in meters, but you could easily use centimeters. The abbreviation for centimeter is *cm*.

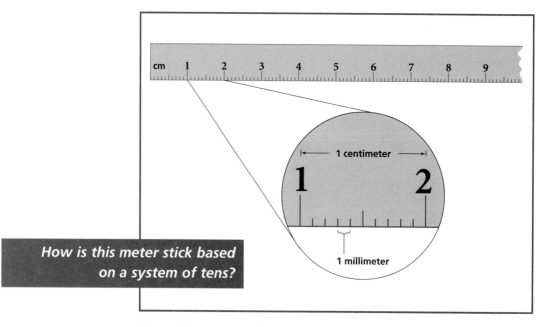

How is this meter stick based on a system of tens?

Sometimes, even the centimeter is too large a unit to measure an object. You need a smaller unit. Again look at the meter stick. Notice that each centimeter is divided into 10 smaller units. Each of these smaller units is a millimeter. A millimeter is 1/1,000 of a meter. You would measure the width of a pencil in millimeters. Use *mm* as an abbreviation for millimeter.

Using meters to measure the distance from your school to your home might be difficult. You need a unit larger than a meter. In that case, you might use the kilometer. A kilometer is 1,000 meters. The abbreviation for kilometer is *km*.

The table to the right summarizes the parts of a meter.

Length Equivalents	
10 millimeters	1 centimeter
1,000 millimeters	1 meter
100 centimeters	1 meter
1,000 meters	1 kilometer

Using Metric Prefixes

Once you understand how the meter stick is divided, you know how to use other units of measurement in the metric system. The prefixes in front of the word *meter* have special meanings. They are used to show how many times the meter is multiplied or divided. Just as a cent is 1/100 of a dollar, a centimeter is 1/100 of a meter. The prefix *centi-* means 1/100. You will learn how to use the prefixes shown in the table with other units of measurement later in this chapter.

Prefix	Meaning	Example
kilo- (k)	1,000 ×	kilometer (km)
centi- (c)	1/100 (0.01)	centimeter (cm)
milli- (m)	1/1,000 (0.001)	millimeter (mm)

Self-Check

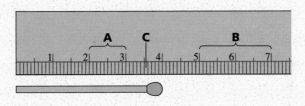

1. Which letter in the illustration above points to 1 millimeter?
2. Which letter points to 1 centimeter?
3. How many millimeters are there in 1 centimeter?
4. How many millimeters are there in 10 centimeters?
5. What is the measurement in millimeters of the match shown?
6. How long is the match in centimeters?

Materials

✓ meter stick

Hands Instead of Feet

Purpose

To create a system of measuring length and to compare it to the metric system

Procedure

1. Copy the data table below on a sheet of paper.

Object	Length in Hands	Length in Centimeters
open book	2	

2. Measure several objects in your classroom. Your teacher will tell you which objects to measure. Each member of the class will measure the same objects.

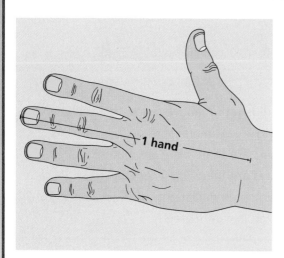

1 hand

3. Use your stretched out left hand as a measuring tool. The length of this hand from your wrist to the end of your longest finger will equal one unit of length in "hands."

4. Measure the length, in hands, of each object. Estimate to the nearest length of a hand. Record this information in the data table.

5. After you have measured all the objects, compare your results with those of at least five other students.

6. Measure the objects again, using a meter stick instead of your hand. Record your measurements in centimeters.

7. Compare these results with those of other students in your group.

Questions

1. Did your length in hands match those of other students? Why or why not?

2. Did your length in centimeters match those of other students? Why or why not?

3. Do you think a system such as the metric system is more useful than one that uses units such as hands? Explain. *yess   persise*

Explore Further

Develop your own system of measurement. Determine the units you will use. Show your system to the class.

How Can You Use Metric Measurements to Find Area?

Objectives

After reading this lesson, you should be able to

▶ explain what area is.

▶ calculate area in metric units.

Area

Amount of space the surface of an object takes up.

You can use measurements of length to calculate other measurements. One example of a calculated measurement is **area.** Area is the amount of space the surface of an object takes up.

Notice that each side of the square in the figure below measures 1 cm. To find the area of the square, multiply the length by the width.

$$\text{area} = \text{length} \times \text{width}$$
$$= 1 \text{ cm} \times 1 \text{ cm}$$
$$= 1 \text{ cm}^2$$

When you calculate area, the units of length and width must be the same. Express the answer in square units. To do this, write a small 2 to the upper right of the unit. In the example above, the unit is read *square centimeter.* *Square centimeter (cm²)* means "centimeter × centimeter." The area of the square is 1 square centimeter.

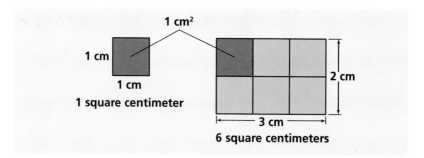

Now look at the rectangle. Its length is 3 cm. Its width is 2 cm. The figure shows that the rectangle contains 6 square centimeters. You can also find the area of the rectangle by using the same formula you used to find the area of the square.

$$\text{area} = \text{length} \times \text{width}$$
$$= 3 \text{ cm} \times 2 \text{ cm}$$
$$= 6 \text{ cm}^2$$

The area of the rectangle is 6 square centimeters.

What is the area of a rectangle with a length of 8.5 mm and a width of 3.3 mm?

$$\text{area} = \text{length} \times \text{width}$$
$$= 8.5 \text{ mm} \times 3.3 \text{ mm}$$
$$= 28.05 \text{ mm}^2$$

The area is 28.05 square millimeters.

Self-Check

Find the area for each of the rectangles in the table. The first one is done for you.

Length	Width	Area (length × width)
8 cm	7.2 cm	8 cm × 7.2 cm = 57.6 cm²
8 m	8 m	6 m × 8 m = 64 m²
3.4 mm	5.2 mm	3.4 mm × 5.2 mm = 18.28²
2.6 m	4.7 m	2.6 m × 4.7 m = 12.22²
13 m	5.1 km	13 m × 5,000 m = 663,000

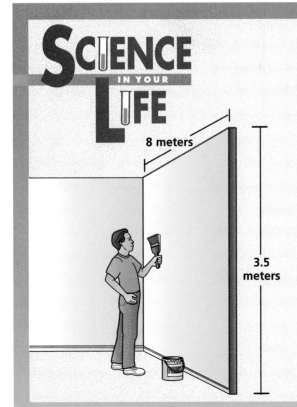

8 meters

3.5 meters

SCIENCE IN YOUR LIFE

Do you have enough paint?

If you have ever gone to a store to buy paint, you know that first you have to figure out how much paint you need. It's easy to do if you use what you learned about calculating area.

Suppose you have a wall that measures 8 m long and 3.5 m high. You want to paint it. The instructions on the paint can say that the paint will cover 32 m² of surface area. Do you have enough paint to cover the wall?

INVESTIGATION

1-2

Counting Squares and Calculating Area

Materials

✓ small sheet of paper

✓ ruler

✓ safety scissors

Purpose
To understand the relationship between area and the number of square units

Procedure

1. Copy the data table below on a sheet of paper.

	Length	Width	Area (length × width)	Total number of squares
Original Paper				
Rectangle 1				
Rectangle 2				

2. Obtain a small sheet of paper from your teacher. The sizes of paper used will not be the same for all students. Use a ruler to measure the length and the width of the paper. Record these two measurements in inches.

3. Calculate the area of the paper. To do so, use the following formula.

$$\text{area} = \text{length} \times \text{width}$$

Record this area. Remember that the units should be square inches (in²).

4. Use the ruler to mark off all four sides of the paper in 1-inch units. Using the ruler as a straightedge, carefully draw straight lines to connect the marks from side to side and from top to bottom. A grid of squares similar to the one on the next page should result.

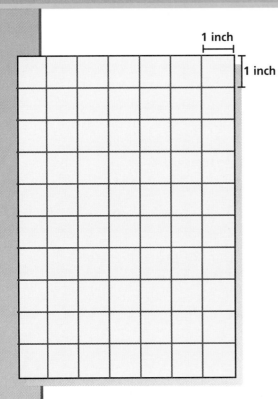

1 inch

1 inch

5. Count the squares on the paper. The area of each square is 1 square inch. That is because area = length × width = 1 in. × 1 in. = 1 in². Since each square is 1 square inch, the area of the sheet of paper is the number of squares × 1 in². Record that number. The answer should be in square inches.

6. Cut the paper into squares along the lines you drew. Be as accurate as you can in cutting.

7. Use all the individual squares to make two smaller rectangles of different lengths and widths. To do this, carefully set the squares down next to each other in rows and columns. Make sure the squares have almost no space between them and that they do not overlap.

8. Measure the length and width of each new rectangle. Find the area of each.

Questions

1. Did the area you found for the original paper in step 6 match the area calculated in step 2? Do you think it should? Explain.

2. How did the sum of the areas of the two new rectangles compare to the total number of squares in the two rectangles? How did it compare to the calculated area of the original sheet of paper? Explain these results.

How Can You Use Metric Measurements to Find Volume?

Objectives

After reading this lesson, you should be able to

▶ explain what volume is.

▶ calculate volume in metric units.

▶ convert metric units of volume.

Volume

The amount of space an object takes up.

Another calculation that you can make using metric measurements is **volume.** Volume describes the amount of space an object takes up.

Volume of a Rectangle

The small box in the figure below measures 1 cm on each edge. You can find out how much space the box takes up—its volume—by using a simple formula.

$$\text{volume} = \text{length} \times \text{width} \times \text{height}$$
$$= 1 \text{ cm} \times 1 \text{ cm} \times 1 \text{cm}$$
$$= 1 \text{ cm}^3$$

The small 3 written to the upper right of the centimeter unit means "cubic." It is read *cubic centimeter* or *centimeter cubed.* Cubic centimeter means "centimeter × centimeter × centimeter." The volume of the small box is 1 cubic centimeter.

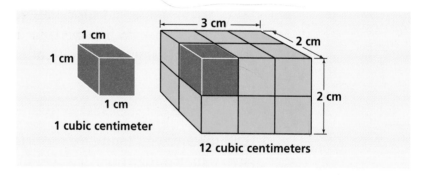

1 cubic centimeter

12 cubic centimeters

Now look at the figure of the larger box. Its length is 3 cm. Its width is 2 cm. Its height is 2 cm. You can see that 12 small boxes will fit into the larger box. If each small box is 1 cm³, then the large box would have a volume of 12 cm³.

You also can use the formula to find the volume of the larger box.

$$\text{volume} = \text{length} \times \text{width} \times \text{height}$$
$$= 3 \text{ cm} \times 2 \text{ cm} \times 2 \text{ cm}$$
$$= 12 \text{ cm}^3$$

Self-Check

1. A box measures 8 cm by 9 cm by 12 cm. What is its volume?
2. What is the volume of a stainless-steel container with a length of 18 mm, width of 20 mm, and height of 10 mm?
3. Find the volume of a cabinet that measures 1.20 m by 5 m by 75 cm. (*Hint:* Convert meters to centimeters. Remember that 1 m = 100 cm.)

1. 864^3_{cm}
2. 3,600
3. 438,000,000

Volume of a Liquid

Liter

Basic unit of volume in the metric system.

You might be familiar with another unit of volume in the metric system—the **liter**. You can see liter containers at the supermarket, especially in the soft-drink section. A liter is slightly more than a quart. The abbreviation for liter is *L*. The liter is often used to measure the volume of liquids.

As you can see in the figure, one liter of water will exactly fill a box that measures 10 cm on each side. A liter takes up the same amount of space as 1,000 cubic centimeters.

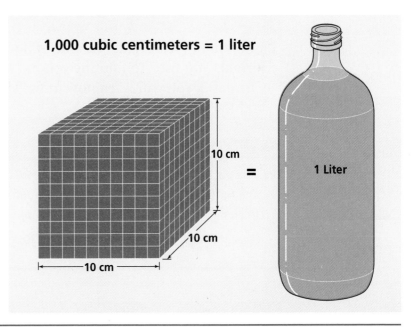

1,000 cubic centimeters = 1 liter

10 cm

10 cm

10 cm

=

1 Liter

Volume Equivalents	
1 liter (L)	1,000 cubic centimeters
1 cubic centimeter (cm³)	1/1,000 liter (0.001 L)
1 milliliter (mL)	1/1,000 liter (0.001 L)
1 milliliter (mL)	1 cubic centimeter (cm³)

You learned earlier in this chapter that you can use the same prefixes you used with the meter to form other units of measurement. The only prefix that is commonly used to measure volume is *milli-*. Recall that *milli-* means 1/1,000. A milliliter is 1/1,000 of a liter. The abbreviation for milliliter is *mL*. There are 1,000 milliliters in a liter. Since there are also 1,000 cubic centimeters in one liter, a milliliter is the same as one cubic centimeter.

Sometimes you will have to convert cubic centimeters to liters. Since one cubic centimeter is 1/1,000 of a liter, you can convert by dividing by 1,000.

Express 1,256 cm³ as liters.

$$1,256 \div 1,000 = 1.256 \text{ L}$$

You can also convert liters to cubic centimeters. Simply multiply by 1,000.

Express 4.3 L as cubic centimeters.

$$4.3 \text{ L} \times 1,000 = 4,300 \text{ cm}^3$$

You cannot measure the volume of liquids by using the formula you used to find the volume of a rectangle. In Chapter 2, you will learn how to use special equipment to find the volume of a liquid.

Self-Check

Convert each of these measurements.

1. 3 L = 3,000 mL
2. 5.5 L = 5,500 mL
3. 3,000 cm³ = 3 L

4. 3,700 cm³ = 3.7 L
5. 0.72 L = 720 mL
6. 350 mL = 350 cm³

How Can You Use Metric Units to Measure Mass?

You learned earlier in this chapter that all matter has mass. Remember that mass is the amount of material an object has. But how can you measure mass?

In the metric system, the **gram** is the basic unit of mass. One gram equals the mass of one cubic centimeter of water. That's about the same mass as a large wooden match or a small paper clip. There are 454 grams in one pound. The abbreviation for gram is *g*.

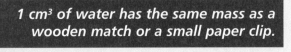

1 cm³ of water has the same mass as a wooden match or a small paper clip.

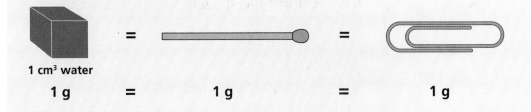

1 cm³ water			
1 g	**=**	**1 g**	**=**	**1 g**

Gram

Basic unit of mass in the metric system.

Mass Equivalents

Recall that the meter sometimes is too large or too small to measure the length of certain objects. The same is true for the gram. For example, a person may have a mass of 85,000 grams. That's a large number!

You can use the same prefixes you use with meters to show parts of a gram or multiples of a gram. The table on the next page shows these units of mass.

Mass Equivalents	
1 kilogram (kg)	1,000 g
1 centigram (cg)	1/100 g (0.01 g)
1 milligram (mg)	1/1,000 g (0.001 g)

To measure the mass of a person, you probably would use kilograms. One kilogram is about 2.2 pounds. However, the mass of a single hair from your head would be measured in smaller units called milligrams. A milligram is 1/1,000 of a gram.

If 1 cubic centimeter of water has a mass of 1 gram, then 1,000 cubic centimeters will have a mass of 1,000 grams, or 1 kilogram (1 kg). Remember that there are 1,000 cubic centimeters in 1 liter. Therefore, as the figure below shows, 1 liter of water will have a mass of 1 kilogram.

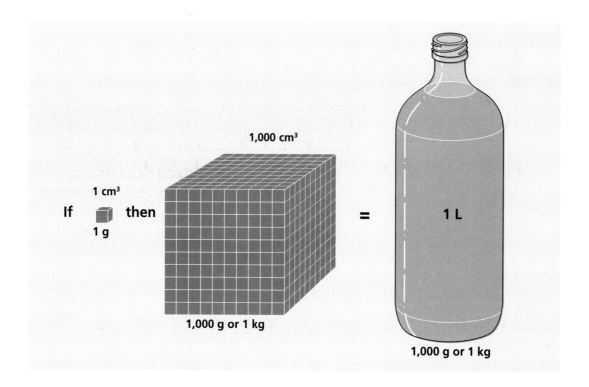

Make these conversions.

1. 6 g = <u>6,000</u> mg
2. 80,000 g = <u>80</u> kg
3. 90 g = <u>9,000</u> cg
4. 3,000 cg = <u>30,000</u> mg
5. 25,300 mg = <s>0.00253</s> kg 0.0253
6. 10 g = <u>10,000</u> mg

25.3

- Physical science is the study of matter and energy.

- Matter is anything that has mass and takes up space. Mass is the amount of material in an object.

- Measurements are important because we cannot always trust observations made with our eyes. Measurements help scientists gather exact information.

- In order for a unit of measurement to be useful, it has to be the same for everyone.

- Scientists use the metric system. The metric system is based on a system of tens.

- The meter is the basic unit of length in the metric system.

- You can measure length with a meter stick. A meter stick is divided into 100 smaller units, called centimeters. Each centimeter is divided into 10 units, called millimeters.

- You can use a system of prefixes in the metric system to show multiples or parts of a unit.

- Area is the amount of space the surface of an object takes up. The formula *length* × *width* is used to calculate area.

- Volume is the amount of space an object takes up. The volume of a rectangle can be calculated by using the formula *length* × *width* × *height*.

- A liter is the basic unit of volume in the metric system.

- You can convert from one unit to another in the metric system.

- The gram is the basic unit of mass in the metric system.

Science Words			
	area, 14	mass, 4	physical science, 4
	chemistry, 5	matter, 4	physics, 5
	English system, 8	meter, 9	unit, 7
	gram, 21	meter stick, 10	volume, 18
	liter, 19	metric system, 8	

Vocabulary Review

Number your paper from 1 to 6. Match each word in Column A with the correct definition in Column B. Write the letter of the definition on your paper.

Column A	Column B
_f_ 1. gram	(a) anything that has mass and takes up space
_e_ 2. liter	(b) the amount of material an object has
_b_ ~~_f_~~ 3. mass	(c) the basic unit of length in the metric system
_a_ 4. matter	(d) the amount of space an object takes up
_c_ 5. meter	(e) the basic unit of volume in the metric system
_d_ 6. volume	(f) the basic unit of mass in the metric system

WORD BANK

centimeter
chemistry
English system
gram
kilogram
liter
metric system
millimeter
physics
unit

Concept Review

Number your paper from 1 to 10. Then choose a word or words from the Word Bank that best complete each sentence. Write the answer on your paper.

1. The unit of length equal to 1/1,000 of a meter is the _mm_.

2. The unit of volume equal to 1,000 cubic centimeters is the _L_.

3. One _kgn g_ is equal to 1,000 grams.

4. There are 10 milliliters in one _cm_.

5. One cubic centimeter of water has a mass of 1 _g_

6. The system of measurement that scientists use is the _MS_.

7. Inches, feet, yards, and miles are all part of the _ES_.

8. The area of physical science that studies matter is _phi_.

9. The area of chemistry that studies energy is _cmistry_

10. A known amount used to measure things is a _unit_

Critical Thinking

Write the answer to each of the following questions.

1. Some ancient civilizations used units of measure based on the length of certain seeds. What kind of problems might you expect with such a system?

Seeds vary in size

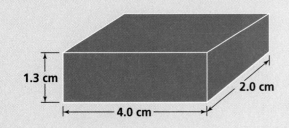

2. Calculate the volume of the rectangular object shown in the figure.

3. For each of the following objects, tell which unit of measurement you would use.

   a. length of an ant   _mɨman_
   b. mass of a postage stamp   _grams_
   c. volume of a large jug of milk   _liters_
   d. mass of a truck   _kilogram_

4. Explain how the metric system is based on a system of tens.

Test Taking Tip   When taking a matching test, match all the items that you know go together. Cross out these items. Then try to match the items that are left.

Chapter 2

The Properties of Matter

If you look at the photograph, you can see a stream of water. How would you describe the water in the stream? Can you find water elsewhere in the photo? The ice, the snow, and even the mist are all water. How would you describe these forms of water? In this chapter, you will learn some ways to describe various substances. You will also learn why ice floats on water.

ORGANIZE YOUR THOUGHTS

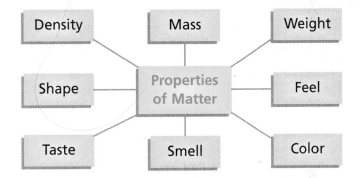

Density · Mass · Weight · Shape · Properties of Matter · Feel · Taste · Smell · Color

Goals for Learning

▶ To describe various objects by listing their properties

▶ To measure the mass of different objects

▶ To measure the volume of a liquid, using a graduated cylinder

▶ To measure the volume of an object, using the displacement of water method

▶ To calculate density

If someone asked you to describe sugar, what would you say? You might say "It is a solid made of small, individual pieces." Each part of that description tells a **property** of sugar. A property is a characteristic that helps identify an object. The above description identifies two properties of sugar.

- ■ It is a solid.
- ■ It is made of small individual pieces.

This description of sugar is correct. But it isn't enough to identify sugar for sure. As you can see in the photo, sand has the same properties. The description could be made more useful by adding other properties. For example, you might add color and taste. Your description of sugar becomes, "It is a white solid made of small, individual pieces that have a sweet taste." Sand could be described as "a tan solid made of small, individual pieces that have no taste."

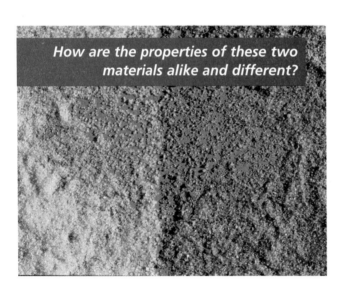

How are the properties of these two materials alike and different?

Some Common Properties

The photo on the next page shows some of the more common properties that you might use to describe matter. Scientists prefer to use some properties more than others. For example, scientists often use mass. The reason is because mass is easily measured. If someone asked you to describe a rock you saw, you might say it was big. But how big is big? And would someone else think the same rock was big? By using specific measurements of mass, everyone can agree on the measurement. Everyone can find the mass of the rock and agree that it is 50 kg. Another property that can easily be measured is volume (length, width, and height).

Which of these properties are easily measured?

Color: yellowish-red

Shape: almost round

Volume: about 20 mL

Feel: fuzzy, soft

Size: similar to a baseball

Mass: about 0.4 kg

Taste: sweet

Smell: pleasant, sweet

Some properties, such as color, aren't measured as easily. Because of this, descriptions based on color can be misunderstood. For example, how would you describe the color of the fruit in the photo above? One person might describe the shade as "pink," while another would call it "yellowish-red." When describing properties, it is important to be as exact as you can and to use measurements whenever possible.

Self-Check

1. For each of the following statements, tell whether it is a good description. Explain your answer.
   a. It was a large, colorful box.
   b. The rock has a mass of 25 kilograms.
   c. The solid that formed was dark, shiny, and lumpy.

2. Choose an object. Write a detailed description of the object. Read your description to the class. Can classmates identify the object from your description?

INVESTIGATION

2-1

Identifying Properties

Purpose
To write clear descriptions of objects

Procedure
1. Copy the data table below on a sheet of paper.

Object number	Properties
1	
2	
3	
4	
5	

2. Obtain a bag from your teacher. You will find five objects in your bag.

3. Carefully study the five objects. On a separate sheet of paper, make a list of the objects in your bag. Number the objects from 1 to 5.

4. Describe each object by writing as many properties as you can. Write the information in your table. Be sure to describe each object clearly and completely. Do not tell what the object is or what is it used for.

5. When you have completed your descriptions, give your descriptions to a classmate. Have your classmate identify the objects, using your descriptions.

Questions

1. How many objects did your classmate identify correctly?

2. What could you have done to make your descriptions more useful?

Explore Further

Work with five other students. Combine the objects from the bags of everyone in your group. Place objects with similar properties in a group. Identify the properties that describe all the objects in each group. Then list the property of each object in a group that makes it different from all the other objects.

You know from Chapter 1 that all matter has mass. Mass is a property of matter that you can measure. For example, the mass of the man in the figure to the left is 65 kg. But what is the man's weight? Are mass and weight the same?

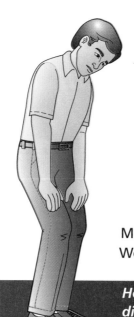

Mass = 65 kg
Weight = ?

How does this man's weight differ from his mass?

Mass and Weight

Mass and *weight* are often used to mean the same thing. However, scientists have different meanings for these two words. Mass is how much matter is in an object. **Weight** is a measure of how hard gravity pulls on an object. The force of gravity depends on the mass of an object. Objects with a large mass will have a strong pull of gravity. You can measure weight with a bathroom scale, like the one to the right.

Weight

The measure of how hard gravity pulls on an object.

This astronaut's weight is less on the moon than on Earth.

The mass of an object never changes under normal conditions. But the weight of an object can change when it is moved to some other place. For example, the pull of gravity on the moon is less than the pull of Earth's gravity. So when the astronaut in the photograph went to the moon, he weighed less on the moon than he did on Earth. But his mass didn't change.

Self-Check

The table below lists some planets of the solar system. It also tells each planet's force of gravity compared to the earth's. Copy the chart on a sheet of paper. Then calculate the weight of a 100-pound person on each of the planets. The first two examples are done for you. Write your answers on your paper.

Planet	Force of gravity compared to Earth	Weight on Earth	Weight on this planet	Method
Earth	1.00	100 lbs	100 lbs	1.00 × 100
Jupiter	2.54	100 lbs	254 lbs	2.54 × 100
Mars	0.379	100 lbs		
Saturn	1.07	100 lbs		
Mercury	0.378	100 lbs		
Venus	0.894	100 lbs		

Measuring Solid Mass

Recall from Chapter 1 that in the metric system, mass is measured in units called grams. The mass of a small paper clip is about 1 g. How many grams do you think a large paper clip might be? How could you find out?

You can use an instrument called a **balance** to measure mass. Balances come in many different kinds. But the simplest kind often looks like the one in the picture below. When you use this kind of balance, you find the mass of an object by balancing it with objects of known masses.

Standard masses are small objects—usually brass cylinders —with the mass stamped on each. You can see some standard masses in the picture. Most people use standard masses when using a balance. You can place standard masses on the pan opposite the object to be massed until the two pans are balanced. The mass of the object is equal to the total of the standard masses.

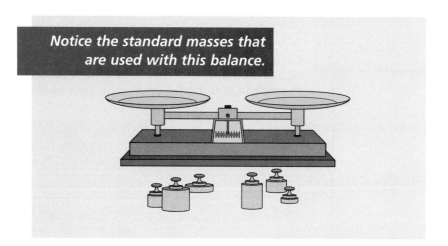

Notice the standard masses that are used with this balance.

Self-Check

1. How does mass differ from weight?
2. What quantity are you measuring when you use a bathroom scale?

How Can You Measure the Mass of a Liquid?

You can find the mass of a solid by using a balance. But how do you find the mass of a liquid? A balance is made to hold solids, not liquids.

To help answer the question, think about the following example. Suppose a boy uses a scale to find his weight. The scale shows that he weighs 100 pounds. Then the boy picks up his dog and weighs himself again while holding the dog. The scale now reads 120 pounds. Why? The answer is that the scale is measuring the weight of both the boy and the dog.

Since the boy knows that his weight is 100 pounds and the weight of the boy and the dog is 120 pounds, he can easily find the weight of the dog.

$$
\begin{array}{ccc}
120\ \text{pounds} & -\quad 100\ \text{pounds} & =\quad 20\ \text{pounds} \\
(\text{weight of boy and dog}) & - (\text{weight of boy}) & = (\text{weight of dog})
\end{array}
$$

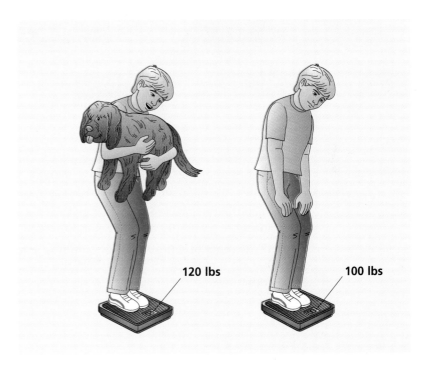

120 lbs   100 lbs

Measuring Liquid Mass

You can use a similar procedure to find the mass of a liquid.

1. Measure the mass of an empty container, such as a beaker.

2. Pour the liquid you want to measure into the beaker.

3. Measure the mass of the liquid plus beaker.

4. Subtract the mass of the empty beaker from the mass of the beaker plus liquid. The answer will be the mass of the liquid.

mass of liquid = mass of liquid plus beaker – mass of beaker

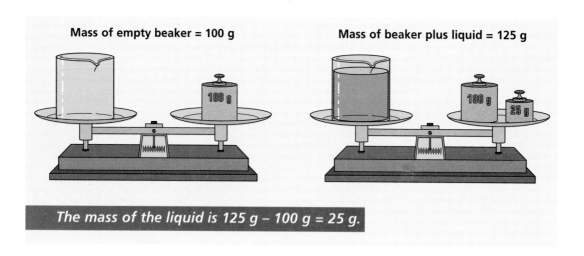

Mass of empty beaker = 100 g   Mass of beaker plus liquid = 125 g

The mass of the liquid is 125 g – 100 g = 25 g.

Self-Check

1. A container has a mass of 150 g. What is the mass of a liquid if the container plus the liquid has a mass of 185 g?

2. A container has a mass of 125 g. When a liquid is added, the mass becomes 163 g. What is the mass of the liquid?

3. If the mass of a liquid is 35 g and it is placed in a beaker having a mass of 75 g, what will the mass of the beaker plus liquid be?

How Can You Measure the Volume of a Liquid?

Objectives

After reading this lesson, you should be able to

▶ explain how to use a graduated cylinder to measure the volume of a liquid.

Graduated cylinder

A round glass or plastic cylinder used to measure the volume of liquids.

Meniscus

The curved surface of a liquid.

In Chapter 1, you learned that the unit of volume in the metric system is the liter. Usually, the liter is too large a unit to use in a laboratory, so scientists often use the milliliter. Remember that 1 milliliter has the same volume as 1 cubic centimeter. Liquid volumes are sometimes measured in cubic centimeters rather than millimeters.

To measure the volume of a liquid, you can use a **graduated cylinder.** Graduated cylinders come in many different sizes. The largest ones usually hold 1 L of a liquid. More common sizes hold 100 mL, 50 mL, or 10 mL. You can see two sizes of graduated cylinders in the figure on page 38.

Measuring with a Graduated Cylinder

To measure the volume of a liquid, follow this procedure.

1. Pour the liquid into the graduated cylinder.

2. Position yourself so that your eye is level with the top of the liquid. You can see the correct position in the figure below.

3. Read the volume from the scale that is on the outside of the cylinder. The top of the liquid usually is curved. This curve is called a **meniscus.** You can see the meniscus in the figure to the left. Read the scale on the bottom of the curve as shown. The volume of this liquid is 16 mL.

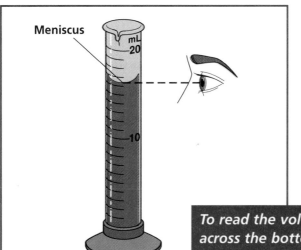

Meniscus

To read the volume of a liquid, sight across the bottom of the meniscus.

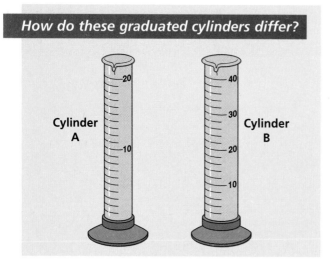

How do these graduated cylinders differ?

Cylinder A

Cylinder B

If you look carefully at the two graduated cylinders to the left, you will see that they are marked differently. Notice that Cylinder A on the left can hold 20 mL of a liquid. Cylinder B on the right can hold 40 mL. The number of spaces between the numbers on the cylinders is also different.

Reading a Scale

In order to measure the volume of a liquid in a graduated cylinder, you need to know what the spaces between each line represent. In other words, you must be able to read the scale. It is easy to do if you follow this procedure.

1. Subtract the numbers on any two long lines that are next to each other. In the figure below, the two long lines are labeled *20* and *10*. When you subtract these numbers (20 mL – 10 mL) you get 10 mL.

2. Count the number of spaces between the two long lines. In the figure, you can see 5 spaces between the two long lines.

3. Divide the number you got in Step 1 by the number you counted in Step 2. This will tell you how much of an increase each line represents from the line below. In the figure below, each space equals 2 mL.

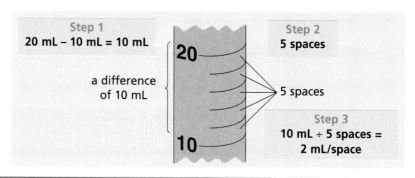

Step 1
20 mL – 10 mL = 10 mL

a difference
of 10 mL

20

10

Step 2
5 spaces

5 spaces

Step 3
10 mL ÷ 5 spaces =
2 mL/space

1. Read the volume of liquid in each cylinder. Write the volume on a sheet of paper.

2. Draw these three cylinders on your paper. Shade each one to show these volumes:

   a. 26 mL   b. 13 mL   c. 8 mL

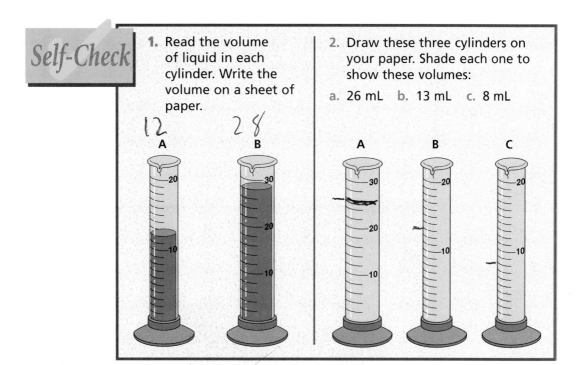

12
28

A   B

A   B   C

SCIENCE IN YOUR LIFE

Is your aquarium large enough?

Suppose you are setting up an aquarium. You have seen 10 fish at the pet store that you would like to include in your aquarium. The store owner tells you that the 10 fish you have chosen will live together well, but they need at least 40,000 cm^3 of water.

45,000
yes

You already own a fish tank that you would like to use. It measures 30 cm wide, 50 cm long, and 30 cm high. Is this tank large enough to provide the fish with the amount of water they need?

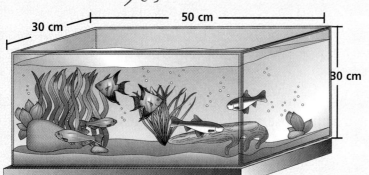

30 cm

50 cm

30 cm

Objectives

After reading this lesson, you should be able to

▶ measure the volume of regularly-shaped solids.

▶ measure the volume of irregularly-shaped solids.

The volume of solid objects cannot be measured using a graduated cylinder. However, you can measure the volume of solids in two different ways, depending on the shape of the solid.

How would you describe the shapes of these objects?

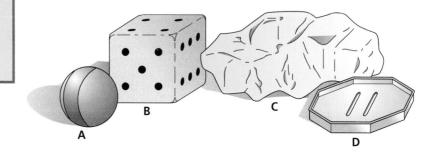

Regular and Irregular Shapes

You can describe some solids as having a regular shape. Objects A and B in the illustration above have a regular shape. When a solid has a regular shape, you can find the volume by using a formula. You have already learned the formula for finding the volume of rectangularly-shaped objects.

volume = length × width × height

Some solids have regular shapes other than rectangular. Examples are spheres and cylinders. You can use different formulas for finding the volumes of objects with these shapes.

Displacement of water

Method of measuring volume of irregularly-shaped objects.

Objects C and D in the illustration have irregular shapes. You cannot use a formula to find the volume of a solid with an irregular shape. Instead, you can use the **displacement of water** method to find the volume of irregularly-shaped objects.

Using Displacement of Water

If a glass is partially filled with water and you place an object in the glass, the level of the water will rise. In fact, the water level will rise by an amount equal to the volume of the object that was placed in the glass. To accurately measure the volume, use a graduated cylinder. The object must be completely under the water.

To measure the volume of a small, solid object, using the displacement of water method, follow the procedure below. Remember to cover the object completely with water when using this method.

Figure A

1. Pour water into a graduated cylinder. Record the volume of the water. (Figure A)

   volume = 10 cm³

2. Place the object in the cylinder. The water level will then rise. Record this new volume. (Figure B)

   volume = 16 cm³

Figure B

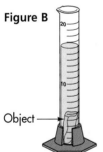

Object →

3. Subtract the volume of the water from the volume of the water and the object. The difference will be the volume of the object.

   16 cm³ – 10 cm³ = 6 cm³

The volume of the object is 6 cm³.

Self-Check

1. What is the volume of an object 10 cm long, 5 cm wide, and 2 cm high? *100 cm³*

2. A stone is placed in a graduated cylinder, which has been filled to the 35-mL mark. The level rises to 42 mL. What is the volume of the stone? *7 mL³ (7 cm³)*

3. A red marble is placed in a graduated cylinder, which has been filled to the 25-mL mark. The level rises to 41 mL. A blue marble is placed in another graduated cylinder, which has been filled to the 25-mL mark. The level rises to 52 mL. Which marble has the greater volume? *Blue marble*

Objectives

After reading this lesson, you should be able to

▶ explain what density is.

▶ calculate density.

▶ explain how to use density to identify a substance.

You probably have heard the riddle, "Which weighs more—a pound of feathers or a pound of lead?" The answer is that they weigh the same—one pound. A pound of lead would be a small cube. A pound of feathers would be much larger.

1 pound of feathers

1 pound of lead

The lead and the feathers have the same weight.

But what if you made 1-cm cubes from both materials? Would they be equally heavy? No, the lead cube would be much heavier. The reason is that lead has more matter packed in the cube than the feathers. The lead has a higher **density.** Density is a measure of how tightly the matter of a substance is packed into a given volume.

Density

A measure of how tightly the matter of a substance is packed into a given volume.

Calculating Density

If you know the volume and mass of a substance, you can find its density. You just have to use the following formula.

$$\text{density} = \frac{\text{mass}}{\text{volume}} \left(\frac{m}{v}\right)$$

Suppose you know the mass of an object is 30 g and its volume is 15 cm³. What is its density?

$$\text{density} = \frac{\text{mass}}{\text{volume}} \left(\frac{m}{v}\right)$$

$$= \frac{30 \text{ g}}{15 \text{ cm}^3}$$

$$= 2 \text{ g/cm}^3$$

One cubic centimeter of this substance has a mass of 2 grams.

Density Is a Property

The density of a particular substance is always the same, no matter how large or what shape the piece of the substance is. As the illustration below shows, the density of lead is always 11.3 g/cm³.

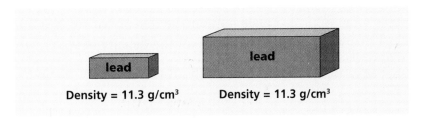

Material	Density (g/cm³)
gold	19.3
mercury	13.6
lead	11.3
silver	10.5
aluminum	2.7
rubber	1.1
water	1.0
cork	0.24
air	0.0013

You can see from the table that different kinds of matter have different densities. Therefore, you can use density to identify a material.

Suppose you have an unknown piece of metal and you want to find out what it is. You can measure its mass and volume, and then use the formula to find its density. Once you know the density, you can use a table like this one to identify the metal.

For example, suppose you have a small piece of metal. You don't know what metal it is. But you measure its mass on a balance. You find its mass is 8 g. Then you use a graduated cylinder to find the volume of the metal. The volume is 3cm³. Using the formula, you find the density of the metal is 2.7. What metal do you have?

Sink or Float

Matter that has a greater density than water will sink in water. Matter with a density that is less than water will float.

Look at the figure. It shows a container of water that holds an ice cube and a silver ball. You know from the table on page 43 that the density of silver is 10.5g/cm³. That density is greater than the density of water, which is 1.0 g/cm³.

But what about the ice cube ? It floats on the water. What does that tell you about the density of ice compared to water?

Why does this ice float while the ball sinks?

Self-Check

1. What is density?

2. Which would have more matter—a 1-cm cube of lead or a 1-cm cube of rubber?

3. Suppose you have a metal bar. Its mass is 57.9 g and its volume is 3 cm³. What is its density?

4. If you cut the metal bar from question 2 in half, what would the density of each half be?

5. What is the metal whose density you calculated in question 2?

6. If you put a piece of cork in a container of water, would it sink or float? Why? (*Hint:* Use the table on page 43 to answer the question.)

INVESTIGATION

Finding Density

Materials

✓ 2 graduated cylinders
✓ balance
✓ oil
✓ water

Purpose
To calculate and compare the densities of oil and water

Procedure
1. Copy the data table below on a sheet of paper.

	Cylinder with water	Cylinder with oil
A. mass of empty cylinder		
B. mass of cylinder and liquid		
C. mass of liquid (B – A)		
D. volume of liquid		
E. density $\left(E = \dfrac{C}{D} \right)$		

2. Obtain two identical graduated cylinders. Use a balance to find the mass of each cylinder. Record the masses on line A of your table.

3. Fill one graduated cylinder with water and the other with oil up to the same mark. You now have equal volumes of water and oil. Record this volume on line D of your data table.

4. Find the mass of the cylinder and the water. Record your data on line B.

5. Subtract the mass of the graduated cylinder from the mass of the graduated cylinder and water (line B – line A). The answer tells you the mass of the water. Record this mass on line C.

6. Repeat steps 4 and 5, using your data for the oil.

7. Use the equation for density to find the densities of the water and the oil.

$$\text{density} = \frac{\text{mass}}{\text{volume}}$$

Questions

1. Which substance—the water or the oil—has the greater density?

2. Liquids with lesser densities will float on liquids with greater densities. If you pour oil and water together, which liquid would float on top?

- Mass measures how much matter is in an object.

- Weight can change when moving from one place to another, but mass generally stays the same.

- Properties are used to describe an object.

- Mass, volume, and density are important properties of matter.

- Mass is measured using a balance. A common unit of mass is the gram.

- Volume of liquids is measured by using a graduated cylinder.

- When measuring the mass of liquids, first measure the mass of an empty beaker. Then pour the liquid into the beaker and measure the mass again. Subtract these two figures to find the mass of the liquid.

- The volume of regularly-shaped objects can be found by using formulas.

- The volume of irregularly-shaped objects is measured by using the displacement of water method.

- Density is a property of matter that tells how tightly the matter is packed into a given volume.

- Density can be used to identify substances.

- Liquids that are less dense than water will float on water. Liquids that are more dense will sink.

Science Words	balance, 34	meniscus, 37
	density, 42	property, 28
	displacement of water, 40	standard mass, 34
	graduated cylinder, 37	weight, 32

Vocabulary Review

Number your paper from 1 to 5. Then choose a word or words from the Word Bank that best complete each sentence. Write the answer on your paper.

WORD BANK

balance ✓

graduated
cylinder ✓

property ✓

volume ✓

weight ✓

1. A characteristic that helps identify an object is a _property_

2. A measure of how hard the earth's gravity pulls on an object is _weight_

3. To measure mass, you use a _balance_

4. The measure of how much space an object takes up is its _volume_

5. Use a _cylinder_ to measure the volume of a liquid.

Concept Review

Number your paper from 1 to 5. Then choose the word or words that best complete each sentence. Write the letter of the answer on your paper.

1. The unit of measure used on graduated cylinders is the _mL_.

    a. gram   b. meter   c. milliliter ✓

2. Displacement of water is a method of measuring _volume_

    a. weight   b. volume ✓   c. mass

3. The mass of an object is measured in _c m_.

    a. grams   b. centimeters ✓ c. meters

4. To read the scale on a graduated cylinder, read the bottom of the _meniscus_

    a. mass   b. meniscus ✓   c. balance

5. When moving from one place to another, _a._.

    a. weight can change ✓

    b. mass can change

    c. neither weight nor mass can change

Critical Thinking

Write the answer to each of the following questions.

1. Would the following statement be a good one for a scientist to use in a report? Explain. *ho*

   not enu "The material was made of small, colorful pieces."

   ph ehfomaS

   tioh

2. Explain how to find the mass of a liquid.

3. How would you measure the volume of each of the objects shown below?

   youse a becar to mesher it

   Put them in watter

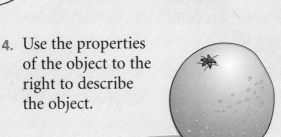

4. Use the properties of the object to the right to describe the object.

5. Suppose scientists have two substances that look alike. How could they use density to see if they are the same substance?

   $$\frac{M}{V}$$

| Test Taking Tip | If you have to choose the correct ending to a sentence, combine the first part of the sentence with each ending. Then choose the one that best fits the sentence.

Chapter

3

The Structure of Matter

When you look at the photograph at the left from a distance, you can see that it appears to be painted. But if you could look very closely at it, you would see that it is made of many tiny pieces of stone. The picture is like matter you can see. Each stone is like a small particle of matter. In this chapter, you will find out about the tiny particles that make up matter.

ORGANIZE YOUR THOUGHTS

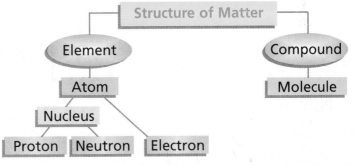

Structure of Matter

Element — Atom — Nucleus — Proton / Neutron / Electron

Compound — Molecule

Goals for Learning

▶ To explain what molecules, elements, and compounds are

▶ To explain how scientists use models

▶ To describe the parts of an atom

▶ To explain the meaning of atomic number and mass number

▶ To calculate the numbers of protons, electrons, and neutrons in an element from its atomic number and mass number

Objectives

After reading this lesson, you should be able to

▶ describe the size of molecules.

▶ explain what a molecule is.

▶ explain how molecules move in each of the three states of matter.

▶ describe what plasma is.

How would you describe the sugar shown in the figure below? You might mention that sugar is a material made of matter. You might tell about its properties, such as its color, taste, or texture. Now think about how you might describe a single grain of sugar. You probably would say that it is very small. But how small is the smallest piece of sugar?

Molecules make up a grain of sugar.

Size of Molecules

Each grain of sugar is made of even smaller particles that are too tiny for you to see. These tiny particles are called **molecules.** Molecules are the smallest particles of a substance that still have the properties of that substance. Each molecule of sugar has exactly the same properties. How small can molecules be? Molecules of some substances are so small that billions of them could be placed side by side on a line one centimeter long.

Molecule

The smallest particle of a substance that has the same properties as the substance.

Describing Molecules

Look at the water spraying out of the fountain in the photograph on the next page. Imagine dividing one drop of this water into smaller and smaller drops. The smallest drop you could make that still had the properties of water would be one molecule of water.

This fountain contains billions of molecules of water.

In general, all water molecules are alike. A water molecule from the fountain is the same as a water molecule in a raindrop, in the ocean, or in the water you drink. The figure below shows a molecule of water. You can see that each water molecule has three parts—one large part and two smaller parts.

If you divided a water molecule into its three parts, it would no longer be a molecule of water. The parts would no longer have the properties of water. When a water molecule is divided into its separate parts, each individual part is called an **atom.** An atom is a building block of matter. A water molecule has three atoms. Each kind of atom has its own properties. All matter is made of atoms.

Atom

The building block of matter.

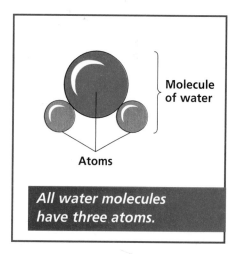

Molecule of water

Atoms

All water molecules have three atoms.

States of Matter

You can describe matter by telling about its properties. For example, you might tell about its mass or density. The form that matter has is another of its properties.

You can see in the photo below three forms of matter. The cars and trees are **solids.** The molecules in a solid attract, or pull toward, each other. In a solid, molecules vibrate, which means that they move back and forth quickly, but stay close together. For this reason, a solid keeps a certain shape and volume.

Solid

Form of matter that has a definite shape and volume.

How many solids, liquids, and gases can you find?

Liquid

Form of matter that has a definite volume but no definite shape.

The water in the picture is a **liquid.** The pull between the molecules is weaker in liquids than it is in solids. The molecules can slide past each other. A liquid has a certain volume, but it can change its shape because its molecules can easily move around. For example, suppose you had a liter of water in a container. If you poured the liter of water into a differently-shaped container, the water would still take up one liter of space. But its shape would be different. It would take the shape of the new container.

Gas

Form of matter that has no definite shape or volume.

Notice the shape of the helium balloons. Helium is a **gas** that fills the balloon. The molecules of a gas are much farther apart than they are in a liquid or a solid. The pull between the molecules in a gas is very weak. A gas takes the same shape as its container because its molecules move around freely. The gas molecules will always fill a container completely. A container of water can be half full, but a container of a gas will always be completely full. The volume of a gas can change.

State of matter

The form that matter has—solid, liquid or gas.

These forms of matter—solid, liquid, and gas—are called the **states of matter.** The drawing summarizes how the molecules move in each of these three states of matter.

Particles move differently in each of the three states of matter.

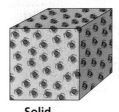 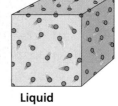 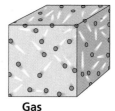

| Solid | Liquid | Gas |

Plasma

Plasma

A very hot gas made of particles that have an electric charge.

Matter can exist in a fourth state of matter called **plasma.** Plasma is a very hot gas made of particles that have an electric charge. The particles of plasma shake violently at very high temperatures. Plasma is very rare on Earth. But all stars, including the sun, are balls of plasma. Scientists estimate that 90 percent of all matter in the universe is plasma.

Self-Check

1. Can you see a single molecule of sugar? Explain.
2. What parts make up a molecule of water?
3. Describe how molecules move in each of the three states of matter.
4. What is plasma?

What Are Elements?

After reading this lesson, you should be able to

▶ explain what an element is.

▶ explain what a natural element is.

▶ give examples of natural elements.

Element

Matter that has only one kind of atom.

In Lesson 1, you learned that atoms are very tiny. In fact, they are one of the smallest particles that make up matter. Remember the balloon that was filled with helium? A balloon as small as a softball would hold many billions of atoms of helium.

One Kind of Atom

Most of the matter you see around you is made up of many different kinds of atoms. However, some matter has only one kind of atom. Matter that is made of only one kind of atom is called an **element**. All atoms of the same element are alike. For example, all atoms of oxygen are the same. The atoms of oxygen are different from the atoms of all other elements.

The foil you might use to wrap a sandwhich is made of atoms of the element aluminum. Gold, silver, and copper are other elements that are used to make jewelry and other common items.

Aluminum, gold, silver, and copper are examples of elements.

Natural Elements

Scientists know of about 109 different kinds of elements. Ninety-two of these elements are called **natural elements.** Natural elements are those that are found in nature. For example, oxygen is an element that you get from the air you breathe. Your body is made of atoms of many different elements. Atoms of the element calcium help keep your bones and teeth strong.

Not all elements are natural elements. Scientists are able to produce a few elements in specialized laboratories. Some of the elements that scientists produce last only a short time—a fraction of a second—before they change into other elements.

The table on this page lists some natural elements. It also tells what some of the elements can be used for. You may be able to think of other uses for some of these elements.

Natural element

An element that is found in nature.

D id You Know?

Look at the tip of your pencil. It is made of a soft, black material that is a form of the element carbon. The small pencil point has billions of carbon atoms.

Some Natural Elements

Name	Used for or found in
copper	coins, frying pans, electrical wire
silver	jewelry, photography
carbon	"lead" pencils, charcoal, diamonds
helium	balloons, airships
nitrogen	air that we breathe, fertilizers
chlorine	bleach, table salt
aluminum	airplanes, cookware, soft-drink cans
neon	"neon" signs
gold	jewelry, seawater, dentistry
mercury	thermometers, drugs, pesticides
iron	steel, eating utensils

Elements in Water

In Lesson 1, you learned that a molecule of water is made of three parts like those in the figure below. These parts are elements. The large part of the molecule, shown in blue, is an atom of the element oxygen. The two small parts, shown in red, are atoms of the element hydrogen. The atoms of the element oxygen are different from the atoms of the element hydrogen.

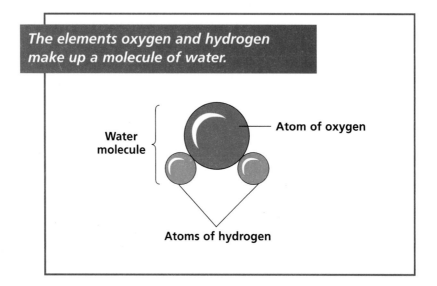

The elements oxygen and hydrogen make up a molecule of water.

Water molecule

Atom of oxygen

Atoms of hydrogen

Self-Check

1. What is an element?
2. What is a natural element?
3. Give three examples of natural elements.
4. Table salt is made up of a sodium atom and two chlorine atoms. Is table salt an element? Explain.

SCIENCE
IN YOUR
LIFE

How are elements important to health?

Your body needs many natural elements in order to stay healthy and work properly. The table lists some of these elements and tells how they are important for your health. The table also lists some foods that contain these elements. Write a menu for a day. Include healthful foods in your menu that provide a variety of natural elements.

Element	Purpose in the body	Food where it is found
calcium	builds and maintains teeth and bones; helps blood clot; helps nerves and muscles work properly	cheese; milk; dark green vegetables; sardines; legumes
phosphorus	keeps teeth and bones healthy; helps release energy from the food you eat	meat; poultry; fish; eggs; legumes; milk products
magnesium	aids breaking down of foods; controls body fluids	green vegetables; grains; nuts; beans; yeast
sodium	controls the amount of water in body; helps nerves work properly	most foods; table salt
potassium	controls the fluids in cells; helps nerves work properly	oranges; bananas; meats; bran; potatoes; dried beans
iron	helps move oxygen in the blood and in other cells	liver; red meats; dark green vegetables; shellfish; whole-grain cereals
zinc	helps move carbon dioxide in body; helps in healing wounds	meats; shellfish; whole grains; milk; legumes

Objectives

After reading this lesson, you should be able to

▶ explain what a compound is.

▶ give examples of compounds.

Compound

A substance formed when atoms of two or more elements join together.

All the substances in the picture are different from the elements you learned about in Lesson 2. The substances in the picture are each made of two or more different kinds of atoms. When two or more atoms of different elements join together, the substance that forms is called a **compound**. A compound has properties that are different from the properties of the elements that form the compound.

All of these substances are compounds.

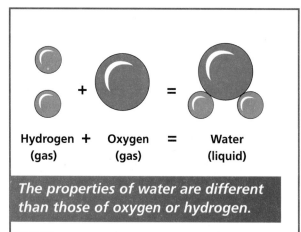

Hydrogen **+** Oxygen **=** Water
(gas) (gas) (liquid)

The properties of water are different than those of oxygen or hydrogen.

Think again about a molecule of water. The drawing shows that an atom of oxygen combines with two atoms of hydrogen to form a molecule of the compound water. Water is different from the elements that form it. Water is a liquid. Both oxygen and hydrogen are gases. You will learn more about breaking down the compound water into its elements when you do the Investigation on pages 62 and 63.

Another compound that probably is familiar to you is table salt. The chemical name of salt is sodium chloride. It is formed when the element sodium is combined with the element chlorine. Sodium chloride is very different from each of the elements it contains. Sodium is a solid. You might be surprised to learn that chlorine is a poisonous gas. However, when chlorine is combined with sodium to form sodium chloride, chlorine no longer has its poisonous property. Remember that a compound can have completely different properties from the elements that form it.

Most kinds of matter on Earth are compounds. In fact, there are more than 10 million known compounds. The table lists some common compounds and tells the elements that make up each compound.

Some Common Compounds

Name	Elements in this compound	Use
table salt	sodium, chlorine	cooking
water	hydrogen, oxygen	drinking
sugar	carbon, hydrogen, oxygen	cooking
baking soda	sodium, hydrogen, carbon, oxygen	baking
Epsom salts	magnesium, sulfur, oxygen	medicine

You might wonder if you can tell by looking at a substance whether it is an element or a compound. An unknown substance must be tested in a laboratory to determine whether it is an element or a compound.

Self-Check

1. Explain what a compound is.
2. Give two examples of compounds.
3. Suppose you test a gas in the laboratory. You learn that the gas is made up of carbon atoms and oxygen atoms. Is the gas a compound? Explain.

3-1

Breaking Down Water

Materials

- ✓ safety goggles
- ✓ beaker or wide-mouth jar
- ✓ water (distilled water preferred)
- ✓ two 50-cm long pieces of copper wire (about 3 cm of insulation removed at ends)
- ✓ one 15-cm long piece of copper wire (about 3 cm of insulation removed at ends)
- ✓ 2 dry-cell batteries (1.5 volt)
- ✓ 1 teaspoon table salt
- ✓ stirring rod

Purpose

To show that water is made from two different substances and is therefore a compound

Procedure

1. Copy the data table below on your paper.

	After 10 minutes
Wire connected to positive (+) terminal	
Wire connected to negative (–) terminal	

2. Put on your safety goggles.

3. Fill a beaker with water.

4. Attach the end of one long copper wire to the negative (–) terminal of one battery, as shown on the next page. Attach the end of the other long copper wire to the positive (+) terminal of the second battery. *Safety Alert: The ends of the wires are sharp. Handle them carefully.*

5. Use the short copper wire to connect the positive (+) terminal of the first battery to the negative (–) terminal of the second battery.

6. Put one end of each longer wire in the beaker so that the ends are about 4 to 5 cm apart, as shown.

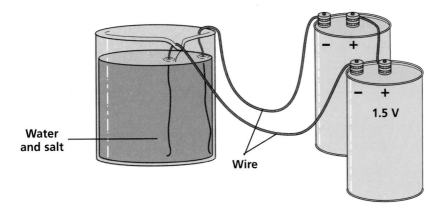

Water and salt

Wire

1.5 V

7. Sprinkle a few grains of salt into the water. Stir with the stirring rod until the salt dissolves. Observe the ends of the wires in the water. Continue adding a few grains of salt to the water. Stir until the salt dissolves. When small bubbles appear at the wire ends, stop adding salt.

8. Observe the ends of both wires in the water for about 10 minutes. Record your observations in the data table.

Questions

1. Which of the wires had more bubbles around it? Identify the wire by telling whether it was connected to the positive (+) terminal or the negative (–) terminal.

2. Describe what you observed at the end of each wire after 10 minutes.

3. The gas you observe comes from the water. The electricity from the batteries breaks down the water into hydrogen gas and oxygen gas. How does this production of gases show that water is a compound?

Objectives

After reading this lesson, you should be able to

▶ describe what a model is and explain how scientists use it.

▶ explain how models of the atom have changed.

▶ describe the electron cloud model.

Since atoms are too small to be seen with the eyes alone, people have wondered for a long time what atoms look like. In fact, scientists have been studying atoms since the 1800s. But if scientists can't see an atom, how do they know what atoms look like?

Using Models

Sometimes scientists can tell what things look like by studying how they act. For example, have you ever seen wind? What does it look like? If you said wind is leaves blowing or your hair getting messed up, you are describing what wind does, not what it looks like. You use the effects of wind to describe it. You know that wind is there because of its effects even though you can't see it. You use evidence.

You can't see the wind, but you can see what it does.

Model

A picture, an idea, or an object that is built to explain how something else looks or works.

Scientists use the same kind of evidence to study things they can't see, such as atoms. Scientists study how atoms act and then decide what an atom must look like. Scientists make **models.** You have probably seen models of cars or airplanes or buildings. In science, a model is an idea, a picture, or an object that is built to explain how something else looks or works. The model may not look exactly like the object it is built to describe, but it helps people understand the way the object acts.

Models of Atoms

Scientists use models of atoms to show how atoms look and act without having to actually see them. Many scientists have developed models of atoms. The first model was developed over 2,000 years ago. But as scientists gather new information about atoms, they change their models.

In the early 1900s, a scientist developed a model of an atom like those shown at the bottom of the page. Although scientists know more about atoms today, this kind of model is still useful for describing atoms.

Nucleus

The central part of an atom.

Proton

A tiny particle in the nucleus of an atom.

Electron

A tiny particle of an atom that moves around the nucleus.

Find the center of each atom. This central part of an atom is called a **nucleus.** The nucleus of an atom contains small particles called **protons.** Protons are labeled with the letter *p.* Another symbol for a proton is a plus (+) sign. Now look in the figures for the letter *e.* This letter stands for **electrons.** Electrons are particles in an atom that move around the outside of the protons. Electrons are smaller than protons. Another symbol for an electron is a minus (–) sign. The protons and electrons of an atom stay together because they attract each other.

Notice that the numbers of protons and electrons in the models are different. Figure A shows a model of an atom of hydrogen. You can see that hydrogen has one proton and one electron. Figure B shows an atom of helium, a gas that is often used to fill balloons. How many protons and electrons does helium have?

These models of atoms show that they are made of protons and electrons.

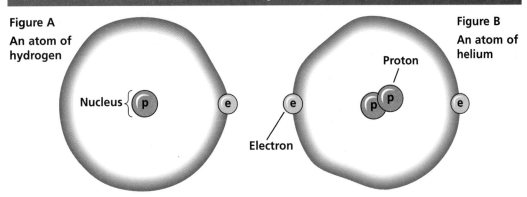

Figure A
An atom of hydrogen

Nucleus { p
e

Figure B
An atom of helium

Proton

Electron

e
p p
e

In 1932, scientists had evidence that the nucleus of an atom had another kind of particle. This particle is called a **neutron.** It is about the same size as a proton. Because of the new evidence, scientists changed the model of the atom. In Figure C, an atom of boron shows how the model changed. Find the neutrons, labeled with the letter *n*.

As you look at Figure C, you can see that the electrons seem to be on certain paths around the nucleus of the atom. Scientists thought that electrons moved in different layers around protons, sometimes jumping from one layer to another.

Today scientists use another model of atoms. You can see this new model—the electron cloud model—in Figure D. The dark center area represents the nucleus. However, you can't see different layers of electrons like you saw in the models in figures A to C. The electron cloud model was developed because scientists have evidence that electrons behave in more complicated ways than they previously thought. Because of this new evidence, scientists are not sure how electrons move around the nucleus. As scientists continue to learn more about atoms, perhaps the model will change again.

How are these two models of the atom different?

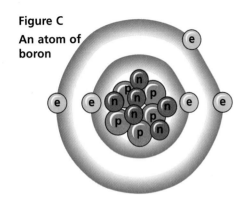

Figure C
An atom of boron

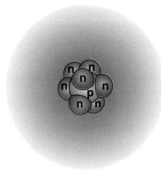

Figure D
Electron cloud model of an atom

You have looked at models showing the number of protons and electrons in the atoms of a few different elements. The table below lists some other elements and tells the numbers of protons and electrons in each. Find the number of protons in the element carbon. How many electrons does carbon have? Compare the numbers of protons and electrons in nitrogen. How many of each does it have? Now look at the numbers of protons and electrons in each of the elements listed. What do you notice? The number of protons in an atom is equal to the number of electrons in the atom.

Number of protons in an atom = Number of electrons in an atom

Element	Number of protons	Number of electrons
hydrogen	1	1
helium	2	2
lithium	3	3
beryllium	4	4
boron	5	5
carbon	6	6
nitrogen	7	7
oxygen	8	8
fluorine	9	9
neon	10	10

Self-Check

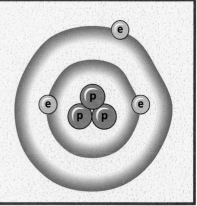

1. If scientists cannot see atoms, how do they know what they look like?

2. How do scientists use models?

3. How many protons are in the element shown in the drawing? How many electrons?

4. What is the name of the element? (*Hint:* Use the table.)

INVESTIGATION

3-2

Making Models of Atoms

Materials

✓ 3 differently-colored pieces of modeling clay

✓ craft sticks

✓ metric ruler

Purpose

To make a model of an atom of a particular element

Procedure

1. Copy the data table below on your paper.

Name of element
Picture of element

2. Choose an element from the table on page 67. Find the numbers of protons, neutrons, and electrons in your element.

3. Place three different colors of modeling clay on your desk. Choose one color of clay for protons. Pull off a small piece of clay for each of the protons in your element. Roll each piece into a ball about 1 cm in diameter.

4. Use another color of clay for neutrons. Make clay balls the same size as you made for protons. Be sure to make the same number of balls as there are neutrons in your element.

5. With the third color of clay, make smaller clay balls to represent electrons. Make the same number of balls as you made for protons.

6. Press the protons and neutrons together gently to make the nucleus of your model atom.

7. Gently put the craft sticks into the nucleus of your model. Put the same number of sticks as there are electrons in your element.

8. Place the clay electrons on the ends of the craft sticks.

9. Write the name of the element in your data table. Then draw a picture of your model.

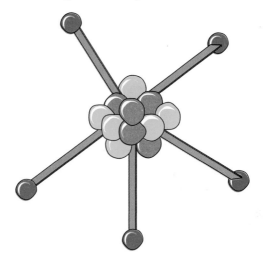

Questions

1. What is the name of your element? How many protons are in the nucleus? How many neutrons?

2. How many electrons does your element have?

3. Write at least four things that your model shows about atoms.

Because more than 100 elements are known, scientists need a way to identify them. One way scientists can identify elements is by knowing their **atomic numbers.**

Atomic Number

The table below lists the same ten elements listed in the table on page 67. You can see that an additional column, labeled Atomic number, has been added to the table. The atomic number of an element tells you how many protons are in each atom of the element.

Atomic number

A number equal to the number of protons in the nucleus of an atom.

Element	Atomic number	Number of protons	Number of electrons
hydrogen	1	1	1
helium	2	2	2
lithium	3	3	3
beryllium	4	4	4
boron	5	5	5
carbon	6	6	6
nitrogen	7	7	7
oxygen	8	8	8
fluorine	9	9	9
neon	10	10	10

Notice that each element has a different number of protons, and therefore a different atomic number. For example, the element hydrogen has 1 proton. Its atomic number is also 1. The drawing on the next page shows an atom of boron. How many protons does boron have? What does the table tell you the atomic number of boron is? For all the elements, the atomic number of the element is equal to the number of protons it has.

Atomic number = Number of protons

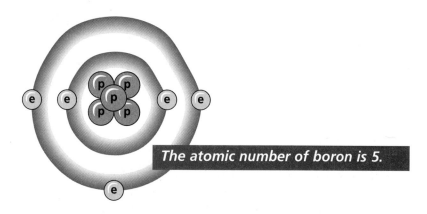

The atomic number of boron is 5.

1. An element has an atomic number of 33. How many protons does it have? 33

2. An element has 26 protons. What is its atomic number? 26

3. Complete the chart.

Element	Atomic number	Number of protons	Number of electrons
sodium	11	11	11
aluminum	13	13	13
chlorine	17	17	17
calcium	20	20	20

The Mass of an Element

You learned in Chapter 1 that mass is the amount of matter in an object. Protons and neutrons have a greater mass than electrons have. In fact, the mass of a proton or a neutron is about 1,800 times the mass of an electron. Yet protons and neutrons are still so small that it would not be possible to measure their mass on a balance scale. Instead, scientists tell about the mass of an element by using its **mass number.** The mass number of an element is equal to the sum of the numbers of protons and neutrons in an atom of the element.

Mass number

A number equal to the sum of the numbers of protons and neutrons in an atom of an element.

Mass number **=** Number of protons + Number of neutrons

The drawing shows an atom of beryllium. You can see that it has 4 protons and 5 neutrons. The atomic number of beryllium is 4, the same as the number of protons. To determine the mass number of beryllium, you add the number of protons, 4, and the number of neutrons, 5. The mass number of beryllium is 9 (4 + 5 = 9).

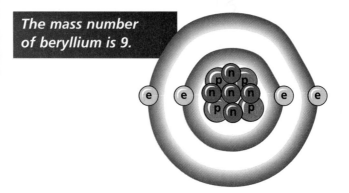

The mass number of beryllium is 9.

You have learned about protons, neutrons, and electrons. You also have learned about atomic numbers and mass numbers of elements. The table below gives a summary of information for the first ten elements.

Element	Atomic number	Mass number	Number of protons	Number of electrons	Number of neutrons
hydrogen	1	1	1	1	0
helium	2	4	2	2	2
lithium	3	7	3	3	4
beryllium	4	9	4	4	5
boron	5	11	5	5	6
carbon	6	12	6	6	6
nitrogen	7	14	7	7	7
oxygen	8	16	8	8	8
fluorine	9	19	9	9	10
neon	10	20	10	10	10

Remember that you can use information you know about an element to determine other information. For example, look at this drawing of an atom of sodium. Find the numbers of protons and neutrons. How many protons are in the nucleus? You know that the number of electrons in an element is equal to its number of protons. How many electrons does sodium have? You also know that the atomic number of an element is equal to the number of protons it has. What is the atomic number of the element sodium?

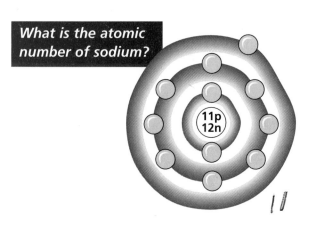

What is the atomic number of sodium?

11p
12n

The box below shows the relationships between the mass number of an element and the numbers of protons and neutrons it has. Notice that Relationship 1 explains how you can find the mass number of an element by adding the number of protons and neutrons it has in its nucleus.

Relationship 1:	**Mass number**	**=**	**Number of protons**	**+**	**Number of neutrons**
Relationship 2:	**Number of neutrons**	**=**	**Mass number**	**–**	**Number of protons**
Relationship 3:	**Number of protons**	**=**	**Mass number**	**–**	**Number of neutrons**

Suppose you know the mass number of an element and the number of protons it has. Can you determine the number of neutrons it has? Find Relationship 2 in the box. This relationship explains how you can use the information you know to find the number of neutrons in the nucleus of an atom.

Finally, suppose you know the mass number of an element and its number of neutrons. For example, the element aluminum has a mass number of 27. You can see in the drawing that aluminum has 14 neutrons in its nucleus. You can use Relationship 3 to determine the number of protons it has. How many protons are in the nucleus of the element aluminum? 13

An atom of aluminum has 13 protons in the nucleus.

13p
14n

Self-Check

Copy the table on a sheet of paper. Fill in the missing numbers. Use the three relationships on page 73 to help you. The first element is done for you.

Element	Atomic number	Mass number	Number of protons	Number of electrons	Number of neutrons
carbon	6	12	6	6	6
silver		108	47	47	61
silicon	14	28	14	14	14
calcium	20	40	20	20	20
iodine	53	127	63	63	84
chlorine	17	35	17	17	18
sulfur	16	32	16	16	16
potassium	19	39	19	19	20

- A molecule is the smallest particle of a substance that still has the same properties of the substance.
- An atom is the basic building block of matter.
- Scientists use models to explain things they can't see.
- Molecules move in different ways in each of the three states of matter—solids, liquids, and gases.
- An element is matter that is made of only one kind of atom. There are 92 natural elements, which are found in nature.
- A compound is formed from two or more atoms of different elements. A compound has properties that are different from the elements that form the compound.
- An atom is made of protons, neutrons, and electrons.
- The number of protons in an atom is equal to the number of electrons.
- The atomic number of an element is equal to the number of protons in its nucleus.
- The mass number of an element is equal to the number of protons plus the number of neutrons.

Science Words		
atom, 53	molecule, 52
atomic number, 70	natural element, 57
compound, 60	neutron, 66
electron, 65	nucleus, 65
element, 56	plasma, 55
gas, 55	proton, 65
liquid, 54	solid, 54
mass number, 71	state of matter, 55
model, 64	

Vocabulary Review

Number your paper from 1 to 7. Then choose a word or words from the Word Bank that best complete each sentence. Write the answer on your paper.

WORD BANK

atom

compound

element

model

molecule

natural element

states of matter

1. A(n) _____ has only one kind of atom.

2. A(n) _model_ is built to explain how something works.

3. The smallest particle of water that still has all the properties of water is a(n) _____ of water.

4. A(n) _7_ is found in nature.

5. A(n) _atom_ is the building block of each kind of matter.

6. Atoms of two elements can join to form a(n) _compound_

7. Solid, liquid, and gas are the _____.

Concept Review

Number your paper from 1 to 6. Then choose the word or words that best complete each sentence. Write the letter of the answer on your paper.

1. All matter is made of _____.

   a. plasma   b. atoms   c. compounds

2. An atom always has the same number of electrons and

   _____.

   a. protons   b. neutrons   c. nuclei

3. Molecules are _____.

   a. large   b. easy to see   c. small

4. An example of an element is _____.

   a. oxygen   b. water   c. sodium chloride

5. Molecules move most freely in _____.

    a. solids   b. liquids   c. gases

6. An example of a compound is _____.

    a. helium   b. hydrogen   c. carbon dioxide

Critical Thinking

Write the answers to each of the following questions.

1. Look at the drawing to the right. Give the following information about the atom: How many protons does it have? How many neutrons? How many electrons? What is the element's atomic number? What is the mass number?

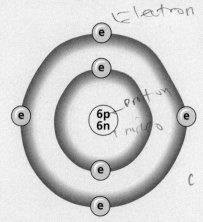

2. Does the drawing below show an atom or a molecule? Explain your answer.

Test Taking Tip | Before you choose an answer to a multiple-choice question, be sure to read each answer choice carefully.

16

S

Sulfur

32.06

Chapter 4

Classifying Elements

Y ou might not recognize the yellow substance in the photo. But you probably have used it before. The substance is sulfur. It is found in the tip of a match. Sulfur is an element. In this chapter you will learn what an element is. You will also learn about the properties of some elements.

ORGANIZE YOUR THOUGHTS

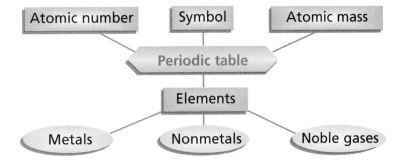

Goals for Learning

▶ To identify the symbols used to represent different elements

▶ To describe the kinds of information about each element that is contained in the periodic table

▶ To explain how elements are organized in the periodic table

▶ To classify elements as metals, nonmetals, or noble gases

Symbol

One or two letters that represent the name of an element.

Think about addressing an envelope for a letter you write to a friend. You probably use an abbreviation to indicate the state to which the letter should be delivered. What is the abbreviation for your state?

Element Symbols

Scientists also use abbreviations to represent each of the 92 natural elements. The abbreviations for elements are called **symbols.** The tables on these pages list some symbols for elements. All these symbols are alike in the following ways.

- All of the symbols have either one or two letters.

- The first letter of each symbol is a capital letter.

- If the symbol has a second letter, the second letter is a small letter.

- No period is used at the end of a symbol.

Table 1

Element name	Element symbol
hydrogen	H
boron	B
carbon	C
nitrogen	N
oxygen	O
fluorine	F
phosphorus	P
sulfur	S
iodine	I
uranium	U

Table 2

Element name	Element symbol
helium	He
lithium	Li
neon	Ne
aluminum	Al
silicon	Si
argon	Ar
calcium	Ca
cobalt	Co
bromine	Br
barium	Ba
radium	Ra

Table 3

Element name	Element symbol
magnesium	Mg
chlorine	Cl
chromium	Cr
manganese	Mn
plutonium	Pu
zinc	Zn
strontium	Sr
platinum	Pt

Table 4

Element name	Element symbol
sodium	Na
potassium	K
iron	Fe
silver	Ag
tin	Sn
tungsten	W
gold	Au
mercury	Hg
lead	Pb
antimony	Sb
copper	Cu

Notice that the symbols in Table 1 use only the first letter of the element name. Look at the symbols in Table 2. This group of symbols uses the first two letters of the element name. The symbols in Table 3 also use two letters. The first letter is the first letter of the element name. The second letter is another letter from the element name.

How do the symbols in Table 4 differ from the other symbols? Most of these symbols come from the Latin names for the elements. For example, the symbol for iron is Fe, which comes from the Latin word *ferrum,* meaning "iron."

In recent years, scientists have made new elements in the laboratory. Some of these elements have symbols with three letters. You can see the symbols for these elements in the table on pages 86 and 87.

Self-Check

1. How are all of the element symbols alike?
2. Write the symbol for each of the following elements.
   a. helium   b. silver   c. carbon   d. chlorine   e. calcium
3. Write the element name for each of the following symbols.
   a. Hg   b. Ne   c. Mn   d. O   e. P

Finding Iron in Your Cereal

Materials

✓ iron-fortified cereal (flakes)

✓ self-sealing sandwich bag

✓ 250-mL beaker

✓ warm water

✓ bar magnet

✓ rubber band

✓ craft stick

✓ white paper

✓ hand lens

Purpose

To observe bits of iron in an iron-fortified cereal

Procedure

1. Copy the data table below on your paper.

Procedure step	Observations
7	
8	
9	

2. Place about a handful of iron-fortified cereal into the sandwich bag. Crush the cereal into a fine powder.

3. Place the cereal into the beaker. Add just enough water to cover the cereal.

4. Use the rubber band to attach the bar magnet to the craft stick.

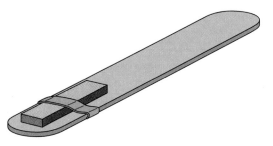

5. Use the magnet end of the stick to stir the cereal-water mixture for about 3 minutes. Allow the magnet to stay in the mixture for about 10 minutes. Then stir again.

6. Remove the stick and the magnet from the mixture and hold them over a sheet of white paper.

7. Use a hand lens to look at the end of the magnet. Write your observations in the data table.

8. Wipe the end of the magnet onto the white paper. Use a hand lens to look at any bits that are on the paper. Write your observations in the data table.

9. Use the magnet to try to pick up bits from the paper. Record your observations.

Questions

1. What did you observe on the end of the magnet?

2. What did you observe on the white paper?

3. Were the bits on the white paper attracted to the magnet?

4. What element from the cereal did you see?

Explore Further

Why might iron be added to cereal? Use an encyclopedia or other reference source to find out.

Periodic table

An arrangement of elements by increasing atomic number.

For many years, scientists noticed that some elements were similar to others. In the mid-1800s, a Russian scientist named Mendeleev designed the first chart that showed some of the similarities among the elements.

How Elements Are Arranged

Mendeleev began by making cards for each element known at that time. Then he organized the elements in order of increasing mass. He placed hydrogen, the lightest element, first. Mendeleev then used the cards to construct a table with rows and columns that organized the elements according to their properties. The cards formed the first **periodic table.**

Mendeleev left blank spaces in his table where he thought an element should fit—even for elements that he didn't know existed. When these elements were later discovered, his unknown elements were found to be in the correct spaces in the table.

The form of Mendeleev's table changed over the years as scientists learned more about atoms. Scientists found that an element's properties are related more closely to its atomic number than to its mass. (Remember that the atomic number of an element tells you the number of protons in its nucleus.) The periodic table used today is an orderly arrangement of all known elements. The elements are arranged according to their atomic number.

Look at the periodic table shown on pages 86 and 87. Notice that elements are arranged from left to right in rows by increasing atomic number. The two separate rows at the bottom of the page are too long to fit into the drawing. Arrows show where the rows belong.

Information in the Periodic Table

You can use the periodic table to learn more about the elements. Each box in the periodic table contains information about one element. The figure below shows the box from the periodic table for the element hydrogen. The symbol for hydrogen, H, is shown in the center of the box. Below the symbol, you can see the name of the element hydrogen.

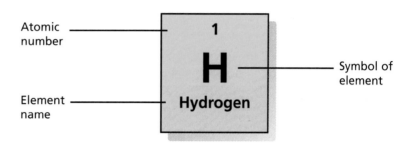

You already learned that the atomic number for hydrogen is 1. Find the atomic number in the box. You can see that the atomic number is shown above the symbol for the element.

The position of an element in the periodic table can tell you many properties of the element. The properties of elements change gradually as you move from left to right across the rows of the table. The properties change because the number of electrons that an atom of an element has increases as you move from left to right. Electrons move around the nucleus of an atom. The number of electrons that surround the nucleus of an atom determines the element's properties. Later in this chapter, you will learn how to determine some properties of an element from its position in the periodic table.

The Periodic Table

Metals

Nonmetals

Noble gases

1	2		3	4	5	6	7	8	9
1 **1** **H** Hydrogen 1.01									
2 **3** **Li** Lithium 6.94	**4** **Be** Beryllium 9.01								
3 **11** **Na** Sodium 22.99	**12** **Mg** Magnesium 24.30								
4 **19** **K** Potassium 39.10	**20** **Ca** Calcium 40.08	**21** **Sc** Scandium 44.96	**22** **Ti** Titanium 47.90	**23** **V** Vanadium 50.94	**24** **Cr** Chromium 52.00	**25** **Mn** Manganese 54.94	**26** **Fe** Iron 55.85	**27** **Co** Cobalt 58.93
5 **37** **Rb** Rubidium 85.47	**38** **Sr** Strontium 87.62	**39** **Y** Yttrium 88.91	**40** **Zr** Zirconium 91.22	**41** **Nb** Niobium 92.91	**42** **Mo** Molybdenum 95.94	**43** **Tc** Technetium 98.91	**44** **Ru** Ruthenium 101.07	**45** **Rh** Rhodium 102.91
6 **55** **Cs** Cesium 132.91	**56** **Ba** Barium 137.33	**71** **Lu** Lutelium 174.97	**72** **Hf** Hafnium 178.49	**73** **Ta** Tantalum 180.95	**74** **W** Tungsten 183.85	**75** **Re** Rhenium 186.21	**76** **Os** Osmium 190.20	**77** **Ir** Iridium 192.22
7 **87** **Fr** Francium 223	**88** **Ra** Radium 226.02	**103** **Lr** Lawrencium 260	**104** **Unq** Unnilquadium 261	**105** **Unp** Unnilpentium 262	**106** **Unh** Unnilhexium 263	**107** **Uns** Unnilseptium 264	**108** **Uno** Unniloctium 265	**109** **Une** Unnilennium 266

6	57 **La** Lanthanum 138.91	58 **Ce** Cerium 140.12	59 **Pr** Praseodymium 140.91	60 **Nd** Neodymium 144.24	61 **Pm** Promethium 145	62 **Sm** Samarium 150.40	63 **Eu** Europium 151.96
7	89 **Ac** Actinium 227	90 **Th** Thorium 232.04	91 **Pa** Protoactinium 231.04	92 **U** Uranium 238.03	93 **Np** Neptunium 237.05	94 **Pu** Plutonium 244	95 **Am** Americium 243.13

# of Elements

			13	14	15	16	17	18
								2 **He** Helium 4.00
			5 **B** Boron 10.81	6 **C** Carbon 12.01	7 **N** Nitrogen 14.01	8 **O** Oxygen 16.00	9 **F** Fluorine 19.00	10 **Ne** Neon 20.17
			13 **Al** Aluminum 26.98	14 **Si** Silicon 28.09	15 **P** Phosphorus 30.97	16 **S** Sulfur 32.06	17 **Cl** Chlorine 35.45	18 **Ar** Argon 39.95
10	11	12						
28 **Ni** Nickel 58.70	29 **Cu** Copper 63.55	30 **Zn** Zinc 65.38	31 **Ga** Gallium 69.74	32 **Ge** Germanium 72.59	33 **As** Arsenic 74.92	34 **Se** Selenium 78.96	35 **Br** Bromine 79.90	36 **Kr** Krypton 83.80
46 **Pd** Palladium 106.42	47 **Ag** Silver 107.87	48 **Cd** Cadmium 112.41	49 **In** Indium 114.82	50 **Sn** Tin 118.69	51 **Sb** Antimony 121.75	52 **Te** Tellurium 127.60	53 **I** Iodine 126.90	54 **Xe** Xenon 131.30
78 **Pt** Platinum 195.09	79 **Au** Gold 196.97	80 **Hg** Mercury 200.59	81 **Tl** Thallium 204.37	82 **Pb** Lead 207.20	83 **Bi** Bismuth 208.98	84 **Po** Polonium 209	85 **At** Astatine 210	86 **Rn** Radon 222

64 **Gd** Gadolinium 157.25	65 **Tb** Terbium 158.93	66 **Dy** Dysprosium 162.50	67 **Ho** Holmium 164.93	68 **Er** Erbium 167.26	69 **Tm** Thulium 168.93	70 **Yb** Ytterbium 173.04
96 **Cm** Curium 247	97 **Bk** Berkelium 247	98 **Cf** Californium 251	99 **Es** Einsteinium 254	100 **Fm** Fermium 257	101 **Md** Mendelevium 258	102 **No** Nobelium 259

Isotopes

Remember that all atoms of one element have the same atomic number. The atomic number tells the number of protons in the nucleus. However, different atoms of one element may have different masses. The reason for this is that almost every element can be found in slightly different forms, which are called **isotopes.** An isotope has the same number of protons and electrons as the original element, but has a different number of neutrons in the nucleus.

The drawings below show three isotopes of hydrogen. The first drawing shows the most common isotope of hydrogen. This isotope has one proton and no neutrons. The second drawing shows **deuterium,** an isotope of hydrogen that has one proton and one neutron. The third drawing shows **tritium,** an isotope of hydrogen that has one proton and two neutrons. Tritium does not occur naturally on Earth. It is made in a laboratory. Remember that each isotope of hydrogen has the same number of protons and therefore the same atomic number.

Isotopes have many uses. In medicine, isotopes can be used to find problems with the organs in your body. Scientists use isotopes to follow the path of certain substances in living things. Another use of isotopes is to find cracks in underderground plumbing pipes.

Isotope
One of a group of atoms of an element with the same number of protons but different numbers of neutrons.

Deuterium
An isotope of hydrogen that has one proton and one neutron.

Tritium
An isotope of hydrogen that has one proton and two neutrons.

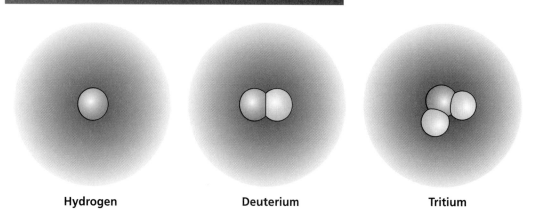

Hydrogen has three isotopes.

Hydrogen   Deuterium   Tritium

Atomic Mass

An element's mass number is the sum of its numbers of protons and neutrons. The sum of the numbers of protons and neutrons is different for hydrogen, deuterium, and tritium. Therefore, each isotope of hydrogen has a different mass number. What is the mass number of each isotope?

Isotopes of most elements do not have names and are identified by their atomic mass. For example, carbon has three isotopes. The most common isotope has a mass number of 12 because it has 6 protons and 6 neutrons. This isotope is called carbon-12. Another isotope of carbon is carbon-13, which has 6 protons and 7 neutrons. Carbon-14 has 6 protons and 8 neutrons.

Look at the box for hydrogen shown below. How does it differ from the box shown on page 85? An additional number appears at the bottom of the box. Notice that the number is not a whole number. This number is the element's **atomic mass,** the average mass for all the isotopes of the element. The average mass is determined by the masses of an element's isotopes and by the amount of each isotope found in nature.

Atomic mass

The average mass of all the isotopes of a particular element.

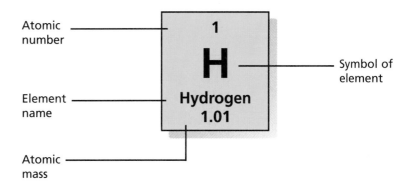

Atomic number

Symbol of element

Element name

1

H

Hydrogen
1.01

Atomic mass

Columns in the Periodic Table

Look at the periodic table shown on pages 86 and 87. You learned that the elements in the periodic table are arranged across in order of increasing atomic numbers. You can also read the periodic table another way—in columns from top to bottom.

Elements that are together in a column are said to be in the same **family.** They have similar properties. In other words, elements in the same family usually react with other kinds of matter in the same way.

Part of the first column from the periodic table is shown on this page. It shows the elements lithium, sodium, and potassium. Now find these three elements in the first column, or Group 1 column, of the periodic table on pages 86 and 87. The elements in Group 1, with the exception of hydrogen, are solids at room temperature. They are soft, shiny, and silvery. These elements react strongly when combined with water, exploding and releasing large amounts of heat.

Now look at the elements in Group 2, or column 2, of the periodic table on pages 86 and 87. The elements in this family are found in minerals in the earth. Magnesium and calcium are the most common elements in this group.

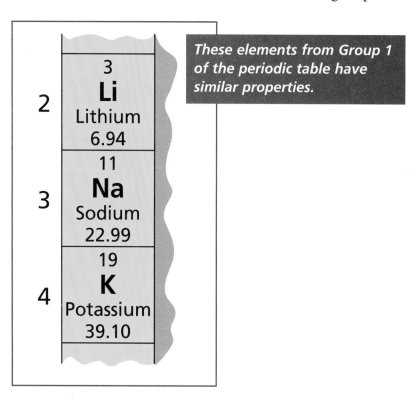

These elements from Group 1 of the periodic table have similar properties.

Look for other families in the periodic table. Fluorine and chlorine—both in Group 17—are poisonous gases. Helium, neon, and argon—elements in Group 18—are all gases that do not usually combine with any other kinds of matter. You will read more about this group of elements in Lesson 3.

As you read the rest of this chapter, continue to refer to the periodic table on pages 86 and 87. You will learn how the periodic table can give you even more information about different elements.

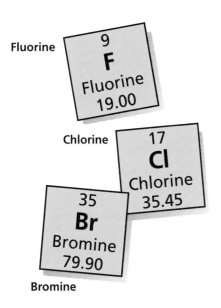

Fluorine

| 9 |
| **F** |
| Fluorine |
| 19.00 |

Chlorine

| 17 |
| **Cl** |
| Chlorine |
| 35.45 |

| 35 |
| **Br** |
| Bromine |
| 79.90 |

Bromine

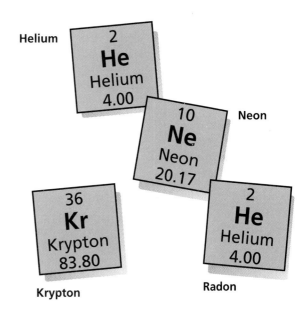

Helium

| 2 |
| **He** |
| Helium |
| 4.00 |

| 10 |
| **Ne** |
| Neon |
| 20.17 |

Neon

| 36 |
| **Kr** |
| Krypton |
| 83.80 |

| 2 |
| **He** |
| Helium |
| 4.00 |

Krypton

Radon

Self-Check

1. How are the elements arranged in the periodic table?

2. Draw the box from the periodic table for hydrogen. Include the symbol for hydrogen as well as its atomic number and atomic mass. Write sentences to explain each piece of information in the box.

3. Explain how elements are grouped in columns in the periodic table.

What Are Metals, Nonmetals, and Noble Gases?

Metal

One of a group of elements that is usually solid at room temperature, often shiny, and carries heat and electricity well.

You have learned about some ways the periodic table provides information about elements. An element's position on the table also tells you whether the element is a metal, a nonmetal, or a noble gas. As you read this lesson, you will find out about each of these three groups.

Metals

Look again at the periodic table on pages 86 and 87. Find the zigzag line near the right side of the chart. Find the elements shown in the green boxes to the left of the zigzag line. These elements are **metals,** a group of elements that share the following properties.

■ Most metals are solid at room temperature. In fact, mercury is the only liquid metal.

■ Most metals can be polished to look shiny.

■ The shape of a metal can be changed. For example, aluminum can be pounded into a thin foil without being broken. Copper is often stretched into very thin wires.

■ Electricity and heat travel well through metals.

Look at the figures on this page. Tell how each figure illustrates one of the properties of metals.

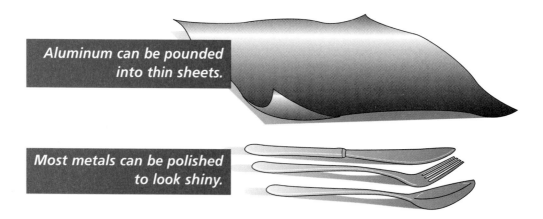

Aluminum can be pounded into thin sheets.

Most metals can be polished to look shiny.

Notice that hydrogen is the only element on the left side of the periodic table that is not considered a metal. As you can see, about 80 percent of all the elements are metals.

Alloys

Heat can be used to change metals into liquids. Melted metals can be combined with other metals. The mixture is cooled until it hardens. In this way, **alloys,** or mixtures of metals, are formed. Alloys have a combination of the properties of the different metals. The table on this page lists some common alloys, the metals that can be combined to form them, and some of their uses.

Alloy

A mixture of two or more metals.

Metal Alloys		
Alloy	Made from	Used for
alnico	aluminum (Al), nickel (Ni), cobalt (Co), iron (Fe), copper (Cu)	magnets
brass	copper (Cu), zinc (Zn)	plumbing fixtures, musical instruments, artwork
bronze	copper (Cu), tin (Sn)	coins, artwork
pewter	copper (Cu), lead (Pb), antimony (Sb), tin (Sn)	trays, pitchers, vases
solder	lead (Pb), tin (Sn)	electrical connections, plumbing connections
stainless steel	iron (Fe), chromium (Cr), nickel (Ni)	eating utensils, kitchen equipment, surgical equipment

Nonmetals

Look again at the periodic table on pages 86 and 87. Find the elements shown in the yellow boxes on the right side of the table. These elements, called **nonmetals,** are elements that do not have the properties of metals.

Most nonmetals are solids or gases at room temperature. Sulfur and carbon are examples of solid nonmetals. You probably know about some of the nonmetal elements that are gases, such as oxygen and nitrogen. Notice on the circle graph below that these two gases make up most of the air. Bromine is the only nonmetal that is liquid at room temperature.

Many metals look somewhat similar. Nonmetals, however, can look very different from one another. For example, oxygen is a colorless gas, while sulfur is a yellow solid.

You can see that nonmetals do not have many properties in common. In fact, the only thing that many nonmetals have in common is that they are not metals. Nonmetals are not shiny. They cannot be pounded into thin sheets or stretched into wires. Except for some forms of carbon and silicon, nonmetals do not carry electricity or heat well. You can learn more about some nonmetals when you read the Science in Your Life feature on the next page.

Nonmetal

One of a group of elements with properties opposite to those of metals.

Did You Know?

Nitrogen and phosphorus are very important to living things. Plants need materials containing these two nonmetals in order to grow. In fact, nitrogen and phosphorus are two of the most important ingredients in fertilizers used in farming.

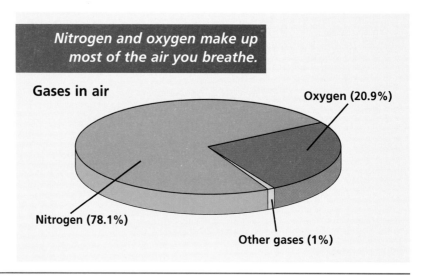

Nitrogen and oxygen make up most of the air you breathe.

Gases in air

Oxygen (20.9%)

Nitrogen (78.1%)

Other gases (1%)

A few elements have some properties of both metals and nonmetals. These elements include silicon, germanium, boron, arsenic, antimony, tellurium, and polonium. You can find these elements next to the zigzag line in the periodic table that separates metals from nonmetals.

When some of these elements are combined with other materials, their ability to carry electricity is increased. This ability makes elements such as silicon useful for electronic devices like the computer.

SCIENCE IN YOUR LIFE

Nonmetals

Look around your classroom. Many of the objects you see contain nonmetal elements. For example, a desk or a chair made of wood contains carbon. Now think of other objects you see or read about in the world around you. You might be surprised to learn how many of them contain nonmetals. The table below lists a few nonmetal elements and gives some of their uses.

Name and symbol	Some uses
carbon, C	pencils, fabrics, cleaning agents, fuel, tires
chlorine, Cl	water purification, bleaching, plastics, dyes, refrigerator coolant
fluorine, Fl	etching glass, refrigerator coolant, toothpaste additive, non-stick coating for pots
iodine, I	ink pigments, disinfectants, halogen lights, ingredient in iodized salt
nitrogen, N	fertilizers, present in air
oxygen, O	present in air, needed for breathing, medical treatments, steelmaking, propellants
sulfur, S	medicines, matches, rubber, dyes, fungicides, cements

Noble Gases

The six elements listed in the last column of the periodic table are called the **noble gases.** These gases are **inert,** which means that they do not react or combine with any other elements under ordinary conditions. Look at Group 18 in the periodic table on pages 86 and 87 to find the names of all the noble gases.

Neon is one noble gas that may be familiar to you. Neon is a gas used for lights such as the ones shown on this page. The neon is sealed in tubes. When electricity is passed through the gas, neon gives off colored light.

Neon gas makes these signs glow.

Self-Check

1. Describe the properties of metals.
2. Explain what a nonmetal is and give some examples of nonmetals.
3. Explain what a noble gas is.

INVESTIGATION

4-2

Electricity and Metals

Materials

✓ safety goggles

✓ sample of sulfur

✓ piece aluminum foil, about 5 cm long

✓ sandpaper

✓ 3 pieces copper wire, each 0.25 m long

✓ electrical tape

✓ 1.5 volt D-cell battery

✓ light bulb in socket

Purpose
To determine which materials carry electricity

Procedure
1. Copy the data table below on your paper.

	Observations
copper wires	
sulfur	
aluminum	

2. Put on your safety goggles.

3. Use sandpaper to remove 3 cm of the insulating coating from each end of the copper wires.
Safety Alert: The ends of the wire can be sharp. Handle them carefully.

4. Make a loop at the ends of each wire.

5. Using electrical tape, fasten a loop from one wire to the flat end of the battery.

6. Fasten the other loop of the wire to the light bulb socket.

7. Tape a loop from the second wire to the other end of the battery.

8. Fasten a loop of the third wire to the other side of the light bulb socket. Your circuit should look like the one in the diagram.

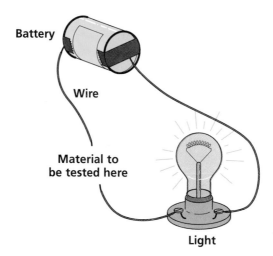

Battery

Wire

Material to be tested here

Light

9. Hold the two unattached loops of copper wire together. Record your observations.

10. Hold the sample of sulfur between the two unattached loops of wire. Record your observations.

11. Repeat step 10 with the sample of aluminum.

Questions

1. What happened to the light bulb when you held the copper wires together?

2. What happened to the light bulb when you held the samples of sulfur and aluminum between the wires?

3. What did you observe about the ability of copper, sulfur, and aluminum to carry electricity?

4. Which materials do you think are metals? Why?

- Each element has a symbol, an abbreviation for its name.

- All known elements are arranged on the periodic table in order of increasing atomic number.

- Information contained in the periodic table about an element includes its name, its symbol, its atomic number, and its atomic mass.

- Almost every element has isotopes, which are different forms of the same element.

- An isotope of an element has the same numbers of protons and electrons as the original element; however, an isotope has a different number of neutrons.

- The atomic mass of an element is an average mass of the various isotopes of the element that exist in nature.

- Elements that have similar properties and are together in a column of the periodic table are in the same family.

- Elements are classified as metals, nonmetals, or noble gases.

- Most metals are solids at room temperature and can be polished. The shape of a metal can be changed, and electricity and heat travel well through metals.

- Metals can be melted and mixed with other metals to form alloys.

- Nonmetals have properties that are different from those of metals. Most nonmetals are solids or gases at room temperature. Most nonmetals have the opposite properties of metals.

- Noble gases are called inert because they do not ordinarily react or combine with other elements.

Science Words		
alloy, 93	metal, 92
atomic mass, 89	noble gas, 96
deuterium, 88	nonmetal, 94
family, 90	periodic table, 84
inert, 96	symbol, 80
isotope, 88	tritium, 88

Vocabulary Review

Number your paper from 1 to 6. Match each word in Column A with the correct definition in Column B. Write the letter of the definition on your paper.

Column A	Column B
_____ 1. symbol	a. average mass for all the isotopes of an element
_____ 2. nonmetal	b. does not combine with other elements
_____ 3. inert	c. abbreviation for an element
_____ 4. alloy	d. formed from melted metals that are mixed together
_____ 5. atomic mass	e. element that does not have the properties of a metal
_____ 6. family	f. elements together in a column of the periodic table

Concept Review

Number your paper from 1 to 8. Then choose the word or words from the Word Bank that best complete each sentence. Write the answer on your paper.

WORD BANK

atomic number

hydrogen

isotope

metals

noble gases

nonmetals

periodic table

tritium

1. The letter H is the symbol for _____.

2. Information about each element is provided in its box in the _____.

3. A(n) _____ is a different form of the same element.

4. Most _____ do not carry electricity well.

5. One isotope of hydrogen is _____.

6. Elements are arranged in the periodic table in order of increasing _____.

7. The six elements listed in the last column of the periodic table are called _____.

8. Most _____ can be polished to look shiny.

Critical Thinking

Write the answer to each of the following questions.

Use the figure from the periodic table shown to answer questions 1 to 4 .

1. What is the name of the element?

2. What is its symbol?

3. What is its atomic number?

4. What is its atomic mass?

5. Why is oxygen classified as a nonmetal instead of a metal?

6. Carbon has an atomic number of 6. How are two carbon atoms with mass numbers 12 and 14 different from each other? What are these atoms called?

Test Taking Tip Take time to organize your thoughts before writing answers to short-answer questions.

Compounds

Perhaps you have seen a fireworks display similar to the one in the photograph. Thousands of years ago, the Chinese combined different elements to make the first fireworks. Today a variety of compounds are used to produce the brilliant colors in fireworks displays. In this chapter, you will find out how different elements are combined to form compounds. You also will learn how some compounds are classified.

ORGANIZE YOUR THOUGHTS

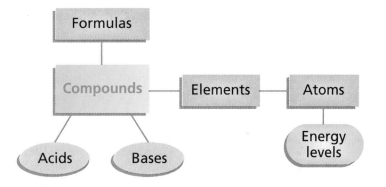

Goals for Learning

▶ To describe compounds
▶ To explain how compounds are formed
▶ To explain what the information in a formula means
▶ To explain how compounds are named
▶ To classify some compounds as acids or bases

What Are Some Characteristics of Compounds?

Only about 90 different elements combine in various ways to form the millions of different compounds you see around you. Do these millions of compounds have any common characteristics? How do these compounds form?

Compounds and Chemical Changes

You learned in Chapter 3 that two or more elements combine to form a compound. For example, hydrogen gas combines with oxygen gas to form the liquid compound water. Water has properties that are different from the elements that form it.

Chemical change

A change that produces one or more substances that differ from the original substances.

When atoms of elements combine to form a compound, a **chemical change** takes place. A chemical change produces new substances with new properties. A chemical change takes place when hydrogen and oxygen combine to form water.

The drawing illustrates another example of a chemical change. As the wood burns, it changes to gases and ash. The ash is a soft, gray powder that cannot burn. Wood and ash are different substances and have different properties.

A chemical change takes place when wood burns.

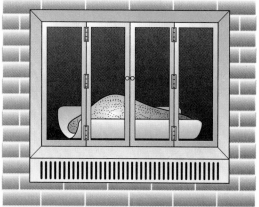

Now think about taking a similar piece of wood and chopping it into tiny pieces. Does a chemical change take place when this happens? Ask yourself if the pieces of wood have properties that are different from the original piece of wood. In this case, they do not. Each small piece is still wood. The pieces just have different sizes and shapes. Changes like this are called **physical changes.** A physical change is a change in which the appearance of a substance changes but the properties stay the same. In a physical change, no new substances are formed.

Characteristics of Compounds

Although there are millions of compounds, they all share some basic characteristics. Any particular compound always contains the same elements. For example, the elements that make up water—hydrogen and oxygen—are always the same. The water can be from a faucet, a river, or a puddle in the road.

Another characteristic of compounds is that the atoms in a particular compound always combine in the same numbers. A molecule of water always contains two hydrogen atoms and one oxygen atom. If you change the molecule by adding another oxygen atom, the compound is no longer water. It becomes hydrogen peroxide, the clear liquid that people can use to clean cuts and other wounds to the skin. Water and hydrogen peroxide are different substances with different properties.

Physical change

A change in which the appearance of a substance changes but the properties stay the same.

Self-Check

Copy the table on a sheet of paper. Identify each change as a chemical change or a physical change. Tell how you know. (*Remember:* In a chemical change, the properties are different after the change.)

Change	Chemical or physical?	How do you know?
melting ice cream		
rusting a nail		
chopping onions		
baking a cake		

INVESTIGATION

Observing a Chemical Change

Materials

✓ safety goggles
✓ 2 small jars with lids
✓ distilled water
✓ 2 plastic spoons
✓ washing soda
✓ Epsom salts
✓ clock

Purpose
To observe physical and chemical changes

Procedure
1. Copy the data table below on your paper.

	Appearance
washing soda in water	
Epsom salts in water	
washing soda and Epsom salts in water	

2. Put on your safety goggles.

3. Fill each jar about halfway with distilled water.

4. Add a spoonful of washing soda to one jar. Place the lid on the jar and shake for about 30 seconds. Record your observations.

5. Use a clean spoon to add a spoonful of Epsom salts to the second jar. Place the lid on the jar and shake for about 30 seconds. Record your observations.

6. Carefully pour the contents of one jar into the other jar. Observe for 5 minutes. Record the results.

Questions

1. What happened when you added the washing soda to water?

2. What happened when you added the Epsom salts to water?

3. What did you observe when you mixed the contents of the jars together in step 6?

4. Did a chemical change or a physical change take place in steps 4 and 5? Explain your answer.

5. Did a chemical change or a physical change take place in step 6? Explain your answer.

Explore Further

Place a small amount of vinegar in a soft-drink bottle. Add a small amount of baking soda. Immediately cover the mouth of the bottle with a balloon. What do you observe happening? Has a chemical change taken place? Explain.

After reading this lesson, you should be able to

- ▶ describe how electrons in an atom are arranged.
- ▶ explain how electrons fill the energy levels.
- ▶ explain how atoms combine to form compounds.
- ▶ explain how ions form chemical bonds.

Energy level

One of the spaces around the nucleus of an atom in which an electron moves.

You now know that compounds form when chemical changes occur. But how do the atoms of elements combine to form compounds? Electrons play an important part when compounds combine. Reviewing the structure of an atom can help you understand how this happens.

Arrangement of Electrons in an Atom

Electrons in an atom move around the nucleus. Each electron moves in its own space a certain distance from the nucleus. This space is called the **energy level.** Within each energy level, electrons may move in all directions.

Compare the drawing of the onion with the model of the atom below. Each energy level of an atom is somewhat like a layer of the onion. Notice that each energy level is labeled with a letter. Level K is closest to the nucleus and is the smallest. Electrons that have the most effect on the properties of an element are those in the outer energy levels. Level O is farthest from the nucleus.

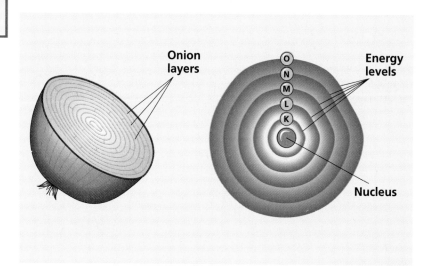

Onion layers · Energy levels · Nucleus

Each energy level can hold only a certain number of electrons. Look at the models of the hydrogen and helium atoms below. The one electron in a hydrogen atom moves around in the first level, called level K. The two electrons in helium also move at level K. Two electrons are the limit for level K.

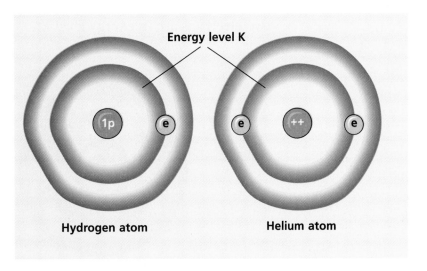

Hydrogen atom   Helium atom

The table shows how many electrons each energy level can hold. Notice that the levels farther from the nucleus can hold more electrons than the levels closer to the nucleus.

Energy levels in an atom

Name	Number of electrons when filled
K	2
L	8
M	18
N	32
O	50

How Electrons Fill Energy Levels

The electrons fill the energy levels in order. Level K is the level closest to the nucleus. It is filled first. Then the second level, level L, is filled. This goes on until all the electrons are in place. For example, the element magnesium has 12 electrons. Notice in the figure that two of these electrons fill level K. Eight more electrons fill level L. The remaining two electrons are in energy level M.

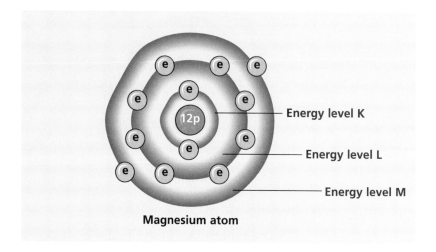

Magnesium atom

Different elements will have electrons in different numbers of levels. Helium has fewer electrons than magnesium. Helium has only two electrons. It will have electrons only in level K. But elements with more electrons will fill more levels. For example, chlorine has 17 electrons. It will have the following.

2 electrons in level K

8 electrons in level L

7 electrons in level M

Level M will not be full because it can hold more than the 7 electrons that it has. Level M can hold as many as 18 electrons. You can see the chlorine atom on the next page.

How Atoms Combine

You learned that compounds form when the atoms of elements combine. Exactly how do the atoms of different elements join together? When atoms form compounds, they share, lend, or borrow electrons that are in their outermost energy level.

An atom has a tendency to fill its outer energy level. An atom becomes more stable when its outermost energy level is filled. Atoms share, lend, or borrow electrons to fill each atom's outer energy level.

Look at the models of atoms in the figures below. Sodium has 11 electrons. Notice that only one of its electrons is in the outer energy level. Sodium tends to lose one electron to another atom to become stable. By losing an electron, the outer level—level L—will have 8 electrons. It will have the most electrons it can hold. On the other hand, the chlorine atom has 7 electrons in its outer energy level—level L. Level L can hold 8 electrons. The chlorine will become more stable if it gains or borrows one electron.

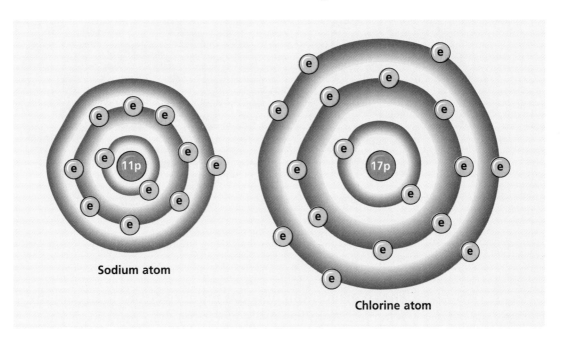

Sodium atom

Chlorine atom

Attraction Between Atoms

Table salt is a familiar compound made from one sodium atom and one chlorine atom. The drawing shows how the sodium atom lends its electron to the chlorine.

Keep in mind that when sodium loses an electron, the number of protons in the nucleus remains the same. As a result, the atom has more protons than electrons. Protons have a positive charge. Electrons have a negative charge. When an atom has equal numbers of electrons and protons, the atom has no charge. But when an atom has more protons than electrons, it has a positive (+) charge.

Look at the drawing. How has the chlorine changed?

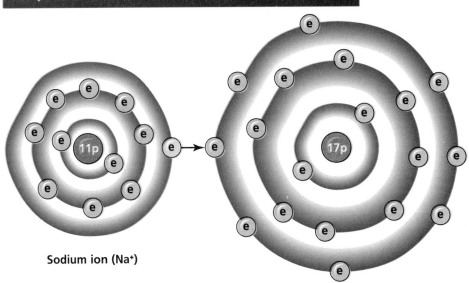

Sodium gives one electron to chlorine to form the compound sodium chloride.

Sodium ion (Na⁺)

Chloride ion (Cl⁻)

The chlorine atom now has more electrons than protons. When an atom has more electrons than protons, it has a negative (−) charge.

Ion

An atom that has either a positive or a negative charge.

Chemical bond

The attractive force that holds atoms together.

An atom that has a charge is called an **ion.** In the sodium chloride example, the chlorine becomes a negative ion. The sodium becomes a positive ion. Positive ions and negative ions strongly attract each other. The diagram shows this attraction between ions. The attractive force between atoms is called a **chemical bond.** The chemical bond between ions keeps the atoms together when they form a compound. For example, a chemical bond keeps sodium and chlorine ions together when they combine to form table salt.

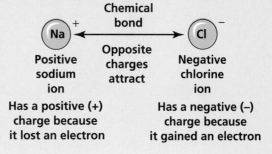

A chemical bond between ions keeps atoms together in a compound.

Chemical bond

Na + ⟵————⟶ **Cl** −

Positive sodium ion

Opposite charges attract

Negative chlorine ion

Has a positive (+) charge because it lost an electron

Has a negative (–) charge because it gained an electron

Self-Check

1. How are electrons arranged around the nucleus of an atom?
2. In what order do electrons fill energy levels?
3. Would an atom with 3 electrons in level M tend to gain or lose electrons? Why? (*Hint:* Use the chart on page 109.)
4. How do atoms of different elements combine?

Objectives

After reading this lesson, you should be able to

▶ explain how to write a chemical formula.

▶ interpret a chemical formula.

▶ explain what a radical is.

▶ give examples of radicals.

Suppose you want to describe a particular beverage such as the one in the drawing. You might tell about its recipe. Notice that the recipe lists all the ingredients. It also tells the amount of each ingredient the drink has.

Recipe

Banana-Strawberry Slush

1 cup sliced bananas
1 cup fresh sliced strawberries
4 mint leaves
1 cup skim milk
1/4 cup crushed ice cubes

Mix all of the ingredients in a blender until slushy. Serve immediately.

You can describe a compound by using the same kind of information you use in a recipe. You can tell what elements form the compound. You can also tell the amount of each element contained in the compound.

Formulas for Compounds

Chemical formula

A way to write the kinds and numbers of atoms in a compound.

Scientists use the symbols for the elements to write a **chemical formula** for each compound. A chemical formula tells what kinds of atoms are in a compound and how many atoms of each kind are present. You know that sodium and chlorine combine to form table salt. The symbol for sodium is Na. The symbol for chlorine is Cl. The chemical formula for table salt is NaCl. The formula shows that sodium and chlorine combine to form table salt.

Scientists use a number called a **subscript** to indicate the number of atoms of each element in a compound. For example, the formula for water is H_2O. The number 2 tells that a water molecule contains two atoms of hydrogen. You can see that the subscript number 2 is smaller than the H and written slightly below the letter.

Notice that no subscript is written after the O. If no subscript number is given after the symbol of an element, the compound has only one atom of that element. The formula H_2O shows that one molecule of water contains three atoms—two of hydrogen and one of oxygen.

Look at the tables to learn the chemical formulas for some other compounds. Read carefully to find out what each formula shows about the compound it represents.

CH_4

Symbol	Element	Subscript	Number of atoms
C	carbon	none	1
H	hydrogen	4	+ 4
			5 Total atoms

$C_{12}H_{22}O_{11}$

Symbol	Element	Subscript	Number of atoms
C	carbon	12	12
H	hydrogen	22	22
O	oxygen	11	+11
			45 Total atoms

Self-Check

Copy the chart on a sheet of paper. Fill in the missing information. Use the periodic table on pages 86 and 87 if you need help naming the elements. The first compound is done for you.

Compound	Symbols	Elements	Subscripts	Number of atoms of each kind
$NaHCO_3$	Na	sodium	none	1
	H	hydrogen	none	1
	C	carbon	none	1
	O	oxygen	3	3
$K_2Cr_2O_7$				
H_2SO_4				
$KClO_3$				

Compounds Containing Radicals

The formulas for some compounds contain groups of two or more atoms that act as if they were one atom. These groups of atoms are called **radicals.** They form compounds by combining with other atoms. During a chemical reaction, the atoms in a radical stay together.

Radical

Group of two or more atoms that acts like one atom.

Household lye is one common substance with a formula that contains a radical. This strong chemical is used to clean drains. The formula for lye is NaOH. The OH is an example of a radical. It contains one atom of oxygen and one atom of hydrogen. The chemical name for this radical is the hydroxyl radical. Other examples of radicals and their names are listed in the table.

Radical	Name
SO_4	sulfate
ClO_3	chlorate
NO_3	nitrate
CO_3	carbonate
PO_4	phosphate
OH	hydroxide

Compounds containing more than one radical are written with the radical in parentheses. A subscript outside of the parentheses tells how many units of the radical are in one molecule of the compound. For example, in the formula $Ba(OH)_2$, the Ba atom combines with two OH radicals as shown in the figure. In $Al(OH)_3$, the Al atom combines with three OH radicals.

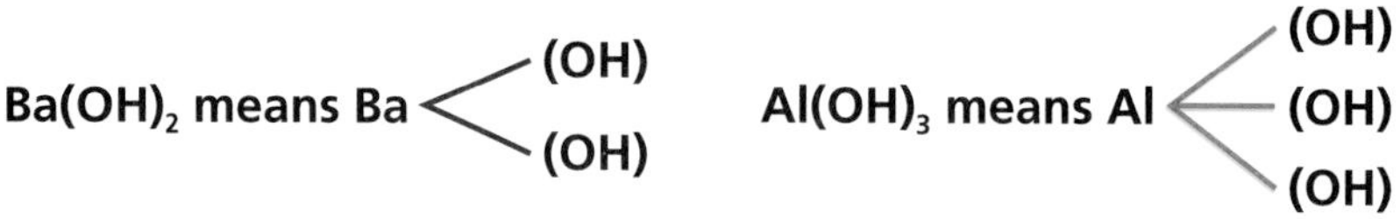

$Ba(OH)_2$ means Ba $<$ (OH) (OH)

$Al(OH)_3$ means Al $\Leftarrow$ (OH) (OH) (OH)

When formulas contain radicals with subscripts, the subscripts multiply the number of atoms inside the parentheses. Examine the first example below. The compound $Ba(NO_3)_2$ is barium nitrate. The nitrate radical is made up of one nitrogen atom and three oxygen atoms. But in barium nitrate, the barium atom combines with *two* nitrate radicals. You can see from the table that the compound has a total of two nitrogen atoms and six oxygen atoms.

$Ba(NO_3)_2$				
Symbol	Element	Subscript	Radical subscript	Number of atoms
Ba	barium	none	not in a radical	1
N	nitrogen	none	2	2 (2×1)
O	oxygen	3	2	$\underline{+6}$ (2×3)
				9 Total atoms

Self-Check

Use the periodic table on pages 86 and 87 to help answer questions 2 and 3.

1. What does a formula tell about a compound?
2. Write a formula for a compound containing one atom of aluminum and three atoms of chlorine.
3. Complete the table for the compound $Al_2(SO_4)_3$.

$Al_2(SO_4)_3$				
Symbol	Element	Subscript	Radical subscript	Number of atoms
Al				
S				
O				$\underline{+}$
				Total atoms

Objectives

After reading this lesson, you should be able to

▶ explain how compounds containing two elements are named.

▶ explain how compounds containing more than two elements are named.

How would you identify yourself to a new acquaintance? You most likely would give your complete name, your first name and your last name. A compound also has a complete name, including a first and last name.

Compounds Containing Two Elements

The name of a compound with two elements combines the names of the elements that form the compound. The number of atoms in the compound is not considered when naming a compound. The following two rules are used to name compounds containing two elements.

■ The first name of a compound is the same as the name of the first element in the compound's formula.

■ The second name of a compound is the name of the second element in the compound's formula with the ending changed to *-ide*. The table shows how names of some elements are written when they are the second elements in a formula.

When naming a compound,

For	Use
chlorine (C)	chloride
iodine (I)	iodide
fluorine (Fl)	fluoride
bromine (Br)	bromide
oxygen (O)	oxide
sulfur (S)	sulfide

You can see how looking at the formula for a compound can help you determine the compound's name. The formula NaCl contains symbols for the elements sodium and chlorine. The first name of the compound is the name of the first element, sodium. Chlorine is changed to chloride to form the second name of the compound. The compound NaCl is named sodium chloride.

Another example is the formula BaO. The first part of the compound's name is the name of the first element, barium. The second element is oxygen. Its name is changed to oxide. The compound name is barium oxide.

Self-Check

Write the names for the following compounds. Use the periodic table on pages 86 and 87 to find the element name for each symbol.

1. $CaBr_2$
2. $AlCl_3$
3. AgI
4. MgO
5. $CaCl_2$

6. BaI_2
7. CaF_2
8. HCl
9. MgS
10. $NaBr$

Compounds Containing More Than Two Elements

A compound that contains more than two elements usually has a radical in its formula. The first name of such a compound is the name of the first element in the formula. The second name of the compound varies according to the radical the formula contains. Review the names for some common radicals in the table on page 116. The subscript numbers in a formula with radicals do not affect the name of the compound.

To find the name of the compound with the formula $Al(OH)_3$, use the name of the first element—aluminum. Then add the name of the OH radical—hydroxide. The name of the compound is aluminum hydroxide.

Identifying radicals accurately is important. The seashells shown on this page contain the compound $CaCO_3$, calcium carbonate. The radical carbonate, CO_3, is listed in the table on page 116. The formula for the compound CO_2 looks similar. However, note that CO_2 has a different subscript—a 2 instead of a 3. In fact, it is the formula for a completely different compound. It is named carbon dioxide, a gas in the air.

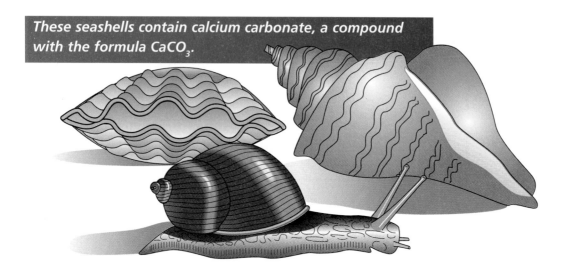

These seashells contain calcium carbonate, a compound with the formula $CaCO_3$.

Self-Check

Write the names for the following compounds. Use the periodic table on pages 86 and 87 to find the element name for each symbol.

1. $Al_2(SO_4)_3$
2. $Ba(OH)_2$
3. $Al(NO_3)_3$
4. K_2CO_3
5. $Mg(OH)_2$
6. $ZnSO_4$

Acid

A compound that reacts with metals to produce hydrogen.

Imagine biting into a lemon. How would it taste? You probably would describe its taste as sour. Then think about a time when you accidentally got soap in your mouth while washing. How did it taste? Soap has a bitter taste. These contrasting tastes, sour and bitter, help illustrate the differences between two groups of substances—acids and bases.

Properties of Acids

What gives a lemon its sour taste? A lemon contains a substance called an **acid.** All acids have the following characteristics.

- All acids taste sour.
- They contain hydrogen.
- They react with metals to produce hydrogen.

Weak acids, such as the citric acid in a lemon, give food a sour, sharp flavor. Vinegar is another familiar substance that contains an acid called acetic acid. The table lists some common acids and tells where they are found.

You can see from the table that you can eat some acids. But other acids are poisonous. Some acids can burn your skin. In fact, even touching a strong acid for a moment can cause a severe burn. You can see why it is wise to never taste or touch an unknown substance.

Common acids		
Name of acid	**Formula**	**Where found**
acetic acid	$HC_2H_3O_2$	vinegar
boric acid	H_3BO_3	eyewashes
carbonic acid	H_2CO_3	rain water, soft drinks
hydrochloric acid	HCl	gastric juice in stomach
citric acid	$H_3C_6H_5O_7$	citrus fruits (oranges, lemons, etc.)
sulfuric acid	H_2SO_4	batteries, acid rain, volcanic smoke

What is acid rain?

Imagine visiting a beautiful lake such as the one in the photograph. You can't wait to get in the water to swim. Maybe you've been thinking about the fish you will catch there. But suppose the water is not safe for swimming. Suppose no fish or plants live there. What has happened? Perhaps the water is polluted.

One cause of water pollution is acid rain. Pollutants in the air from industry and vehicles can combine with water vapor in the air to form harmful acids. These acids fall back to earth in rain or snow.

People first noticed the effects of acid rain in the 1960s. They noticed that fish in some lakes in Europe and North America were dying. Next, they noticed that some forests showed signs of damage. They saw fewer trees and needles shedding or turning yellow.

Some rainfall can contain more acid than vinegar. Some acid rain has 500 times more acid than nonpolluted rain. Acid rain can reduce fish populations in waterways. It can destroy crops and forests. It can remove important nutrients from the soil. Acid rain has eaten away at important statues and buildings.

People can help reduce acid rain. Factories can release fewer pollutants into the air. Driving automobiles less can help reduce acid rain. Scientists are working to solve the problem of acid rain.

Acid rain can turn a healthy lake into a dead lake.

Properties of Bases

Why does soap have such a bitter taste? Soap belongs to a group of compounds called **bases.** All bases have the following characteristics.

- All bases taste bitter.

- They contain the OH radical.

- They feel slippery.

Many common bases are weak, so weak that you can eat them! For example, magnesium hydroxide is a weak base that is used in some medicines. However, strong bases, such as sodium hydroxide, or lye, can cause severe burns. Many bases can be poisonous. The table below lists some common bases and tells where they are found.

Common bases		
Name of base	**Formula**	**Where found**
aluminum hydroxide	$Al(OH)_3$	deodorants, antacids, water purification
magnesium hydroxide	$Mg(OH)_2$	laxatives, antacids
potassium hydroxide	KOH	soap, glass
sodium hydroxide	NaOH	drain cleaner, soap making
calcium hydroxide	$Ca(OH)_2$	mortar

Testing Acids and Bases

Tasting or feeling a substance to determine if it is an acid or a base usually is not safe. But you can use another characteristic of both acids and bases. You can find out how they react to **indicators.** Indicators change color to identify acids or bases. Litmus is a common indicator used in the laboratory. Litmus turns from blue to red in acids. It turns from red to blue in bases. You will be using an indicator in Investigation 5-2.

Some indicators tell you the **pH** of a substance. The pH is a number that tells whether the substance is an acid or a base. Acids have a pH from 0 to 7. Bases have a pH from 7 to 14. Some substances are neither acids nor bases. These substances are said to be neutral. They have a pH of 7. You can see the pH of some common substances in the scale on this page.

You can use indicators to tell how strong an acid or a base is. The lower the pH number of an acid, the stronger the acid is. For example, your stomach produces acid that is very strong. Its pH is 1. Milk is only slightly acidic. Its pH is 6.9. The higher the pH of a base, the stronger the base. Lye has a pH around 13. It is a strong base. Liquid soaps are much weaker bases.

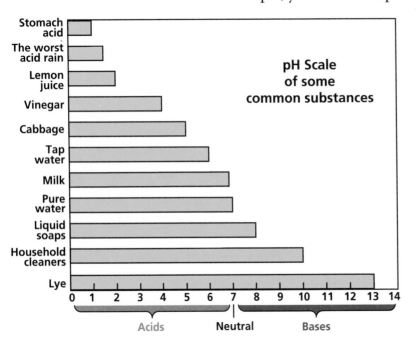

Number a sheet of paper from 1 to 10. Tell whether each of the following is a property of an acid or a base.

1. Tastes sour
2. Is slippery
3. Has a pH of 3
4. Has a pH of 11
5. Contains the OH radical
6. Tastes bitter
7. Turns litmus from red to blue
8. Contains hydrogen
9. Turns litmus from blue to red
10. Reacts with a metal to produce hydrogen

INVESTIGATION

5-2

Identifying Acids and Bases

Materials

✓ safety goggles

✓ 8 small paper cups

✓ marker

✓ baking soda

✓ white vinegar

✓ aspirin tablet

✓ lemon juice

✓ weak ammonia solution

✓ soap

✓ soft drink

✓ milk of magnesia

✓ spoon

✓ graduated cylinder

✓ red-cabbage juice

Purpose

To use an indicator to test for acids and bases

Procedure

1. Copy the data table below on your paper.

Substance	Color after cabbage juice is added	Acid or base
baking soda		base
vinegar		acid
lemon juice		
weak ammonia		
aspirin		
soap		
soft drink		
milk of magnesia		

2. Put on your safety goggles.

3. Use a marker to label each cup with the name of one substance from the table. Use these labels: baking soda (base), vinegar (acid), lemon juice, weak ammonia solution, aspirin, soap, soft drink, and milk of magnesia.

4. Add a small amount of each substance to the cup labeled with its name. Use a spoon to crush the aspirin tablet before adding it to the cup.

5. The cabbage juice will be the acid-base indicator. Record the color of the cabbage juice in the data table.

6. Add 20 mL of cabbage juice to the cup labeled baking soda (base). Stir. Notice the color of the liquid in the cup. Record this color in the data table. Baking soda is a base. Any substance that changes to a color similar to the liquid in the baking soda cup after you add cabbage juice is a base.

7. Add 20 mL of cabbage juice to the vinegar (acid) cup. Record the results in the data table. Vinegar is an acid. Any substance that changes to a color similar to the liquid in the vinegar cup after you add cabbage juice is an acid.

8. Add 20 mL of cabbage juice to each of the remaining cups and stir. Determine whether each cup contains an acid or a base. Record your results.

Questions

1. Which of the substances are acids?

2. Which of the substances are bases?

3. Are some bases stronger than others? Explain your answer.

- A compound forms when two or more elements combine. A chemical change takes place when elements combine to form a compound. In a chemical change, new substances with new properties are formed.

- A physical change is a change in which the appearance of a substance changes but the properties stay the same.

- Molecules of the same compound always contain the same elements. The atoms in the molecules of the same compound always combine in the same numbers.

- An electron moves in a certain energy level around the nucleus of an atom. Each energy level can hold only a certain number of electrons. Electrons fill the energy levels in order.

- Different elements have electrons in different numbers of levels. Atoms share, borrow, or lend electrons to other atoms in order to form compounds.

- An atom that has a charge is called an ion. Ions with opposite charges attract each other.

- A chemical formula is used to show what kinds of atoms and how many atoms of each kind are in a compound.

- A radical is a group of elements that behaves as if it were one element.

- In naming a compound, use the name of the first element and the name of the second element with the ending changed to -*ide*.

- Acids are compounds that contain hydrogen, react with metals to form hydrogen, and have a sour taste.

- Bases are slippery compounds that contain the hydroxyl radical, and have a bitter taste.

- Indicators can be used to test for acids and bases.

Science Words		
acid, 121	indicator, 123
base, 123	ion, 113
chemical bond, 113	pH, 124
chemical change, 104	physical change, 105
chemical formula, 114	radical, 116
energy level, 108	subscript, 115

Vocabulary Review

Number your paper from 1 to 9. Then choose a word or words from the Word Bank that best complete each sentence. Write the answer on your paper.

1. In the formula H_2O, the _____ indicates how many atoms of hydrogen are contained in the compound.

2. When an iron pot becomes rusty, a(n) _____ takes place.

3. The compound sodium hydroxide contains the hydroxyl _____.

4. In the compound sodium chloride, the sodium _____ has a positive charge.

5. A(n) _____ is a compound that contains hydrogen.

6. A(n) _____ holds atoms in a compound together.

7. Each _____ of an atom holds only a certain number of electrons.

8. The _____ for sodium chloride is NaCl.

9. A(n) _____ is a compound that contains the radical OH.

Concept Review

Number your paper from 1 to 9. Then choose the word or words that best complete each sentence. Write the letter of the answer on your paper.

1. The name of the compound MgS is _____.
   a. magnesium sulfide
   b. magnesium sulfate
   c. magnesium sulfur

2. Each electron moves in a certain _____ around the nucleus.
   a. proton
   b. atomic number
   c. energy level

3. An atom that has more protons than electrons has _____.
   a. a negative charge
   b. a positive charge
   c. no charge

4. An atom tends to share, lend, or borrow an electron from its _____ energy level.
   a. outer   b. middle   c. inner

5. A(n) _____ tells what elements and how many atoms of each element are in a compound.
   a. symbol   b. ion   c. formula

6. A molecule of water always contains two hydrogen atoms and _____ oxygen atom(s).
   a. one   b. two   c. three

7. The first energy level to be filled with electrons is _____.
   a. level A   b. level K   c. level M

8. A _____ in a compound remains together when a chemical change takes place.
   a. radical   b. base   c. chemical bond

9. Sodium hydroxide, NaOH, is a(n) _____.
   a. acid   b. ion   c. base

Critical Thinking

Write the answer to each of the following questions.

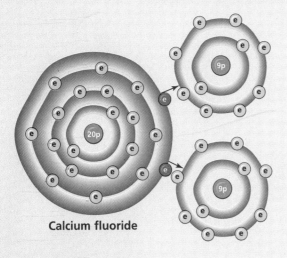

Calcium fluoride

1. Look at this drawing of the atoms in the compound calcium fluoride. Explain what the drawing is illustrating.

2. When you digest food, your body changes the food into nutrients. The nutrients are carried through your bloodstream to your body cells. What type of change happens to the food? Explain your answer.

Test Taking Tip — When answering multiple choice questions, first eliminate those you know are incorrect.

How Matter Changes

Look at the glow of the molten iron ore (Fe_2O_3) going into the blast furnace in the photograph. What is happening to the iron ore? A simple chemical reaction is taking place to produce pure iron (Fe). As you will see in this chapter, when chemical reactions take place, new substances are formed. In this chapter, you will learn about some kinds of chemical reactions.

ORGANIZE YOUR THOUGHTS

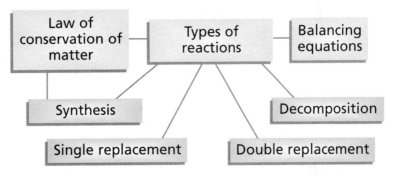

Law of conservation of matter — Types of reactions — Balancing equations

Synthesis

Single replacement

Decomposition

Double replacement

Goals for Learning

▶ To explain what a reaction is

▶ To describe what occurs when something dissolves

▶ To state the law of conservation of matter

▶ To interpret and write balanced chemical equations

▶ To name and explain the four main types of chemical reactions

Objectives

After reading this lesson, you should be able to

▶ explain what a reaction is.

▶ explain the difference between solutions, solutes, and solvents.

Hundreds of years ago, people known as alchemists tried to change different materials into gold. Imagine being able to change iron or lead into solid gold!

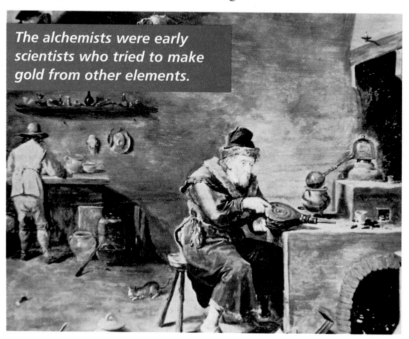

The alchemists were early scientists who tried to make gold from other elements.

Unfortunately for the alchemists, they never succeeded. Today, scientists know that chemically changing one element into another is not possible. But during a chemical change, elements can be combined to form compounds. The elements in compounds can be rearranged to form new compounds. When elements combine or rearrange, they are said to react. The process is called a **chemical reaction.** For some reactions, it is necessary to heat the substances. In other cases, the substances must be mixed with water for a chemical reaction to take place.

Chemical reaction

Chemical change in which elements are combined or rearranged.

Substances do not always react. Many elements and compounds can be mixed together and nothing at all happens. A **mixture** is formed when substances are simply stirred together and no new substance is formed. When you stir sugar and cinnamon together, you form a mixture.

Mixture

A combination of substances in which no reaction takes place.

Dissolve
Break apart.

Solute
The substance that is
dissolved in a
solution.

Solution
A mixture in which
one substance is
dissolved in another.

Solvent
The substance in
which the dissolving
occurs in a solution.

Dissolving

Many reactions take place only when the substances have been **dissolved** in other liquids. To dissolve means to break up substances into individual atoms or molecules. An example of dissolving occurs when sugar is placed in water. The sugar mixes with the water and seems to disappear. But the sugar is still there. The pieces of the sugar have been broken down into tiny particles—molecules.

When a substance is thoroughly dissolved in another, the result is a mixture called a **solution.** The substance that dissolves is called the **solute.** When you dissolve sugar in water, the solute is sugar. The substance in which the dissolving is done is called the **solvent.** In the sugar-water solution, water is the solvent. Can you think of other examples of solutions, solutes, and solvents?

Types of Solutions		
Substance (solute)	Dissolved in (solvent)	Examples
liquid	liquid	alcohol in water
	gas	water vapor in air
	solid	ether in rubber
gas	liquid	club soda in water (CO_2 in water)
	gas	air (nitrogen, oxygen, other gases)
	solid	hydrogen in palladium
solid	liquid	salt in water
	gas	iodine vapor in air
	solid	brass (copper and zinc)

A solution does not always have to be a solid dissolved in a liquid. Solutions can also be formed by dissolving substances in solids and gases. The table gives some examples of solutions.

Self-Check

1. What metal were the alchemists trying to produce? Did they succeed?
2. What are two things a scientist can do to cause some substances that are mixed together to react?
3. Suppose you dissolve salt in water. Name the solvent and the solute.

INVESTIGATION

6-1

Separating a Mixture

Materials

✓ 2 g table salt (sodium chloride, NaCl)
✓ 2 g sand
✓ spoon
✓ sheet of paper
✓ 200 mL water
✓ graduated cylinder
✓ 2 beakers
✓ stirring rod
✓ circular piece of filter paper or paper towel
✓ funnel

Purpose
To use dissolving to separate a mixture

Procedure
1. Copy the data table below on a sheet of paper.

	Observations
salt	
sand	
mixture of salt and sand	
solution of salt, sand, and water	
filter paper	
sides of beaker	

2. Place about one spoonful of sand and one spoonful of salt in separate piles on a sheet of paper. Observe the appearance of the salt and of the sand. Record your observations in the data table.

3. Thoroughly mix the salt with the sand. Describe the resulting mixture. Record your observations.

4. Using a graduated cylinder, measure 200 mL of water. Pour the water into a beaker.

5. Place the salt-sand mixture in the beaker containing the water.

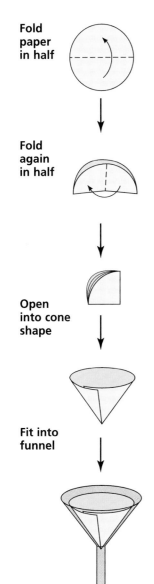

Fold paper in half

Fold again in half

Open into cone shape

Fit into funnel

6. Stir the solution with the stirring rod. Observe the liquid in the beaker. Record your observations.

7. Fold the filter paper and fit it inside the funnel.

8. Hold the funnel over a second beaker. Slowly pour the solution from the first beaker into the funnel. Allow the second beaker to catch the liquid as it passes through the funnel.

9. Observe the filter paper. Record your observations.

10. Let the second beaker and its contents sit in a warm place for several days.

11. After all the liquid has evaporated, observe the sides of the beaker. Record your observations.

Questions

1. In steps 5 and 6, what happens to the salt when the water is added to the mixture?

2. In step 6, does the sand dissolve? How do you know?

3. In step 8, where is the salt after you pour the solution into the second beaker? How do you know?

4. In step 9, which material remains on the filter paper? How do you know?

5. In step 11, what substance forms on the side of the beaker?

6. What is the solvent in this Investigation?

7. What is the solute?

Explore Further

Suppose you had a mixture of iron filings and sugar. How would you separate it? Write a procedure.

Objectives

After reading this lesson, you should be able to

▶ explain how chemical equations describe a chemical reaction.

▶ balance chemical equations.

Chemical equation

A statement that uses symbols, formulas, and numbers to stand for a chemical reaction.

You know that chemical symbols and formulas can be used to represent substances. These symbols can be used to describe reactions as well. A **chemical equation** is a statement that uses symbols, chemical formulas, and numbers to stand for a chemical reaction. You can see an example of a simple chemical equation below. The chemicals involved are described by using their symbols and formulas. Below the equation, you can see the description in words.

Reactants		Products
$HCl + NaOH$	$\rightarrow$	$NaCl + H_2O$

hydrogen chloride plus sodium hydroxide   yields   sodium chloride plus water

Notice that the arrow symbol ($\rightarrow$) stands for "yields" or "makes." The chemicals on the left side of the arrow are called **reactants.** They are the substances that are reacting together. The chemicals on the right side of the arrow are called **products.** They are the substances that form from the reactants. In the above example, HCl and NaOH are the reactants. The products are NaCl and H_2O.

Self-Check

1. Copy the table on a sheet of paper. Then complete the table. The first one is done for you.

Reaction	Reactants	Products
a. $Fe + S \rightarrow FeS$	Fe, S	FeS
b. $H_2SO_4 + Zn \rightarrow ZnSO_4 + H_2$		
c. $Mg + S \rightarrow MgS$		
d. $AgNO_3 + NaCl \rightarrow NaNO_3 + AgCl$		

2. Write the following chemical equations in words.
   a. $Mg + S \rightarrow MgS$
   b. $Ca + O_2 \rightarrow CaO_2$

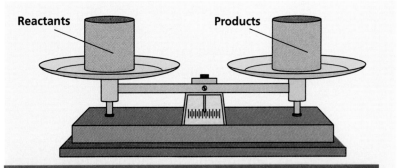

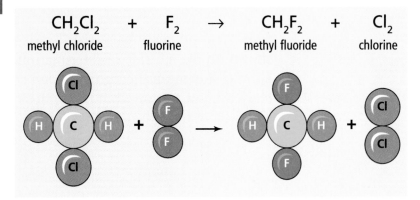

Law of Conservation of Matter

The reactants present *before* a reaction can be quite different from the products present *after* the reaction. But the kinds of atoms do not change during the reaction. Different substances are formed, but the same atoms are there. The atoms are just rearranged. In the reaction below, methyl chloride and fluorine react to form methyl fluoride and chlorine. Notice how the atoms rearrange themselves.

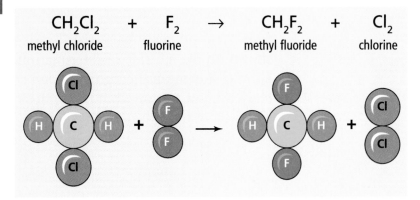

$$CH_2Cl_2 \quad + \quad F_2 \quad \rightarrow \quad CH_2F_2 \quad + \quad Cl_2$$

methyl chloride   fluorine   methyl fluoride   chlorine

The same numbers and kinds of atoms are present before and after a reaction. Mass does not change during the reaction. The mass of the reactants equals the mass of the products. This fact illustrates the **law of conservation of matter.** The law states that matter cannot be created or destroyed in any chemical change. This law is also sometimes called the law of conservation of mass.

Law of conservation of matter

Matter cannot be created or destroyed in any chemical change.

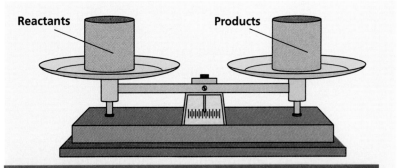

Reactants   Products

The total mass of the reactants in a chemical reaction always equals the total mass of the products.

Balancing Equations

To satisfy the law of conservation of matter, a chemical equation must show the same number of each kind of atom on both sides of the equation. Scientists say that the equation must be **balanced** to keep the number of atoms the same.

Look at the following equation. It shows that hydrogen plus oxygen makes water.

$$H_2 + O_2 \rightarrow H_2O$$

This equation is not balanced. Two oxygen atoms are shown on the left side of the equation. Only 1 oxygen atom is shown on the right. The left side of the equation has a total of 4 atoms, but the right side has only 3 atoms. These facts are summarized below.

$$H_2 + O_2 \qquad \rightarrow \qquad H_2O$$

H 2 atoms	H 2 atoms
O 2 atoms	O 1 atom
Total of 4 atoms	Total of 3 atoms

You can see that there are 4 atoms in the reactants and only 3 in the products. The law of conservation of matter says that atoms do not disappear in chemical reactions. You cannot change the formulas for the reactants or products. How do you balance the equation? To balance an equation means to show the same number of each kind of atom on both sides of the equation.

To make the two sides come out even, you can place numbers called **coefficients** before the formulas. Coefficients multiply the numbers of molecules or other formula units. For example, $2H_2O$ would mean 2 water molecules.

By changing coefficients, the numbers of atoms can be changed. By writing $2H_2O$, you are saying that 4 atoms of hydrogen and 2 atoms of oxygen are in the products. If you write $3H_2O$, you are saying that 6 atoms of hydrogen and 3 atoms of oxygen are in the products.

Balance

To keep the number of atoms the same on both sides of the equation.

Coefficient

A number placed before a formula in a chemical equation.

By placing a 2 in front of the H_2O, you have made the number of oxygen atoms equal on both sides of the equation. But the number of hydrogen atoms is not equal.

$$H_2 + O_2 \rightarrow 2H_2O$$

H 2 atoms	H 4 atoms
O 2 atoms	O 2 atoms
Total of 4 atoms	Total of 6 atoms

You can see that there are 2 hydrogen atoms in the reactants. There are 4 hydrogen atoms in the product. Therefore, you need 2 more hydrogen atoms in the reactants. Again you can change the number of atoms by using a coefficient. You can balance this equation like this.

$$2H_2 + O_2 \rightarrow 2H_2O$$

H 4 atoms	H 4 atoms
O 2 atoms	O 2 atoms
Total of 6 atoms	Total of 6 atoms

The equation is now balanced. The coefficients show that there are 2 molecules each of hydrogen and water. Since the oxygen has no coefficient, it means that there is 1 molecule. The equation tells you that whenever hydrogen and oxygen combine to form water, 2 molecules of hydrogen will combine with 1 molecule of oxygen to produce 2 molecules of water.

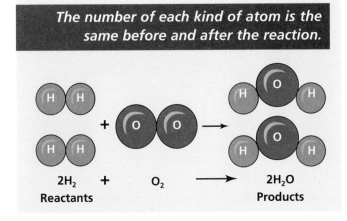

The number of each kind of atom is the same before and after the reaction.

$$2H_2 + O_2 \rightarrow 2H_2O$$
Reactants → Products

Self-Check

Study the following equation. Then answer the questions on a sheet of paper.

$$2Na + Cl_2 \rightarrow 2NaCl$$

1. What are the reactants?
2. What is the product?
3. Is the equation balanced? Explain.

What Are Synthesis and Decomposition Reactions?

There are millions of different chemical reactions that can take place. Even chemists cannot learn all of them. How can you make sense out of all those possibilities? It turns out that most reactions can be grouped into four major types. You will learn about two of these types of reactions in this lesson.

Synthesis Reactions

The first type of reaction is called a **synthesis reaction.** The word *synthesis* means "to combine parts." In a synthesis reaction, two or more elements combine to form a compound. An example of a synthesis reaction is combining iron and sulfur. Iron is a metal used in making steel. Sulfur is a yellow nonmetal that is used in making some medicines. You can see these two elements in the figures below.

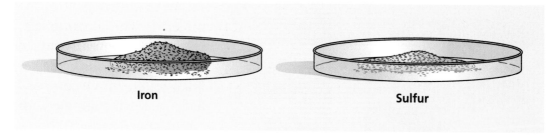

Iron   Sulfur

Suppose you mix iron (in the form of slivers called filings) with sulfur powder. No reaction takes place. The combination of iron and sulfur is an example of a mixture. A mixture is formed when substances are simply stirred together and no new substance is formed.

A mixture keeps the properties of the separate substances. In fact, you could separate the iron and sulfur in the mixture by placing a magnet in the mixture. The iron is attracted to a magnet, but the sulfur is not. The mixture is separated quite easily. The iron is pulled away by the magnet.

A mixture of iron and sulfur can be separated by a magnet.

Now suppose you heat the mixture of iron and sulfur. A reaction will occur. A new compound called iron sulfide (FeS) will form. A compound has been formed from two elements. Therefore, the reaction is a synthesis. Iron sulfide has properties different from those of either iron or sulfur. If a magnet is placed near the iron sulfide, the compound will not be attracted to it. Notice in the photo that the color of iron sulfide is gray-black. The yellow color of sulfur and the silvery color of iron are gone. The properties have changed because a new substance has been formed.

Here is the balanced chemical equation for this synthesis reaction.

Fe	+	S	→	FeS
iron (grey solid)	plus	sulfur (yellow solid)	yields	iron sulfide (grey-black solid)

Decomposition Reactions

Sometimes in a chemical reaction a compound breaks down into two or more simple substances. This type of reaction is called a **decomposition reaction.** For example, sugar is a compound you are familiar with. Its formula is $C_6H_{12}O_6$. When sugar is heated, it is broken down into carbon (C) and water (H_2O). Carbon is a black solid. Water is a compound made of hydrogen and oxygen. The carbon and the water contain the same atoms that were in the sugar. This reaction is shown below.

> **Decomposition reaction**
>
> A reaction in which a compound breaks down into two or more simple substances.

$$C_6H_{12}O_6 \quad \rightarrow \quad 6C \quad + \quad 6H_2O$$

sugar	carbon	water
(white solid)	(black solid)	(colorless liquid)

Another example of a decomposition reaction occurs when the compound mercuric oxide is heated. The chemical equation for the reaction is shown below. The upward arrow ($\uparrow$) after the O_2 indicates that oxygen is a gas that is given off.

$$2HgO \quad \rightarrow \quad 2Hg \quad + \quad O_2\uparrow$$

mercuric oxide	mercury	oxygen

Self-Check

1. Copy the following equations on a sheet of paper. Then tell if each is a synthesis reaction or a decomposition reaction.
   a. $2MgO \rightarrow 2Mg + O_2\uparrow$
   b. $2Hg + O_2 \rightarrow 2HgO$
   c. $C + O_2 \rightarrow CO_2$
   d. $BaCl_2 \rightarrow Ba + Cl_2$
   e. $2H_2O \rightarrow 2H_2 + O_2$

2. Write the products of the following synthesis reactions.
   a. $2Na + Cl_2 \rightarrow$ _____
   b. $Mg + Cl_2 \rightarrow$ _____
   c. $CO + O_2 \rightarrow$ _____

3. Complete the following decomposition reactions.
   a. $CaCO_3 \rightarrow$ _____ $+ CO_2$
   b. $2FeO \rightarrow$ _____ $+ O_2$
   c. $2NaCl \rightarrow$ _____ $+ Cl_2$

What Are Single-Replacement Reactions and Double-Replacement Reactions?

You now know about two kinds of reactions—synthesis reactions and decomposition reactions. Two other kinds of reactions are common.

Single-Replacement Reactions

Look at the photographs below. The photograph on the left shows a container of a silver nitrate solution and a copper wire. The photograph on the right shows what happens if the copper wire is placed in the solution of silver nitrate. Notice the silver metal that forms on the wire. A chemical reaction has taken place. The equation for the reaction is shown below.

$$Cu + 2AgNO_3 \rightarrow 2Ag + Cu(NO_3)_2$$

Notice that copper (Cu) has replaced the silver (Ag) in the silver nitrate. A new compound, copper nitrate—$Cu(NO_3)_2$—is formed. The silver is set free. That is the kind of change that occurs in a **single-replacement reaction.** A single-replacement reaction is a reaction in which one element replaces another in a compound.

Single-replacement reaction

Reaction in which one element replaces another in a compound.

In this single-replacement reaction, the copper replaces the silver.

Double-Replacement Reactions

The fourth kind of chemical reaction is the **double-replacement reaction.** In this kind of reaction, the elements in two compounds are exchanged.

An example of a double-replacement reaction is the reaction between sodium chloride (NaCl) and silver nitrate ($AgNO_3$). The reaction is shown in the following chemical equation.

$$NaCl + AgNO_3 \rightarrow NaNO_3 + AgCl\downarrow$$

Sodium chloride plus silver nitrate has formed two new compounds—sodium nitrate ($NaNO_3$) and silver chloride (AgCl). The elements in the two compounds have exchanged places. That is what makes the reaction a double replacement.

The downward-pointing arrow ($\downarrow$) after the AgCl means that this substance is a solid that forms and settles out of the solution. A solid formed in this way is called a **precipitate.**

The table below summarizes the four kinds of chemical reactions.

Type	General form
Synthesis	A + B $\longrightarrow$ AB
Decomposition	AB $\longrightarrow$ A + B
Single replacement	A + BC $\longrightarrow$ B + AC
Double replacement	AB + CD $\longrightarrow$ AD + CB

1. Identify each of the following reactions as either synthesis, decomposition, single replacement, or double replacement.

   a. $Pb(NO_3)_2 + 2KI \rightarrow 2KNO_3 + PbI_2$

   b. $S + O_2 \rightarrow SO_2$

   c. $BaCl_2 \rightarrow Ba + Cl_2$

   d. $Cl_2 + 2NaBr \rightarrow 2NaCl + Br_2$

   e. $2Fe_2O_3 + 3C \rightarrow 4Fe + 3CO_2$

   f. $CaCO_3 \rightarrow CaO + CO_2$

2. Complete each of the following single-replacement reactions.

   a. $Cu + HgCl \rightarrow$ _____ + _____

   b. $K + NaCl \rightarrow$ _____ + _____

   c. $2NaBr + Cl_2 \rightarrow$ _____ + _____

   d. $Zn + 2HCl \rightarrow$ _____ + _____

   e. $K + NaCl \rightarrow$ _____ + _____

3. Complete each of the the following double-replacement reactions.

   a. $KOH + HBr \rightarrow$ _____ + HOH

   b. $BaCl_2 + Na_2SO_4 \rightarrow$ _____ + _____

   c. $AgNO_3 + NaBr \rightarrow$ _____ + _____

   d. $HCl + NaOH \rightarrow$ _____ + _____

4. What does the downward-pointing arrow ($\downarrow$) mean in the following reaction?

   $BaCl_2 + NaSO_4 \rightarrow BaSO_4\downarrow + 2NaCl$

How does film work?

When you take a photo, you capture an image on film, almost as if by magic. But how does that "magic" really happen? The answer has to do with a chemical reaction.

When you take a picture with a camera, you push the button that releases the shutter. The shutter opens. Light enters the camera and reaches the film.

Film that produces black-and-white photos has a material that is sensitive to light. White silver bromide (AgBr) often is used as the coating. When light hits the silver bromide, it breaks down easily into its elements. These elements are silver and bromine (Ag and Br_2). The silver bromide breaks down only on the areas of the film that light has struck.

When the film is developed, the areas where silver bromide was hit by light turn dark. The rest of the film stays light. The brightest objects photographed look darkest on the film. That is because the brightest objects sent the most light onto the film. The developed film is thus a "negative." It looks the opposite of the original scene. Look at the negative shown below.

The final photo print, also shown below, is made by sending light through the negative. The light hits a special white paper that turns dark in light. The dark parts on the negative send the least light through to the paper. In those areas, the white paper stays light. The negative makes something that is the opposite of itself. The result is an image that resembles the scene that was photographed.

Negative

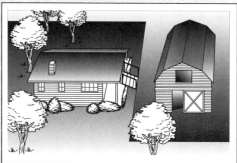

Print of photograph

Observing Different Kinds of Reactions

Materials

- ✓ safety goggles
- ✓ small piece of steel wool
- ✓ tongs
- ✓ Bunsen burner
- ✓ hydrogen peroxide solution (H_2O_2)
- ✓ 4 test tubes
- ✓ test-tube rack
- ✓ manganese dioxide (MnO_2)
- ✓ wooden splint
- ✓ match
- ✓ copper sulfate solution ($CuSO_4$)
- ✓ iron nail
- ✓ sodium carbonate solution (Na_2CO_3)
- ✓ calcium chloride solution ($CaCl_2$)

Purpose

To study the four main types of chemical reactions

Procedure

1. Put on your safety goggles.
2. Copy the data table below on a sheet of paper.

Reaction	Observations
1	
2	
3	
4	

Reaction 1

3. Pick up a small piece of steel wool with a pair of tongs. Use the tongs to touch the steel wool to the flame of the Bunsen burner. *Safety alert: Be careful not to burn yourself.* Record what happens.

Reaction 2

4. Half-fill a test tube with hydrogen peroxide (H_2O_2) solution. Add a tiny piece of manganese dioxide (MnO_2). The manganese dioxide will simply speed up the reaction. It is not a reactant itself. Observe what happens over the next few minutes.

5. Once the reaction is occurring quickly, use a match to light a wooden splint. *Safety alert: Be careful not to burn yourself.* Blow out the splint and immediately insert it into the test tube so that the glowing end is slightly above the liquid level. Record what happens.

Reaction 3

6. Half-fill a test tube with copper sulfate ($CuSO_4$) solution. Gently place an iron nail into the test tube. Record what happens.

Reaction 4

7. Add sodium carbonate (Na_2CO_3) solution to a test tube until it is one-third full.

8. Add calcium chloride ($CaCl_2$) solution to another test tube until it is one-third full.

9. Pour the contents of the second test tube into the first. Record what happens.

Questions

Copy the data table on a sheet of paper. Complete the table.

Reaction	Equation	Type of reaction
1	$4Fe + 3O_2 \rightarrow 2Fe_2O_3$	
2	$2H_2O_2 \rightarrow 2H_2O + O_2$	
3	$Fe + CuSO_4 \rightarrow FeSO_4 + Cu$	
4	$Na_2CO_3 + CaCl_2 \rightarrow 2NaCl + CaCO_3$	

- A chemical reaction involves a change of substances into other substances.

- Reactions can be represented by chemical equations, which should be balanced for atoms.

- The law of conservation of matter states that matter cannot be created or destroyed in any chemical change.

- A combination of materials in which no reaction takes place is called a mixture.

- The four main types of chemical reactions are synthesis $(A + B \rightarrow AB)$, decomposition $(AB \rightarrow A + B)$, single replacement $(A + BC \rightarrow B + AC)$, and double replacement $(AB + CD \rightarrow AD + CB)$.

- In a synthesis reaction, elements combine to form a compound.

- In a decomposition reaction, a compound breaks down into simpler substances.

- In a single-replacement reaction, one element replaces another in a compound.

- In a double-replacement reaction, elements in two compounds are exchanged.

Science Words	
balance, 138	mixture, 132
chemical equation, 136	precipitate, 144
chemical reaction, 132	product, 137
coefficient, 138	reactant, 137
decomposition reaction, 142	single-replacement reaction, 143
dissolve, 133	solute, 133
double-replacement reaction, 144	solution, 133
law of conservation of matter, 137	solvent, 133
	synthesis reaction, 140

Vocabulary Review

Number your paper from 1 to 10. Then choose a word or words from the Word Bank that best complete each sentence. Write the answer on your paper.

1. A substance formed in a chemical reaction is called a _____.

2. A number placed before a formula in a chemical equation is called a _____.

3. Any change in which substances turn into other substances is called a _____.

4. A substance that dissolves another is called a solvent

5. A mixture in which one substance is dissolved in another is called a solution

6. The solve states that material cannot be created or destroyed in any chemical change.

7. A substance that is dissolved in another is called a s____.

8. A substance that changes to produce another substance is called a _____.

9. A combination of substances in which no reaction takes place is called a _____.

10. A _____ uses symbols, formulas, and numbers to stand for a chemical reaction.

Concept Review

Copy the following table on your paper. Look at each chemical equation in the left column. In the right column, describe the kind of reaction the chemical equation represents—synthesis, decomposition, single replacement, or double replacement.

Chemical equation	Kind of reaction
1. $2SO_3 \rightarrow 2SO_2 + O_2$	
2. $AgNO_3 + NaI \rightarrow AgI + NaNO_3$	
3. $Zn + SnCl_2 \rightarrow ZnCl_2 + Sn$	
4. $C + O_2 \rightarrow CO_2$	

Number your paper from 5 to 7. Then choose the words that best complete each sentence. Write the letter of the answer on your paper.

5. In the reaction $C + H_2O \rightarrow CO + H_2$, the reactants are _____.
   a. C and CO
   b. C and H_2O
   c. CO and H_2
   d. H_2O and H_2

6. When sugar is dissolved in water, _____.
   a. water is the solute
   b. sugar is the solvent
   c. sugar is the solute
   d. there is no solvent

7. The coefficients in the expression $5Na_2HPO + 3C_6H_{10}$ are _____.
   a. 2, 4, 6, and 10
   b. 3 and 2
   c. 5, 2, 1, and 4
   d. 5 and 3

Critical Thinking

Write the answer to each of the following questions.

1. Balance the following equation by adding coefficients: $Al + O_2 \rightarrow Al_2O_3$. Then identify the reactant(s) and the product(s).

2. Explain the difference between a single-replacement reaction and a double-replacement reaction.

3. Look at the photograph shown to the left. Explain what is happening.

Test Taking Tip   Read test questions carefully to identify those questions that require more than one answer.

Chapter

7

Motion

Motion—it's happening all the time. People walking and skateboarding. Cars rushing along the highway. Rivers flowing. Leaves rustling in the wind. All these things involve motion. You cannot escape motion even if you try to sit completely still. The chair you are sitting on rests on a rapidly spinning Earth. Earth is moving around the sun. Movement may seem confusing. But once you know what happens when things move, you'll find that motion is not hard to understand.

ORGANIZE YOUR THOUGHTS

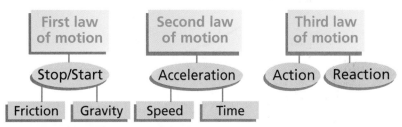

First law of motion — Stop/Start — Friction, Gravity

Second law of motion — Acceleration — Speed, Time

Third law of motion — Action, Reaction

Goals for Learning

▶ To define motion and speed

▶ To calculate speed, distance, and time

▶ To use a graph to describe motion and make predictions

▶ To calculate acceleration and deceleration

▶ To explain what force is

▶ To explain and apply Newton's three laws of motion

▶ To explain what gravity is

▶ To explain the law of universal gravitation

Motion

A change in position.

Elapsed time

Length of time that passes from one event to another.

The earth travels in space. A car carries you from place to place. You walk to the store. An amusement park ride spins you around. What do all these actions have in common? In each case, objects are changing position in space. We say they are moving. **Motion** is simply a change of position.

All change, including change in position, takes place over time. So to help you understand motion, you will begin by learning how the passage of time is measured.

Elapsed Time

Suppose you have just taken an airplane trip from New Orleans to New York in the same time zone. Your flight began at 8:00 P.M. It ended at 11:00 P.M. How long did this trip take?

To answer this question, you calculate the **elapsed time.** Elapsed time is the amount of time that passes from one event to another. To calculate elapsed time, just subtract the time of the earlier event from the time of the later event.

In the case of the flight, subtract the departure time from the arrival time.

```
  11:00    arrival time
 – 8:00    departure time
   3       hours travel time = elapsed time
```

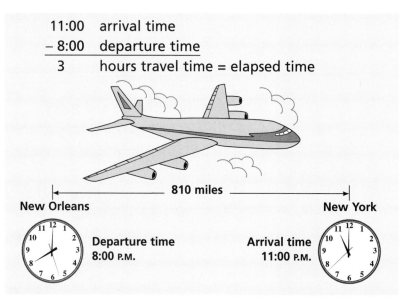

New Orleans ├─────────── 810 miles ───────────┤ New York

Departure time
8:00 P.M.

Arrival time
11:00 P.M.

Speed

Once you know that something is moving, it's natural to wonder how fast it's going, or what its **speed** is. Speed tells how fast an object is moving. The more distance a moving object covers in a given time, the greater is its speed. For example, a cheetah can travel at a speed of 100 kilometers per hour. But an ant can cover only 36 meters in an hour. The cheetah has greater speed than the ant.

Notice that speed uses two units—**distance** and time. Distance is the length of the path traveled by the object in motion. You can use the following formula to find the speed of an object.

$$\text{speed} = \frac{\text{distance}}{\text{time}}$$

Suppose the airplane mentioned on the previous page traveled 810 miles between the two cities. The elapsed time for the trip was 3 hours. You can use the formula to calculate the speed of the airplane.

$$\text{speed} = \frac{810 \text{ miles}}{3 \text{ hours}}$$

$$\text{speed} = \frac{270 \text{ miles}}{1 \text{ hour}}$$

The speed of the airplane is 270 miles per hour. This means that each hour, the plane traveled 270 miles.

In the example, it is unlikely that the airplane traveled at a constant speed of 270 miles per hour during the entire flight. The plane starts and stops very slowly. Between the beginning and the end of the trip, the speed varies during the flight. The speed calculated is actually the average speed. The actual speed at any particular moment could be more or less than the average speed.

Speed does not have to be measured in miles per hour.

Think about a race at a track meet where the distance around the track is 400 meters. Suppose a runner completes the race in 40 seconds. What was the runner's speed?

$$\text{speed} = \frac{\text{distance}}{\text{time}}$$

$$\text{speed} = \frac{400 \text{ meters}}{40 \text{ seconds}}$$

$$\text{speed} = \frac{10 \text{ meters}}{1 \text{ second}}$$

The average speed of the runner is 10 meters per second. The runner covers an average distance of 10 meters each second.

Self-Check

Copy the following table. Calculate the average speed for each of these examples. The first one is completed for you.

Distance Traveled	Time	Average Speed
30 miles	5 hours	6 miles/hour
100 yards	13 seconds	
10 centimeters	5 seconds	
380 kilometers	2 hours	
3,825 feet	30 minutes	
15 inches	4 hours	
82 miles	10 hours	
10,000 meters	36 minutes	
23 feet	6 minutes	
120 kilometers	2 hours	

Calculating Distance

Suppose you are going on a trip by car. You know you can travel about 50 miles an hour on the roads you will be using. You also know you can travel about 6 hours a day. You would like to know how far you can go in one day. In other words, you would like to calculate distance. Since you already know your speed and your time, you can use the formula for finding speed to calculate distance. To do so, all you have to do is rearrange the formula this way.

$$\text{speed} = \frac{\text{distance}}{\text{time}}$$

$$\text{distance} = \text{speed} \times \text{time}$$

$$\text{distance} = \frac{50 \text{ miles}}{1 \text{ hour}} \times 6 \text{ hours}$$

$$\text{distance} = 300 \text{ miles}$$

Calculating Time

Sometimes you might want to figure out how long it will take to cover a certain distance. Suppose you have a job marking the lines on a sports field. The distance to be marked is 80 meters. You mark at a speed of 50 meters per minute. How much time will it take you to mark the whole line? The formula for speed also can be rearranged to solve for the time.

$$\text{speed} = \frac{\text{distance}}{\text{time}}$$

$$\text{time} = \frac{\text{distance}}{\text{speed}}$$

$$\text{time} = \frac{80 \text{ meters}}{50 \text{ meters}/1 \text{ minute}}$$

When you divide by a fraction, you invert the fraction and multiply.

$$\text{time} = \frac{80 \text{ meters}}{1} \times \frac{1 \text{ minute}}{50 \text{ meters}}$$

$$\text{time} = \frac{80 \text{ minutes}}{50}$$

$$\text{time} = 1.6 \text{ minutes}$$

It would take you 1.6 minutes to mark the whole line.

Self-Check

Find the answer for each word problem. Show your work. Use one of these formulas:

$$\text{distance} = \text{speed} \times \text{time}$$

$$\text{time} = \frac{\text{distance}}{\text{speed}}$$

1. A train's average speed is 120 kilometers per hour. Its elapsed time is 2 hours. How far did it travel?

2. A student rides her bike to school. Her school is 5 miles from her home. She travels at an average rate of 16 miles per hour. How much time is needed for this trip?

3. Suppose it takes a plane 5 hours to travel from Philadelphia to San Francisco. It travels at an average speed of 850 miles per hour. What is the distance between the two cities?

4. A rocket can travel at an average rate of 18,000 miles per hour. How far will the rocket travel in 4.5 hours?

5. A man rode on a motorcycle for 2 hours. His average speed was 45 miles per hour. How far did he travel?

How Can You Use a Graph to Describe Motion?

Objectives

After reading this lesson, you should be able to

▶ use a graph to describe motion.

▶ make predictions about distance, using a distance-time graph.

▶ explain what is meant by varying speed.

▶ explain how to recognize varying speed on a distance-time graph.

Sometimes it is useful to use a graph to show motion. Suppose that a car traveled for 5 hours. The following table shows the elapsed time and the distance traveled by the car.

Elapsed Time (hours)	Distance Traveled (kilometers)
0	0
1	50
2	100
3	150
4	200
5	250

The same information that is in the table above is shown on the line graph below. The graph shows distance and time. Points have been plotted for the car. For example, the first point is the one that shows a distance of 50 km at a time of 1 hour.

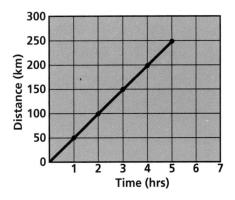

Notice that the line on the graph above is straight, not curved. That means that the car is traveling at a **constant speed.** Constant speed is speed that does not change. For example, observe the first point for the car on the graph. It shows that 50 kilometers are covered in 1 hour. What is the car's speed?

Constant speed

Speed that does not change.

$$\text{speed} = \frac{\text{distance}}{\text{time}}$$

$$\text{speed} = \frac{50 \text{ kilometers}}{1 \text{ hour}}$$

$$\text{speed} = 50 \text{ kilometers/hr}$$

The car's speed during the first hour is 50 kilometers per hour. Likewise, during the second hour, the car's speed would be 50 kilometers per hour.

$$\text{speed} = \frac{\text{distance}}{\text{time}}$$

$$\text{speed} = \frac{100 \text{ kilometers}}{2 \text{ hours}}$$

$$\text{speed} = 50 \text{ kilometers/hr}$$

If you continue to calculate the speed at each of the times, you will find that the car travels at a speed of 50 kilometers per hour each hour. The car is traveling at a constant speed.

Finding Unknown Distances

Suppose you want to know the distance traveled by the car at the end of 4.5 hours. You can use a graph to find the distances at times that are not shown. Use the method below.

1. Copy the graph onto a sheet of paper.

2. Find the time of 4.5 hours along the time axis. This is halfway between 4 hours and 5 hours.

3. Draw a vertical (up-and-down) line from this point on the time axis up to the plotted line.

4. From the point where the vertical line touches the plotted line, draw a horizontal (side-to-side) line to the distance axis.

5. Estimate the distance on the scale. It is the point where the horizontal line touches the distance axis. The distance is about 225 kilometers.

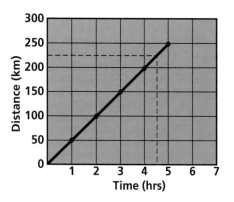

Predicting Distances

You know from the graph how far the car travels in 5 hours. But what if you need to predict where the car will be at some later time? You can use the graph to make this kind of prediction.

For example, suppose you would like to know how far the car will travel in 6 hours. Follow the steps below.

1. Copy the graph onto a sheet of paper.

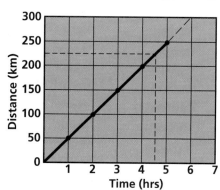

2. Extend the plotted graph line, as shown.

3. Draw a vertical line from the 6-hour line to the plotted line.

4. From the point where the vertical line and the extended graph line touch, draw a horizontal line to the distance axis. Then read the approximate distance. It is about 300 kilometers.

Self-Check

1. Make a line graph for the data in the following table.

Elapsed Time (hours)	Distance Traveled (kilometers)
0	0
1	100
2	200
3	300
4	400
5	500

2. Use your graph to find the distance traveled for each of these times.

   a. 4.5 hours

   b. 7 hours

   c. 10 hours

Velocity

So far we have talked only about the speed of motion. But what about the direction of motion? That can be important, too. For example, you might tell someone that you drove your car north at 90 kilometers per hour. You are telling about the **velocity** of the car. Speed tells how fast an object moves. Velocity tells both the speed and the direction.

Look at the picture below. Suppose you walk 5 kilometers in an hour in an eastward direction. Your velocity would be 5 kilometers per hour eastward.

As you walk, you pass another person traveling westward at 5 kilometers per hour. Both you and the other person have the same speed—5 kilometers per hour. However, your velocities are different because you are going in different directions.

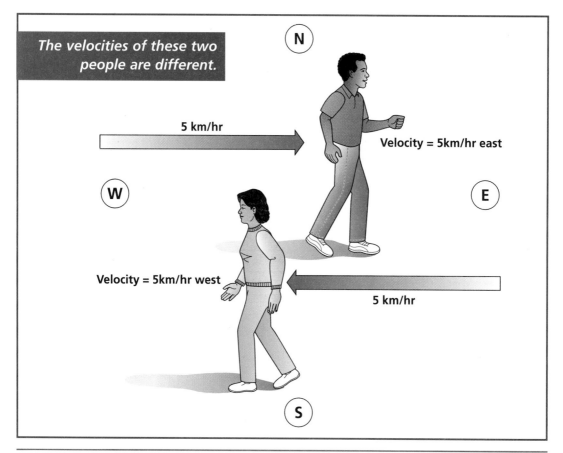

The velocities of these two people are different.

N

5 km/hr

Velocity = 5km/hr east

W

E

Velocity = 5km/hr west

5 km/hr

S

Varying Speed

Few objects move at constant velocity or speed. Look at the following graph. It shows the changes in speed as a family drives a car along a road. Notice that the plotted line in this graph is not straight. This tells you that the car's speed was not constant. But you can still use the information in the graph to find the average speed of the car. You can see that at the end of 6 hours, the car had traveled 300 kilometers. The average speed is shown below.

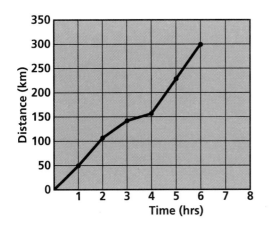

$$\text{speed} = \frac{\text{distance}}{\text{time}}$$

$$\text{speed} = \frac{300 \text{ kilometers}}{6 \text{ hours}}$$

$$\text{speed} = 50 \text{ kilometers/hr}$$

Self-Check

1. Explain how you can tell whether speed is constant or varying by looking at a graph of distance versus time.

2. Make a line graph of distance versus time for the data in the following table.

Elapsed Time (minutes)	Distance Traveled (meters)
0	0
1	200
2	340
3	580
4	760
5	900

7-1

INVESTIGATION

Finding Speed

Purpose
To calculate speed by measuring distance and time, and to use a graph to show motion

Materials
✓ meter stick
✓ ball
✓ stopwatch or watch that shows seconds

Procedure
1. Copy the data table below on your paper.

Length (meters)	Time (seconds)	Speed (distance/time)

2. Work in a very large room, a long corridor, or outdoors, as directed by your teacher. With a partner, measure the length of the space assigned to you. Record that length.

3. Practice gently pushing a ball at the starting point, at ground level. The ball should roll fast enough to cover the whole distance assigned to you. It should not move so fast as to go out of control or create a safety problem. Make sure no one is in your path.

4. Have your partner practice using a stopwatch or watch that shows seconds to measure how many seconds it takes for the ball to roll from the beginning to the end point. Once you have practiced, push the ball again in the same way. Have your partner measure the time. Record the time in your data table.

5. Use your data to calculate the average speed of the ball, in meters per second. Use this formula.

$$\text{speed} = \frac{\text{distance}}{\text{time}}$$

Questions

1. Make a graph with distance in meters on the vertical (up-and-down) axis. Place time in seconds on the horizontal (left-to-right) axis. Extend the axes twice as far as you need to in order to graph your data. Plot one point where 0 seconds crosses 0 meters, to show the beginning of the roll. Plot a second point, using the distance and time values you recorded. Connect the two points with a straight line.

2. Use the graph you made to estimate the distance the ball traveled after it had been moving for half the recorded time.

3. Extend the graph. Estimate the distance the ball would have gone if it had traveled for twice the recorded time.

Objectives

After reading this lesson, you should be able to

▶ explain what acceleration is.

▶ perform calculations involving acceleration.

▶ explain what deceleration is.

▶ perform calculations involving deceleration.

A car stopped at a traffic light is not moving. But when the light turns green, the driver steps on the gas pedal. The car moves forward. Its speed increases. If the car moves away quickly, its velocity changes quickly. Some people might say that it has good "pickup."

Acceleration

Rate of change of velocity.

In science, the word **acceleration**—rather than pickup—is used to describe a change in velocity. Acceleration also tells the rate at which velocity is changing. You can find the acceleration of an object by using this formula.

$$\text{acceleration} = \frac{\text{change in velocity}}{\text{change in time}}$$

An automobile starts from a stopped position. At the end of 5 seconds, it has a speed of 40 km/hr. What is its acceleration?

Step 1: Find the change in speed. To do so, subtract the beginning speed from the final speed.

40 km/hr	final speed
− 0 km/hr	original speed
40 km/hr	change in speed

Step 2: Divide the change in speed by the time required to make the change, 5 seconds. The result is the acceleration.

$$\text{acceleration} = \frac{\text{change in speed}}{\text{change in time}}$$

$$\text{acceleration} = \frac{40 \text{ km/1 hr}}{5 \text{ sec/1}}$$

$$\text{acceleration} = \frac{40 \text{ km}}{1 \text{ hr}} \times \frac{1}{5 \text{ sec}}$$

$$\text{acceleration} = 8 \text{ km/hr per sec}$$

The answer is read *8 kilometers per hour per second.* This means that the auto's speed increases by 8 km per hour during every second of the acceleration.

Acceleration can also refer to a change in direction. For example, suppose a car moves at a constant speed around a curve. The car is accelerating because the direction in which it is traveling is changing.

Deceleration

Deceleration
Rate of slowdown.

You have read that acceleration is a change in velocity. The examples of acceleration you have read about have involved increases in speed. Objects can also slow down. When they slow down, they are said to decelerate. **Deceleration** is the rate of slowdown. The sky diver in the photo accelerates until the parachute opens. Then the sky diver decelerates.

This sky diver is decelerating.

Because deceleration is a form of acceleration, you can use the formula for acceleration to find deceleration. The result is a negative number instead of a positive number. A negative number is a number that is less than zero.

To understand deceleration, think about this example. A car is traveling at 20 km/hr. The driver suddenly puts on the brakes. The car comes to a complete stop 4 seconds later. Calculate the acceleration.

Step 1: The original speed was 20 km/hr. The final speed is 0 km/hr. Therefore, the change in speed is calculated as follows.

0 km/hr	final speed
−20 km/hr	original speed
−20 km/hr	change in speed

Step 2: Divide the change in speed by the change in time to obtain the acceleration.

$$\text{acceleration} = \frac{-20 \text{ km/1 hr}}{4 \text{ sec/1}}$$

$$\text{acceleration} = \frac{-20 \text{ km}}{1 \text{ hr}} \times \frac{1}{4 \text{ sec}}$$

$$\text{acceleration} = -5 \text{ km/hr per sec}$$

The acceleration is −5 km/hour for each second. The minus (−) sign in front of the 5 means that the number is less than zero. Therefore, this can also be expressed as a deceleration of 5 km per hour per second. The word *decelerating* already expresses the idea of negative acceleration. So, the negative sign does not have to be used if the answer is given as deceleration rather than acceleration.

Complete the table by finding the acceleration for each of the following. Some of your answers might be negative numbers. They express deceleration in terms of negative acceleration.

Beginning Speed	Ending Speed	Elapsed Time	Acceleration
40 km/hr	50 km/hr	5 sec	2 km/hr per sec
20 km/sec	109 km/sec	4 sec	
20 km/hr	55 km/hr	7 sec	
0 m/sec	10 m/sec	10 sec	
30 mm/sec	22 mm/sec	0.2 sec	
20 mm/sec	22 mm/sec	0.2 sec	
25 cm/sec	10 cm/sec	0.5 sec	
60 km/hr	70 km/hr	2 sec	
30 m/min	60 m/min	10 sec	
5 cm/sec	10 cm/sec	0.5 sec	

SCIENCE IN YOUR LIFE

How good is the pickup?

A car's pickup is its ability to accelerate. The ability to accelerate rapidly can be important in terms of safety. It can help avoid accidents such as rear-end collisions.

A car's pickup is often reported in terms of the time the car takes to go from 0 to 60 miles per hour. But it may be reported in other ways. You might hear acceleration referred to in kilometers per hour per second, especially for foreign cars.

Suppose you were considering buying a car and had narrowed the choice to three models: a German car, an American car, and a Japanese car. You decide to make your final decision on the basis of pickup. You find out that the German car can go from 0 to 100 km/hour in 8 seconds. The American car can go from 0 to 80 km/hour in 6 seconds. The Japanese car can go from 0 to 120 km/hour in 11 seconds. Calculate the acceleration of each, in km/hour per second. Which one has the best pickup? Assume constant acceleration in each case.

Force

A push or a pull.

Friction

Force that opposes motion and that occurs when things slide or roll over each other.

Sir Isaac Newton was a scientist who lived about 350 years ago. He studied changes in the motion of objects. From his studies, he was able to propose three laws to explain motion.

The First Law of Motion

If you wanted to move a large box that is resting on the floor, you would have to push or pull it. We call this push or pull a **force.** Whenever any object changes its velocity or accelerates, a force causes the change in motion.

Newton's first law of motion states that if no force acts on an object at rest, it will remain at rest. The law also says that if the object is moving, it will continue moving at the same speed and in the same direction if no force acts on it.

The second part of the law may be difficult to understand. For example, a car on flat ground will roll to a stop if you take your foot off the gas pedal. The car slows down because an invisible force is at work. This invisible force is called **friction.** It occurs when things slide or roll over each other. Friction resists the movement of one surface past another. The rougher the surfaces are, the greater the friction.

You can see in the picture below how friction helps stop a moving car. Notice the air resistance. Air resistance is a form of friction. It occurs when molecules of air touch the surface of the car.

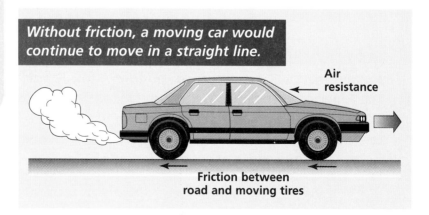

Without friction, a moving car would continue to move in a straight line.

Air resistance

Friction between road and moving tires

An object tends to resist changes in its motion. This tendency to resist changes in motion is called **inertia.** Inertia causes objects at rest to stay at rest. It also causes moving objects to keep moving.

The inertia of an object depends on its mass. The greater the mass of an object, the greater the force needed to cause a given change in its motion. For example, suppose you tried to push two rocks—a large one and a small one—across the ground. You would notice that if you apply the same push (force) to both rocks, the smaller rock will move faster after a certain amount of time. To make both rocks move at the same speed, you would have to push the large rock harder. The large rock has more mass than the small rock. Therefore, it has more inertia.

The Second Law of Motion

Newton's second law of motion says that the amount of force needed to produce a given change in the motion of an object depends on the mass of the object. The larger the mass, the more force is needed to give it a certain acceleration.

Suppose you drive a truck to a brickyard to pick up some bricks. After the bricks are loaded into the truck, you leave the brickyard. On the drive home, you notice that it takes longer to reach the same speed than it did when the truck was empty. What causes the difference? The truck full of bricks has more mass than the empty truck. So if you apply the same force to the truck both times (push the gas pedal the same amount), the truck with the bricks (more mass) will take longer to reach a given velocity.

Newton's second law can be written as follows.

$$\text{force} = \text{mass} \times \text{acceleration,}$$
$$\text{or } F = ma$$

A small force acting on a large mass will cause very little change in motion. A large force acting on a small mass will cause a much larger change in motion, that is, a greater acceleration.

The Third Law of Motion

The picture below illustrates Newton's third law of motion. The law says that if an object exerts a force on a second object, the second object will always exert a force on the first object. This force will be equal to the force exerted by the first object. But the force will be in the opposite direction. This law is sometimes stated: For every action, there is an equal and opposite reaction.

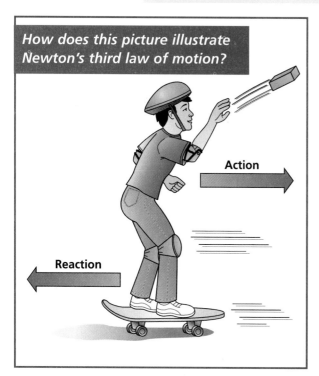

How does this picture illustrate Newton's third law of motion?

Action

Reaction

The boy in the picture is standing on a skateboard, holding a large brick in his hand. When he throws the brick forward, the boy and the skateboard move in the opposite direction from the brick—backwards. This is an example of action and reaction. The action is throwing the brick. The reaction is the force of the brick on the boy. The boy is standing on the skateboard. Therefore, the skateboard moves backward. The action of throwing the brick causes the equal and opposite reaction of the skateboard moving backwards.

Self-Check

1. What are Newton's three laws of motion?
2. When a marble is rolled along a floor, what forces cause it to slow down and stop?
3. If an object is at rest, what must happen for it to begin moving?

Gravity

Force of attraction between any two objects that have mass.

One force with which you are probably familiar is the force of **gravity.** You might know that gravity keeps you from flying off the earth. If you are like many people, you might think of gravity as the pull exerted by Earth on other objects. But gravity is a force of attraction between any two objects that have mass.

The Law of Universal Gravitation

The gravitational force caused by an object depends on its mass. An object like Earth has a large mass. So it also produces a large gravitational force. Smaller objects, such as people, trees, and buildings, have much smaller gravitational forces because they have less mass. These forces are so small that they are very difficult to observe.

Mass isn't the only thing that affects the pull of gravity. The distance between objects also determines how strong the force is due to gravity. The greater the distance between objects, the smaller the gravitational force is between them.

Think about an astronaut. When the astronaut is on Earth, gravity keeps him or her from flying off the earth. The earth pulls on the astronaut. But the astronaut also pulls on the earth. The earth's gravity is strongest near the earth's surface. As the astronaut travels away from the earth in a spaceship, the pull of Earth's gravity gets weaker. But no matter how far from the earth the astronaut travels, the earth still exerts a force. In fact, Earth's gravity extends millions of kilometers into space.

Law of universal gravitation

Gravitational force depends on the mass of the two objects involved and on the distance between them.

Sir Isaac Newton, who stated the three laws of motion, put these ideas about gravity together in the **law of universal gravitation.** That law says two things. First, gravitational force depends on the mass of the two objects involved. Second, the gravitational force depends on the distance between the objects.

Gravity and Acceleration

Have you ever jumped off a low diving board and then a high one? If so, you might have noticed that when you jumped from the higher board, you were moving faster when you struck the water. And you hit the water harder. That is because the force of gravity causes an object to speed up as it falls.

Gravity causes all objects to have the same acceleration as they fall. But another force—air resistance—also acts on a falling object. (Recall that air resistance is a form of friction. It is caused by molecules of air rubbing against a moving object.) Air resistance causes objects to fall at different speeds. The amount of air resistance acting on a moving object depends on the shape of the object. You can see in the picture that a sheet of paper will fall slower than a small stone. The reason is because the mass of the paper is spread out over a wider, thinner area than that of the stone. More molecules of air hit the surface of the paper.

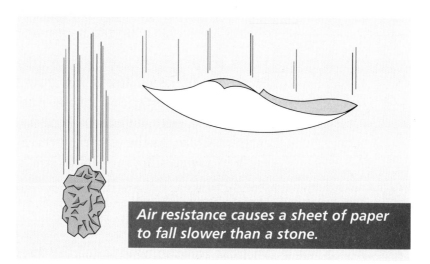

Air resistance causes a sheet of paper to fall slower than a stone.

1. What two factors affect the pull of gravity?
2. Gravity is a measure of the pull of gravity on an object. Use this information to explain why an astronaut weighs less on the moon than on Earth.
3. How does gravity affect acceleration?

INVESTIGATION

Newton's Third Law of Motion

Purpose
To demonstrate action and reaction

Procedure

Part A

1. Copy the data table below on your paper.

Observations	
Part A	**Part B**

2. Put on your safety goggles.

3. Thread the string through the two straws.

4. Tie the ends of the string to the backs of two chairs.

5. Blow up the balloon. Hold the end closed. Have a classmate use masking tape to attach the balloon to one of the straws, as shown in Figure A. Position the balloon near the end of the string.

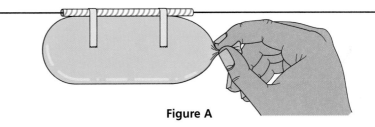

Figure A

Materials

✓ safety goggles
✓ string, 3 meters long
✓ 2 straws
✓ 2 chairs
✓ long balloon
✓ masking tape
✓ table tennis ball

6. Release the balloon. Observe what happens. Record your observations in your data table.

Part B

7. Blow up the balloon again. Hold the end closed. Have a classmate attach the balloon to the straw again.

8. Have another classmate attach a table tennis ball to the second straw, as shown in Figure B. Place the ball behind the open end of the balloon.

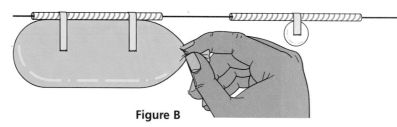

Figure B

9. Release the balloon. Observe what happens. Record your observations.

Questions

1. In Part A, in what direction does the escaping air move?

2. In Part A, in what direction does the balloon move?

3. How does Part A demonstrate Newton's third law of motion?

4. In Part B, in what direction does the balloon move?

5. In Part B, in what direction does the ball move?

6. In Part B, use Newton's third law of motion to explain why the ball moves the way it does.

- Motion is a change of position.
- Elapsed time is the time between events. It is calculated by subtracting the time of the earlier event from the time of the later event.
- Speed is the rate at which the position of an object changes. It is equal to distance divided by time.
- The formula for speed can be rearranged for calculation of distance or time.
- Graphs of distance versus time can be used to describe motion and to make predictions about distances.
- Velocity tells about the speed and direction of a moving object.
- Objects may travel at varying speed rather than constant speed.
- Acceleration is the rate of change of velocity. Acceleration equals the change in velocity divided by the change in time.
- Deceleration is the rate of slowdown. Deceleration occurs whenever acceleration is negative. It is usually calculated as negative acceleration.
- A force is a push or a pull.
- Newton's first law of motion states that an object remains at rest or keeps moving at constant speed unless an outside force acts on it.
- Newton's second law of motion states that the amount of force needed to change the motion of an object depends on the mass of the object.
- Newton's third law of motion states that for every action there is an equal and opposite reaction.
- Gravity is a force of attraction between any two objects that have mass. According to the law of universal gravitation, the greater the masses are, the greater the force is. The greater the distance is, the less the force is.
- Gravity causes all falling objects to have the same acceleration. Air resistance acts on falling objects to slow them down.

Science Words		
	acceleration, 166	gravity, 173
	constant speed, 159	inertia, 171
	deceleration, 167	law of universal gravitation, 173
	distance, 153	motion, 152
	elapsed time, 152	speed, 153
	force, 170	velocity, 162
	friction, 170	

Vocabulary Review

Number your paper from 1 to 9. Then choose a word or words from the Word Bank that best complete each sentence. Write the answer on your paper.

WORD BANK

acceleration

deceleration

first law of motion

friction

gravity

inertia

law of universal gravitation

second law of motion

third law of motion

1. The _____ states that force equals mass times acceleration.

2. The tendency of an object to resist changes in its motion is called _____.

3. The _____ states that for every force there is an equal and opposite force.

4. A force of attraction that acts between any two masses is _____.

5. The rate of slowdown is called _____.

6. The _____ states that an object remains at rest or moves at constant speed unless an outside force acts on it.

7. A force that opposes motion and that occurs when things slide or roll over each other is _____.

8. The _____ states that the force of attraction between two objects depends on their masses and their distance apart.

9. The rate of change of speed is called _____.

Concept Review

Number your paper from 1 to 5. Then choose the word or words that best complete each sentence. Write the letter of the answer on your paper.

1. To calculate acceleration, you must divide _____.
   a. change in speed by change in distance
   b. change in speed by change in time
   c. change in distance by change in time

2. To calculate force, you must _____.
   a. multiply mass by acceleration
   b. divide mass by acceleration
   c. multiply distance by mass

3. To calculate speed, you must _____.
   a. divide distance by time
   b. divide time by distance
   c. multiply time and distance

Critical Thinking

Write the answer to each of the following questions.

1. The figure below shows the motion of a bicycle. Calculate the speed of the bicycle.

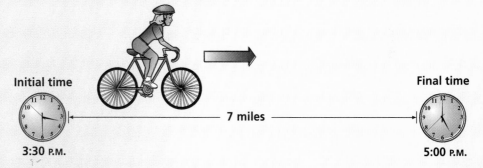

Initial time

3:30 P.M.

7 miles

Final time

5:00 P.M.

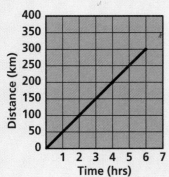

2. The graph shows distance and time for 6 hours for a train moving at constant speed. How could you use the graph to predict how far the train will have gone at the end of 7 hours?

3. How far would the train in question 2 have traveled at the end of 7 hours?

Test Taking Tip   If you have time, compute problems a second time. Then check your original answer.

Work and Machines

8

I magine what life would be like without machines. There would be no tools, no cars, no appliances. Most tasks would be much harder and take more time. Some would be impossible. In this chapter, you will explore the nature of work and machines. You will also learn about the role machines have in your daily life.

ORGANIZE YOUR THOUGHTS

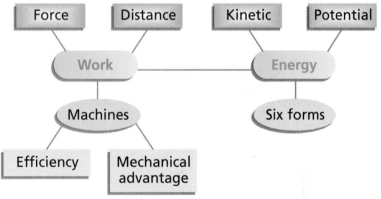

Goals for Learning

▶ To explain what work is and to calculate work
▶ To explain what energy is
▶ To name six forms of energy
▶ To describe six types of simple machines
▶ To describe the classes of levers
▶ To calculate efficiency and mechanical advantage

Work

What happens when something changes its motion in the direction of the force being applied.

You probably do some "work" around your home. What things do you consider work? You might think of ironing clothes, washing dishes, taking out the garbage, and sweeping the floors. In everyday language, we use the word *work* as another word for *labor*.

Work

To scientists, however, **work** is what happens when a force makes something move in the direction of the force. A force is a push or a pull.

Suppose you struggled for an hour to lift a very heavy box, but you could not budge it. No work was done in the scientific sense, because the box did not move. If you rolled a ball down a ramp, however, work was done. The reason is the ball changed its direction due to the force of gravity.

When you apply force to lift a heavy object, you do work.

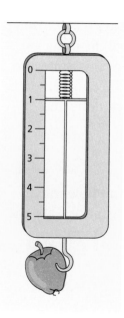

Measuring Work

How can you measure work? You can start by measuring how much force is used to do the work. Spring scales, like the one shown to the left, are used to measure force. In the metric system, force is measured in newtons. The spring scale shows that the apple is exerting a force of 1 newton.

To measure work, you must also measure the distance (in meters) through which the force acted. To find out how much work was done, use this formula.

work = force × distance

Your answer will be in newton-meters. Scientists have a simpler name for a newton-meter. It is called a **joule.** So when calculating work, your answer will be in joules.

Joule

Metric unit of work.

Suppose a woman is pushing a bike. She uses a force of 2 newtons and pushes the bike a distance of 10 meters. How much work did she do?

work = force × distance
work = 2 newtons × 10 meters
work = 20 newton-meters
work = 20 joules

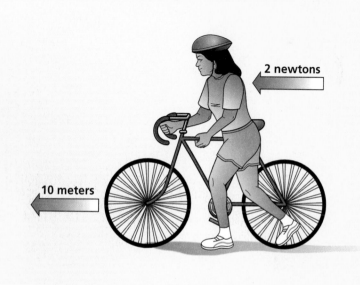

2 newtons

10 meters

Because force, distance, and work are always related, you can calculate any one of them if you know the other two. For example, if you know how much work was done and you know the distance, you can find out how much force was used. Simply take the amount of work done and divide it by the distance.

$$\text{force} = \frac{\text{work}}{\text{distance}}$$

If you know how much work was done and how much force was needed, you can calculate the distance. Take the amount of work done and divide it by the amount of force that was used.

$$\text{distance} = \frac{\text{work}}{\text{force}}$$

Self-Check

1. What is the metric unit of work?
2. What must you know to find the amount of work done on an object?
3. A man pushed a table, using a force of 8 newtons. He moved the table 13 meters. How much work did he do?
4. One person solved 40 math problems in her head, and the other person picked up a kitten. Which one did more work, in the scientific sense?

Energy

The ability to do work.

Kinetic energy

Energy of motion.

Potential energy

Stored energy.

Have you ever tried to play a radio with a "dead" battery? The radio would not play because the battery had no more energy stored inside. In science, **energy** is defined as "the ability to do work." Without energy, no work could be done.

Kinetic and Potential Energy

A moving object has the energy of motion, called **kinetic energy.** When a car is moving, it can do work. It can overcome road friction and air resistance and keep going forward. The amount of kinetic energy a moving object has depends on the object's mass and speed. The greater the mass or speed, the greater the kinetic energy.

Some objects are not moving, but they have the potential to move because of their position. These objects have stored energy. This stored energy is called **potential energy.** A book sitting on the floor has no potential energy. It cannot do work. But if you set the book so that it hangs over the edge of a table, the book has stored energy. It can do work by falling to the floor. Then the potential energy changes to kinetic energy. If you place the book over the edge of a higher table, the book has more potential energy because it can fall farther. The spring of a mousetrap is another example of potential energy. It can do work as it snaps shut.

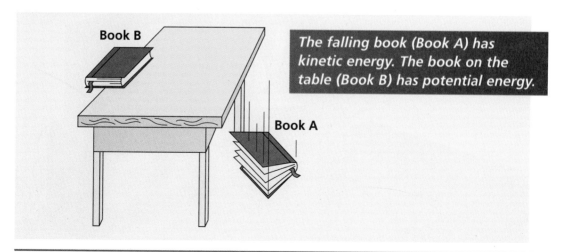

Book B

Book A

The falling book (Book A) has kinetic energy. The book on the table (Book B) has potential energy.

The Forms of Energy

The energy you use to do work exists in six main forms. These six forms of energy can be stored. They can also produce motion. That is, each form of energy can be potential or kinetic.

Chemical energy is stored in the bonds between atoms. When substances react, they can release some of the chemical energy in the substances and warm the surroundings. For example, burning coal produces heat.

Heat energy is associated with the moving particles that make up matter. The faster the particles move, the more heat energy is present. All matter has some heat energy. You will learn more about heat in Chapter 9.

Mechanical energy is the energy in moving objects. Objects, such as a moving bicycle, wind, and a falling rock, have mechanical energy in kinetic form. Sound is a form of mechanical energy that you will learn about in Chapter 10.

Nuclear energy is energy that is stored in the nucleus, or center, of an atom. It can be released in devices such as nuclear power plants and atomic weapons.

How many forms of energy can you find in this room?

Radiant energy is associated with light. Some energy that Earth receives from the sun is in the form of light energy. You will learn more about light in Chapter 10.

Electrical energy is energy that causes electrons to move. Electrons are the negatively charged particles in atoms. Appliances, such as refrigerators and vacuum cleaners, use electrical energy. You will learn about electricity in Chapter 11.

Generator

Device used to convert mechanical energy to electrical energy.

Energy can be changed from one form to another. At an electric power plant, for example, chemical energy is converted to heat energy when fuel is burned. The heat energy is used to make steam. The steam turns a turbine and produces mechanical energy inside a **generator.** The generator converts mechanical energy to electrical energy. The electrical energy is sent to your home and you can use it to do work.

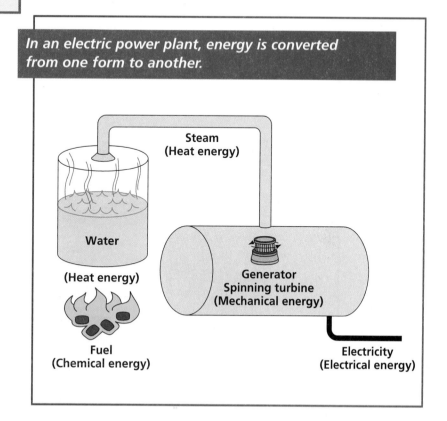

In an electric power plant, energy is converted from one form to another.

Steam
(Heat energy)

Water

(Heat energy)

Generator
Spinning turbine
(Mechanical energy)

Fuel
(Chemical energy)

Electricity
(Electrical energy)

The Law of Conservation of Energy

Energy might change its form, but it does not disappear. You can add energy to an object or take energy away from it, but the total amount of the energy does not change. The **law of conservation of energy** states that energy cannot be created or destroyed. A book falling from a table illustrates the law of conservation of energy. As the book falls, its potential energy decreases and its kinetic energy increases. The amount of energy stays the same.

Self-Check

1. What is energy?
2. What is the difference between kinetic and potential energy?
3. Explain the law of conservation of energy.
4. Each illustration shows an example of energy changing form. List the energy changes that take place in each example.

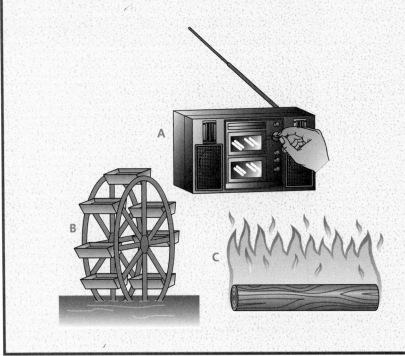

SCIENCE IN YOUR LIFE

How can energy change forms?

Have you ever ridden a roller coaster? A roller coaster is a good example of how energy can change from one form to another. When you first climb into the car at the bottom of the hill, the car has no potential energy. A chain must pull you up the first big hill. That chain changes electrical energy into potential energy. When the cars are at the top, they can fall downward. Potential energy changes to kinetic energy as the cars plunge down one hill and up the next hill. The cars slow as they reach the top of the hill. The kinetic energy that pushed them up the hill has changed back to potential energy. That stored energy converts to kinetic energy as the cars zoom down again.

You might notice that the hills get smaller and smaller during the ride. Although energy is not actually lost, friction converts some of it to other forms of energy, such as heat energy. The heat energy warms the tracks and the air but is not useful for propelling the cars forward.

Mass, Height, and Energy

Materials

- ✓ paper cup
- ✓ safety scissors
- ✓ 2 books
- ✓ grooved ruler
- ✓ small marble
- ✓ large marble

Purpose
To demonstrate how mass affects potential and kinetic energy

Procedure
1. Copy the data table below on a sheet of paper.

Object	Distance cup moved
small marble	
large marble	

2. Cut a 2.5-cm square window from the lip of the cup, as shown in Figure A below.

3. Place one end of the ruler on the edge of a book to form a ramp, as shown in Figure B. The ruler's groove should be on top.

Figure A

Figure B

4. Place the cup upside down over the other end of the ruler. The ruler should touch the back of the cup.

5. Measure the distance from the edge of the book to the back edge of the cup. Mark the base line at the back edge of the cup.

6. Set the small marble at the top of the ruler's groove. Let it roll down by itself. Do not push it.

7. Observe what happens to the cup. Measure the distance from the edge of the book to the back edge of the cup. Record this distance in the data table.

8. Reset the cup at the base line. Repeat steps 6 and 7, using the large marble. Measure and record the distance.

Questions

1. Which marble pushed the cup farther from the ramp?

2. What conclusion can you draw about the effect of mass on kinetic energy?

Explore Further

How does the height of the ramp affect potential energy. Repeat the Investigation using ramps of different heights.

Objectives

After reading this lesson, you should be able to

▶ explain what a simple machine is.

▶ describe how a lever works.

▶ distinguish among the three classes of levers.

▶ analyze work and efficiency for levers.

Effort force

Force applied to a machine by the user.

Fulcrum

Fixed point around which a lever rotates.

Lever

Simple machine containing a bar that can turn about a fixed point.

Simple machine

Tool with few parts that makes it easier or possible to do work.

Have you ever tried to open a paint can, using only your fingers? It is hard, if not impossible, to do so. With a screwdriver, you can easily pry the lid from the can. A screwdriver, used in this way, is an example of a **simple machine.** Simple machines make it easier or possible to do work. Simple machines change the size or direction of the force you apply, or the distance through which the force moves.

The Lever

A **lever** is a simple machine. Levers can have many shapes. In its most basic form, the lever is a bar that is free to turn around a fixed point. The fixed point is called a **fulcrum.**

In the figure below, the woman is using a lever to move a boulder. Notice that the lever changes the direction of the force the woman applies. She pushes down, but the boulder moves up. The force the woman applies to the machine is called the **effort force** (F_E).

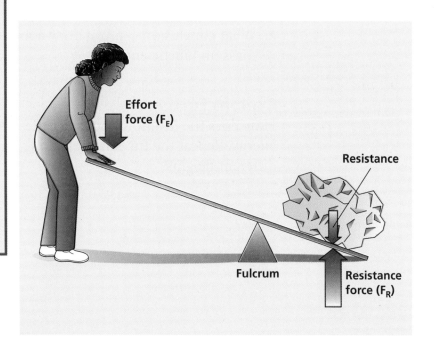

The object to be lifted is called the resistance. In this example, the boulder is the resistance. Gravity is pulling down on the boulder, so the machine must exert a force upward to lift it. The force the machine uses to move the resistance is called the **resistance force** (F_R). The force the machine exerts is greater than the force the woman exerts. In other words, using the lever makes the woman's job easier. The lever takes the amount of force she exerts and increases that force.

Resistance force

Force applied to a machine by the object to be moved.

The Three Classes of Levers

Levers can be grouped into three classes. The classes of levers are based on the position of the resistance force, the fulcrum, and the effort force. The figure below illustrates a first-class lever.

In a first-class lever, the fulcrum is positioned between the effort and the resistance. A first-class lever changes the direction of a force and can also increase the force.

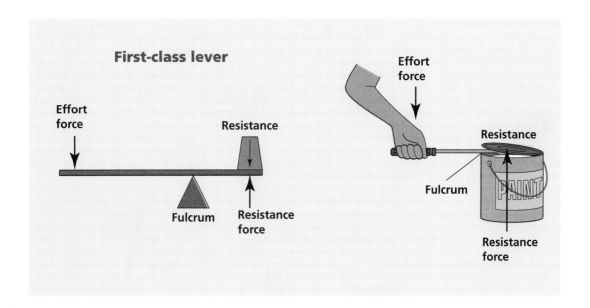

In a second-class lever, shown below, the resistance is positioned between the effort and the fulcrum. Second-class levers always increase the force applied to them. They do not change the direction of the force. Wheelbarrows, paper cutters, and most nutcrackers are examples of second-class levers.

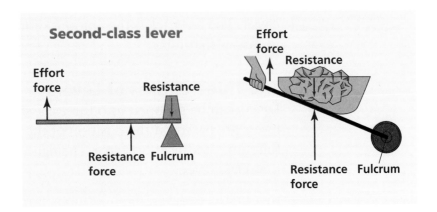

The diagram below shows a third-class lever. Notice that the effort is between the fulcrum and the resistance. Third-class levers increase the distance through which the force moves, which causes the resistance to move farther or faster. A broom is an example of a third-class lever. You use effort force on the handle between the fulcrum and the resistance force. When you move the handle of the broom a short distance, the brush end moves a greater distance.

Did You Know?

The ancient Egyptians understood the principle of the lever. They used a lever called a shadoof to lift heavy buckets of water for irrigation, possibly as early as 1,500 B.C. The shadoof is still used today in Egypt, India, and other countries.

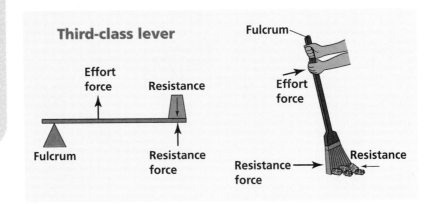

Work and Efficiency for a Lever

Energy cannot be created or destroyed. Because energy is the ability to do work, work cannot be created either. No simple machine can do more work than the person using it supplies. What machines can do is increase or change the direction of the force a person exerts. Lesson 1 explained that work = force × distance. Some machines allow a person to use less force to do the same amount of work. But in return, that person must exert the force over a greater distance.

In the figure below, a lever is being used to move a boulder. The distance the effort moves is called the effort distance (d_E). The distance the resistance moves is called the resistance distance (d_R). Notice that the effort distance is much greater than the resistance distance.

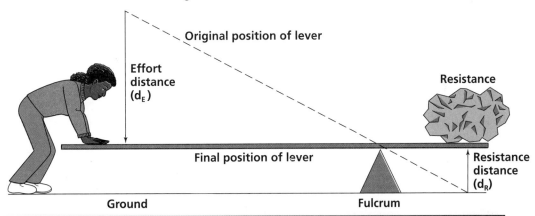

The woman exerts a smaller force over a greater distance, while this lever exerts a greater force over a smaller distance.

Work input	The amount of work a person puts into a machine is called the **work input.** The work input equals the person's effort force multiplied by the distance of that effort.
Work put into a machine by its user.	work input = $F_E \times d_E$

The amount of work actually done by the machine is called the **work output.** The work output equals the resistance force multiplied by the distance the resistance moved.

Work output	
Work done by a machine against the resistance.	work output = $F_R \times d_R$

Work output can never be greater than work input because energy cannot be created. But in reality, work output is always less than work input. No machine can do quite as much work as a person puts into it. Machines cannot destroy energy, but they change some of it to heat and other forms of energy that cannot do useful work.

<table>
<tr><td>Efficiency
How well a machine performs.</td></tr>
</table>

The **efficiency** of a machine measures how much useful work it can do compared with how much work was put into it. You can find the efficiency of a machine by using this formula.

$$\text{efficiency} = \frac{\text{work output}}{\text{work input}} \times 100$$

Efficiency is written as a percent. Multiplying by 100 tells you what percent of the work input is converted to work output. All machines have efficiencies that are less than 100 percent.

Suppose a woman uses a lever to lift a crate. She applies 120 newtons of effort force. She pushes her end of the lever 1.0 meter. The machine exerts 400 newtons of resistance force. It lifts the crate 0.2 meter. What is the work input, the work output, and the efficiency of the lever?

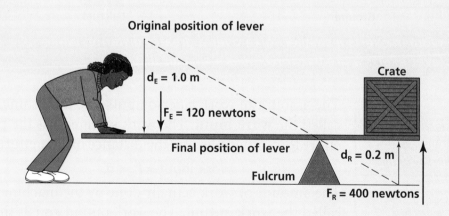

Original position of lever

$d_E = 1.0$ m

$F_E = 120$ newtons

Final position of lever

Crate

$d_R = 0.2$ m

Fulcrum

$F_R = 400$ newtons

work input = effort force (F_E) × effort distance (d_E)
work input = 120 newtons × 1.0 m
work input = 120 joules

work output = resistance force (F_R) × resistance distance (d_R)
work output = 400 newtons × 0.2 m
work output = 80 joules

$$\text{efficiency} = \frac{\text{work output}}{\text{work input}} \times 100$$

$$\text{efficiency} = \frac{80 \text{ joules}}{120 \text{ joules}} \times 100$$

efficiency = 66⅔%

Self-Check

1. Draw a first-class, second-class, and third-class lever. Show the fulcrum, effort force, and resistance for each.
2. What is work input? Work output?
3. What does efficiency tell you about a machine?

After reading this lesson, you should be able to

▶ explain and calculate mechanical advantage.

▶ use effort arm and resistance arm to determine the mechanical advantage of a lever.

Mechanical advantage

Factor by which a machine multiplies the effort force.

Usually, simple machines are used to make tasks easier by multiplying the force you apply. You can figure out how much easier.

Mechanical Advantage

The number of times a machine multiplies your effort force is called the **mechanical advantage** of the machine. You can find a machine's mechanical advantage (MA) with this formula.

$$\text{mechanical advantage} = \frac{\text{resistance force}}{\text{effort force}}, \; or \; \text{MA} = \frac{F_R}{F_E}$$

Suppose the machine pictured below lifts a resistance weighing 30 newtons when you apply an effort force of only 10 newtons. What is the machine's mechanical advantage?

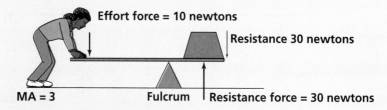

Effort force = 10 newtons

Resistance 30 newtons

MA = 3   Fulcrum   Resistance force = 30 newtons

$$\text{MA} = \frac{F_R}{F_E}$$

$$\text{MA} = \frac{30 \text{ newtons}}{10 \text{ newtons}}$$

$$\text{MA} = 3$$

The mechanical advantage is 3. The machine has multiplied your effort force by 3. This makes the object easier for you to lift.

Some machines are not used to multiply effort force. Instead, people use them to increase the distance or speed the resistance will move, or to change the direction of a force. Rather than increasing your effort force, they may even reduce it.

Effort arm	# Effort Arm and Resistance Arm
Distance between the fulcrum and the effort force of a lever.	You can increase the mechanical advantage of a lever simply by moving the fulcrum closer to the resistance and farther from the effort force. Another way to find the mechanical advantage of a lever is to measure the **effort arm.** The effort arm is the distance between the fulcrum and the effort force. Measure the resistance force and the **resistance arm.** The resistance arm is the distance between the fulcrum and the resistance force. Then divide the effort arm by the resistance arm.
Resistance arm	
Distance between the fulcrum and resistance force of a lever.	

$$MA = \frac{\text{effort arm}}{\text{resistance arm}}$$

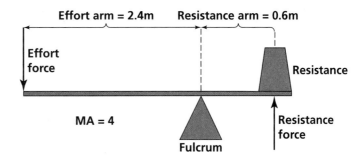

Effort arm = 2.4m   Resistance arm = 0.6m

Effort force

Resistance

MA = 4

Resistance force

Fulcrum

What is the mechanical advantage of the lever pictured above?

$$MA = \frac{\text{effort arm}}{\text{resistance arm}}$$

$$MA = \frac{2.4 \text{ m}}{0.6 \text{ m}}$$

$$MA = 4$$

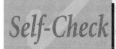

Self-Check

1. What is mechanical advantage?
2. How do you find the mechanical advantage of most simple machines?
3. How can you find the mechanical advantage of levers?
4. What is the mechanical advantage of a lever with an effort arm of 16 cm and a resistance arm of 2 cm?

INVESTIGATION 8-2

Finding the Mechanical Advantage of a Lever

Purpose
To find the mechanical advantage of levers

Procedure

1. Copy the data table below on a sheet of paper.

Fulcrum position	Resistance force	Effort force	Resistance arm	Effort arm
50 cm				
80 cm				
20 cm				

2. Use a spring scale to hold up a 200-g weight. Record the weight (the resistance force) in newtons.

3. Using a rubber band, attach the 200-g weight to the top side of a stiff meter stick, at the 0-cm end.

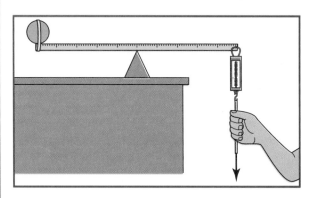

4. Work at a table or desk. Place the weighted meter stick on a fulcrum so that it is positioned under the stick's 50-cm mark. The end of the stick without the weight should extend beyond the edge of the table, as shown in the diagram.

5. Use a spring scale to gently pull down on the 100-cm end of the stick until it is level at both ends. On the spring scale, read the effort force you apply to make the stick level. Record that force, in newtons, on the 50-cm line of the data table.

6. Record the length of the resistance arm (the distance from the weight to the fulcrum). Then record the effort arm (the distance from the fulcrum to the spring scale).

7. Follow the basic procedure used in steps 4 to 6 except position the fulcrum under the 80-cm mark. Record the values in the data table.

8. Place the fulcrum under the 20-cm mark. Repeat the basic procedure in steps 4 to 6. Record the values.

Questions

1. Where was the fulcrum placed when you had to apply the most force? The least force?

2. On a sheet of paper, calculate the mechanical advantage of the three levers. Use this formula.

$$MA = \frac{\text{effort arm}}{\text{resistance arm}}$$

3. Which setup showed the greatest mechanical advantage? The least?

4. How do the mechanical advantages you calculated in step 3 compare to your answers to question 1?

5. How does the position of the fulcrum affect a lever's mechanical advantage?

There are six types of simple machines, including the lever. In this lesson, you will learn about the other five types.

The Pulley

A **pulley** is a wheel with a rope, chain, or belt around it. The figure shows a single pulley.

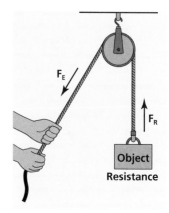

A single pulley changes the direction of the force you apply, but it does not multiply that force. The mechanical advantage equals 1. You can use this type of pulley to lift a heavy object by pulling down instead of lifting up.

The pulley shown above is called a fixed pulley because it is fixed or attached at the top. The wheel is free to spin, but it cannot move up and down.

The pulley shown below is a movable pulley. As effort is applied to a movable pulley, the entire pulley and the object attached will rise. You can use this type of pulley to make a lifting job easier. Because the rope supports the pulley from two directions, you need to apply only half as much force to lift the object. Therefore, the pulley has a mechanical advantage of 2.

Pulley

Simple machine made up of a rope, chain, or belt wrapped around a wheel.

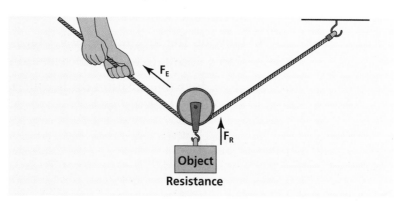

There is a price to pay for making the object easier to lift. You must pull twice as far on the rope as the object actually moves. For example, to lift the object 1 meter, you must pull up a distance of 2 meters on the rope. The direction of the force is not reversed. To lift the object, you must pull up on the rope, not down.

Pulleys can be combined in different ways. Look at the examples to the left. Note the number of supporting ropes pulling up on the object. Note the mechanical advantage (MA) of each pulley system. The MA of a pulley system is usually about equal to the number of ropes that pull upward. In the left pulley system, two ropes pull up on the object. Mechanical advantage equals 2. In the right pulley system, three ropes pull up, so MA equals 3.

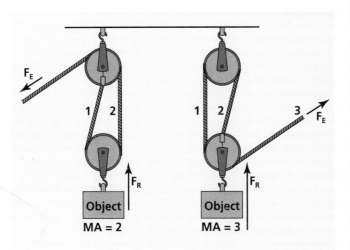

1. What is a pulley?
2. What is the difference between a fixed pulley and a movable pulley?
3. In each of the pulleys shown, what is the mechanical advantage?

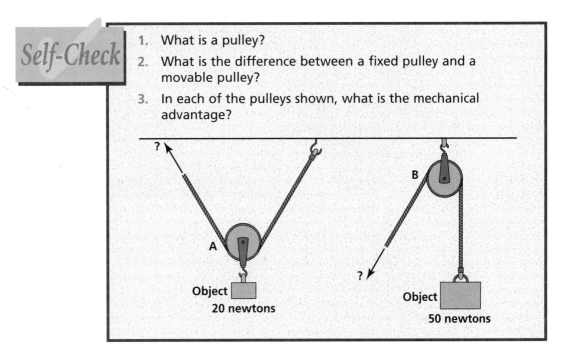

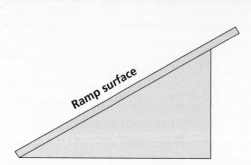
The Inclined Plane

The **inclined plane** has no moving parts, but it is a machine.

Inclined planes, such as the one pictured to the left, decrease the force you need to move an object. Once again, you pay for this decrease in effort force by an increase in the distance the object has to be moved. For example, if a delivery person needs to put a box on a truck that is 1 meter from the ground, he might use an inclined plane, or ramp, to make his job easier. Rather than lifting the box 1 meter straight up, he can push it up the ramp. It takes less force to push an object than to pick it up. However, he must move the object farther, as shown in the figure below.

An inclined plane is a ramp up which an object can be pushed.

Ramp surface

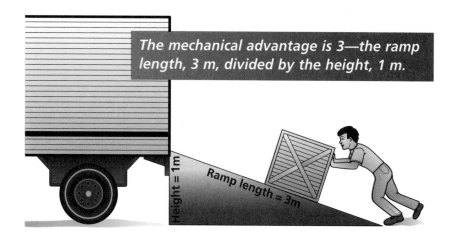

The mechanical advantage is 3—the ramp length, 3 m, divided by the height, 1 m.

Height = 1m
Ramp length = 3m

The mechanical advantage of an inclined plane is the length of the slanted surface, divided by the vertical (up and down) height. The more gradual the slant, the greater the mechanical advantage, but the farther the object must go.

The Screw

Another kind of simple machine, the **screw,** is a form of inclined plane. Think of a screw as a straight piece of metal with an inclined plane wrapped in a spiral around it. The ridges formed by this spiral are called threads.

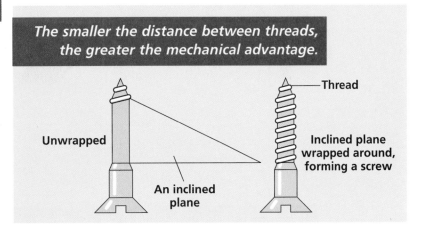

The smaller the distance between threads, the greater the mechanical advantage.

Unwrapped

An inclined plane

Thread

Inclined plane wrapped around, forming a screw

Screws make it easier to fasten objects together. The mechanical advantage of a screw depends on the distance between the threads. The smaller the distance, the more times the inclined plane is wrapped around, and the greater is the mechanical advantage.

Inclined planes

This person is using a wedge tool called an adze to split a log.

The Wedge

A **wedge** is an inclined plane that moves when it is used. It is thick at one end and thinner at the other. A wedge is often made up of two inclined planes joined together. Both edges are slanted. A wedge can be used for jobs like splitting wood apart. A force applied to the thick end is multiplied and acts at the thin end, piercing the wood. The thinner and more gradual the wedge, the greater is the mechanical advantage.

The Wheel and Axle

An automobile steering wheel and a doorknob are examples of a simple machine called a **wheel and axle.** In this machine, a wheel is attached to a shaft called an axle, as shown below.

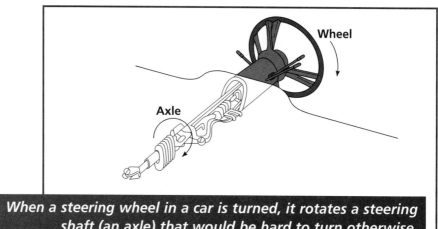

Wheel

Axle

When a steering wheel in a car is turned, it rotates a steering shaft (an axle) that would be hard to turn otherwise.

A wheel and axle increases the force you apply to the wheel. The multiplied force can then turn something else attached to the axle. The mechanical advantage of a wheel and axle depends on the size of the wheel compared to the thickness of the axle. The bigger the wheel is in comparison to the thickness of the axle, the greater is the mechanical advantage.

Self-Check

1. What is an inclined plane? How can you find the mechanical advantage of an inclined plane?
2. Screws and wedges are variations of what simple machine?
3. Which will have a greater mechanical advantage: a screw with closely spaced threads or one with widely spaced threads?
4. Which will have a greater mechanical advantage: a thin, gradual wedge or a thick, greatly sloping one?

- Work is what happens when a force makes something move in the direction of the force.

- Energy is the ability to do work.

- Kinetic energy is energy of motion. Potential energy is stored energy.

- The six main forms of energy are chemical, heat, mechanical, nuclear, radiant, and electrical. Energy can change from one form to another.

- Energy cannot be created or destroyed.

- Simple machines make doing work easier by changing the size or direction of a force or the distance through which a force acts.

- Resistance force is the force applied by a machine against a resistance. Effort force is the force applied to a machine by the person using it.

- A lever is a bar that turns about a fulcrum.

- Levers are divided into three classes, according to the relationship between the effort, fulcrum, and resistance.

- The mechanical advantage of a machine is the number of times by which the machine multiplies effort force.

- A pulley is made up of a rope, chain, or belt wrapped around a wheel.

- An inclined plane is a ramp.

- A screw and a wedge are special forms of inclined planes.

- A wheel and axle is a wheel attached to a shaft.

Science Words

efficiency, 196
effort arm, 199
effort force, 192
energy, 185
fulcrum, 192
generator, 187
inclined plane, 204
joule, 183
kinetic energy, 185
law of conservation
  of energy, 188
lever, 192

mechanical advantage, 198
potential energy, 185
pulley, 202
resistance arm, 199
resistance force, 193
screw, 205
simple machine, 192
wedge, 205
wheel and axle, 206
work, 182
work input, 195
work output, 195

Vocabulary Review

Number your paper from 1 to 12. Then choose a word or words from the Word Bank that best complete each sentence. Write the answer on your paper.

WORD BANK

effort force

energy

inclined plane

kinetic energy

mechanical
    advantage

nuclear energy

potential energy

resistance force

simple machine

wheel and axle

work

work input

1. _____ is the ability to do work.

2. Resistance force divided by effort force equals _____.

3. A(n) _____ is a ramplike simple machine.

4. Force multiplied by distance equals _____.

5. _____ is energy associated with the center of an atom.

6. Effort force multiplied by effort distance equals _____.

7. _____ is stored energy.

8. _____ is the force applied by a machine against the resistance.

9. _____ is energy of motion.

10. A(n) _____ is a tool with few parts.

11. _____ is the force applied to a machine by the user.

12. A(n) _____ has a wheel attached to a shaft.

Concept Review

Number your paper from 1 to 6. Then choose the answer that best completes each sentence. Write the letter of the answer on your paper.

1. A paper cutter is an example of a _____ lever.
    a. first-class   **b.** second-class   **c.** third-class

2. Light is an example of _____ energy.
    a. radiant   **b.** mechanical   **c.** nuclear

3. A machine that has a work output of 4 and a work input of 8 has an efficiency of about _____.
    a. 50 percent   **b.** 200 percent   **c.** 40 percent

4. A pulley that has five upward-pulling ropes has a mechanical advantage of approximately _____.
   a. 1/5   b. 5   c. 10

5. A screw contains a(n) _____.
   a. axle   b. wheel   c. inclined plane

6. When energy changes from one form to another, the total amount of energy _____.
   a. decreases   b. increases   c. remains the same

Critical Thinking
Write the answer to each of the following questions.

1. Suppose some grease is being warmed on an electric stove and catches fire. The hot smoke causes a battery-powered fire detector to sound a siren and flash a warning light. Trace the conversions between energy forms involved.

2. What class of lever is shown in the diagram below? How can you tell?

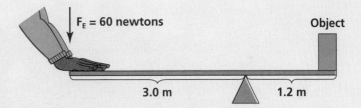

F_E = 60 newtons   Object

3.0 m   1.2 m

Test Taking Tip   Be sure you understand what the test question is asking. Reread it if you have to.

Chapter

9

Heat

Imagine curling up in front of this fire on a chilly night. The light from the fire would probably cast an inviting glow throughout the room. The heat from the fire might make your fingers and toes feel warm. In this chapter, you'll find out about heat. You'll learn different ways to measure heat. You will also find out how heat moves from one place to another.

ORGANIZE YOUR THOUGHTS

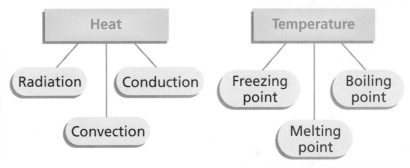

Heat
- Radiation
- Conduction
- Convection

Temperature
- Freezing point
- Melting point
- Boiling point

Goals for Learning

▶ To explain how heat energy can be produced

▶ To explain how heat changes matter

▶ To explain how temperature is measured

▶ To explain the difference between temperature and heat

▶ To calculate heat gained or lost

▶ To explain how matter is heated by conduction, convection, and radiation

Objectives

After reading this lesson, you should be able to

▶ define heat.

▶ explain how heat energy can do work.

▶ explain how heat is produced.

▶ describe some sources of heat.

Heat

A form of energy resulting from the motion of particles in matter; heat energy flows from a warmer object to a cooler object.

What happens if you hold an ice cube in your hand as this picture shows? Your hand is warmer than the ice cube. The warmth from your hand causes the ice cube to melt. **Heat** causes the ice to melt. Heat is a form of energy that results from the motion of particles in matter. Heat energy flows from a warmer object, such as your hand, to a cooler object, such as the ice cube.

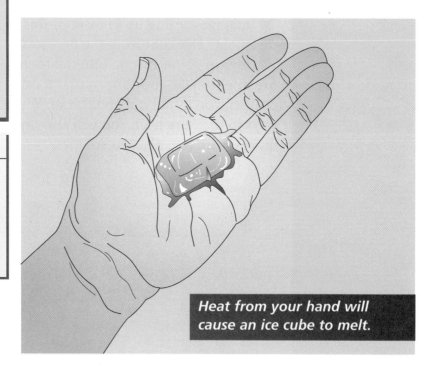

Heat from your hand will cause an ice cube to melt.

You learned in Chapter 8 that heat is a form of energy. Energy can do work. Therefore, heat can do work. Machines can change heat energy into useful mechanical energy. For example, a steam engine uses the heat energy contained in steam to move the parts of the engine. An automobile engine also uses heat energy. Burning fuel produces hot gases that make the engine work.

Sources of Heat

What produces heat energy? Remember that all matter is made of atoms and molecules. These tiny particles are always moving. This motion of particles in matter is a measure of the heat energy. The faster the particles move, the more heat energy they have.

Imagine going outside on a summer day. You feel heat from the sun. The sun is the earth's most important **heat source.** A heat source is a place from which heat energy comes. The motion of the atoms and molecules in the sun gives off the heat energy that warms you.

You might recall from Chapter 8 that energy comes in different forms. Other forms of energy can be changed into heat energy. For example, hold your hands as shown in the picture and then rub them together rapidly. Notice that your hands begin to feel warm. Friction between your hands is a form of mechanical energy—the energy of motion—that produces heat.

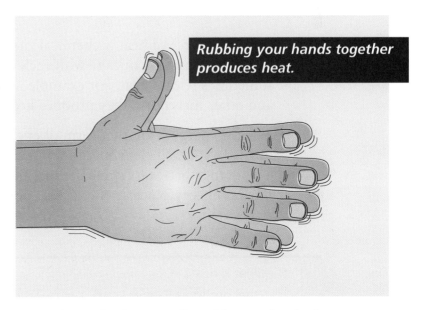

Rubbing your hands together produces heat.

Sometimes the heat produced by mechanical energy can cause harmful effects. For example, the oil-well drills used to drill through rock produce much heat. Workers must cool the drills with water to keep them from melting.

Electricity is also a heat source. Look at the toaster. When energy from an electric current passes through the wires of the toaster, the wires become hot. This energy can toast bread. What other appliances can you name that change electricity into heat energy?

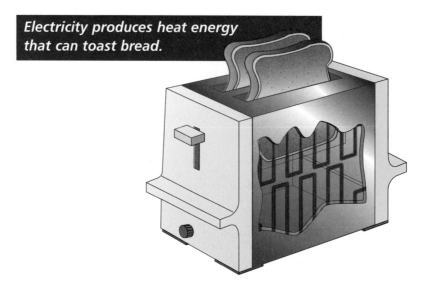

Electricity produces heat energy that can toast bread.

Another source of heat is chemical energy. When substances react chemically with each other, they sometimes release heat. For example, when natural gas and other fuels burn, they produce heat.

Nuclear energy is another form of energy you have learned about. Nuclear energy is released when atoms split or join together. Stars shine because their atoms release nuclear energy. Nuclear energy also produces heat.

Self-Check

1. What is heat?
2. What produces heat energy?
3. Give an example of how another form of energy can be changed into heat energy.

Objectives

After reading this lesson, you should be able to

▶ describe how heat affects solids.

▶ describe how heat affects liquids.

▶ describe how matter expands and contracts.

Evaporate

To change from a liquid to a gas.

Matter exists in different states. In a solid, the particles are closer together than they are in a liquid or a gas. The particles also move slower in the solid. Heat can cause particles to move faster and move farther apart. Heat can change matter from one state to another.

Changing From a Liquid to a Gas

You might have noticed that if you boil water for a period of time, the amount of water gradually decreases. What happens to the water? Heat makes the water molecules move faster. As the molecules move faster, they bump into each other more often and push each other apart. As a result, the water **evaporates,** or changes from a liquid to a gas.

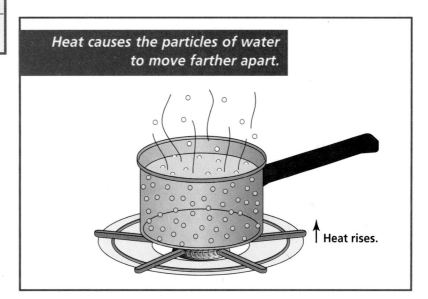

Heat causes the particles of water to move farther apart.

↑ Heat rises.

Changing From a Solid to a Liquid

What happens to an ice cube (a solid) if it is left in a warm room? It melts. But why does it melt? Heat speeds up the moving molecules in the ice cube. The molecules move apart. The solid ice cube changes to liquid water.

Expand	# Expanding and Contracting Matter
To become larger in size.	Heat causes particles in matter to push each other farther apart. Then the matter **expands,** or fills up more space. The figure shows a joint in a metal bridge. Summer heat makes the material in the bridge expand. What might happen if the bridge had no expansion joint?

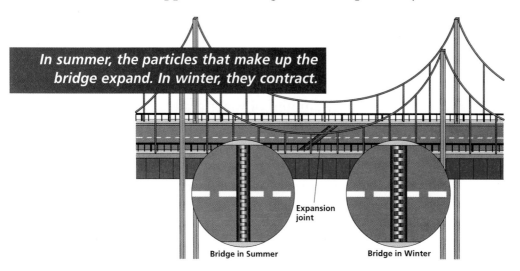

In summer, the particles that make up the bridge expand. In winter, they contract.

Expansion joint

Bridge in Summer   Bridge in Winter

Solids, liquids, and gases do not expand equally. In most cases, liquids expand more than solids. Gases usually expand the most.

<table>
<tr><td>Contract
To become smaller in size.</td><td>Sometimes, matter loses heat. Particles in matter move more slowly and stay closer together as they lose heat. The matter contracts, or takes up less space. In the figure, notice the joint in the bridge in winter. The material in the bridge contracts in cold weather. Water is a material that behaves differently. Cooled water contracts until it reaches 4°C. Below this temperature, water expands until it freezes at 0°C.</td></tr>
</table>

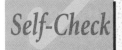

Self-Check

1. What happens to an ice cube when it is heated?
2. What happens when water in a puddle evaporates?
3. How does heat affect the amount of space matter fills?

Observing and Comparing Expansion and Contraction

Materials

✓ safety goggles
✓ balloon
✓ flask
✓ masking tape
✓ 2 buckets
✓ cold water
✓ warm water
✓ paper towels

Purpose
To observe and compare expansion and contraction of gases

Procedure
1. Copy the data table below on your paper.

	Changes in balloon
in warm water	
in cold water	
at room temperature	

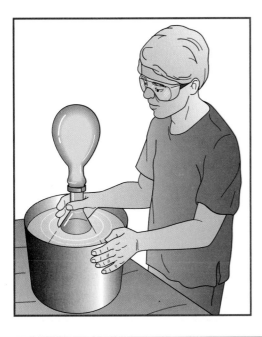

2. Put on your safety goggles.

3. Carefully stretch the opening of the balloon over the opening of the flask. Use masking tape to tape the balloon to the flask.

4. Fill one bucket with cold water.

5. Fill the other bucket with hot water. *Safety Alert: Do not use water hot enough to cause a burn.* Place the flask in the bucket of hot water. Keep the flask in the water until the flask becomes hot.

6. Observe the balloon. Record in your data table any changes you see.

7. Remove the flask from the bucket of hot water. Place the flask in the bucket of cold water. Keep the flask in the cold water until the flask becomes cold. Record any changes to the balloon.

8. Take the flask out of the water and dry it. Watch the balloon as the flask returns to room temperature. Record any changes to the balloon.

Questions

1. What happened to the balloon when the flask was heated?

2. What happened to the balloon as the flask cooled?

3. What caused the changes you observed in the balloon?

After reading this lesson, you should be able to

▶ explain how temperature is measured.

▶ compare and contrast temperature scales.

▶ describe freezing point, melting point, and boiling point.

Suppose you place your hand into a bowl of cool water such as the one in the picture. Heat energy from your hand flows into the water and makes the water warmer.

Heat from your hand will increase the temperature of the cool water.

Temperature

A measure of how fast an object's particles are moving.

The more your hand heats the water, the faster the water particles move. **Temperature** measures how fast an object's particles are moving. The faster an object's particles move, the higher its temperature is.

Touching an object does not always give an accurate measurement of the object's temperature. For example, if you place your hand in cold water, heat energy from your hand moves to the water and your hand becomes cooler. If you move the same hand out of the cold water and into a container of lukewarm water, the water will feel hotter than it actually is because your hand is cool.

Thermometer
A device that measures temperature.

Thermometers

You often can't rely on your sense of touch to accurately tell temperature. So how can you measure temperature accurately? A **thermometer** is a measuring instrument used to measure temperature. The pictures show different kinds of thermometers.

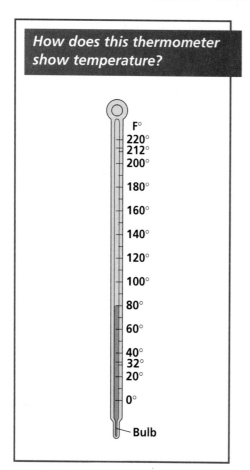

How does this thermometer show temperature?

F°
220°
212°
200°
180°
160°
140°
120°
100°
80°
60°
40°
32°
20°
0°

Bulb

The kind of thermometer shown to the left is a glass tube with a small amount of liquid inside. The liquid is usually mercury or alcohol. As the thermometer measures higher temperatures, heat causes the particles of liquid to expand, or move farther apart. As the liquid expands, it moves up the tube. The more heat that passes to the liquid, the more the liquid will expand and the higher the liquid moves in the tube. When the liquid stops expanding, it stops beside a number on the tube. This number tells the temperature of the substance touching the bulb of the thermometer.

The picture below shows an electronic thermometer. Many doctors and medical workers use this kind of thermometer to take people's temperatures. It measures temperatures very quickly.

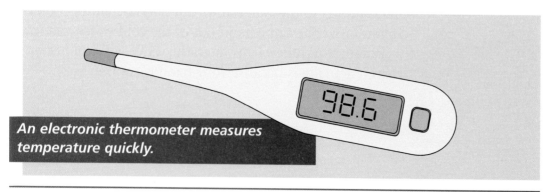

An electronic thermometer measures temperature quickly.

Temperature Scales

Two common scales are used to measure temperature. People in the United States usually use the **Fahrenheit scale.** Fahrenheit is abbreviated as F. People in most other countries use the **Celsius scale.** Celsius is abbreviated as C. Scientists use the Celsius scale.

Look at the thermometers on this page to compare the Fahrenheit scale with the Celsius scale. Find the equally-spaced units on each scale. For both temperature scales, temperature is measured in units called **degrees** (°). The temperature shown on the Fahrenheit scale is 68 degrees Fahrenheit. It is written as 68°F. The same temperature in the Celsius scale is 20 degrees Celsius. It is written as 20°C.

Any temperature below zero degrees is written with a minus (−) sign. For example, a temperature of 10 degrees below zero on the Celsius scale is written as −10°C. The table on the next page shows how temperatures on the Fahrenheit scale and the Celsius scale are written. The table also shows how to read the temperatures on each scale.

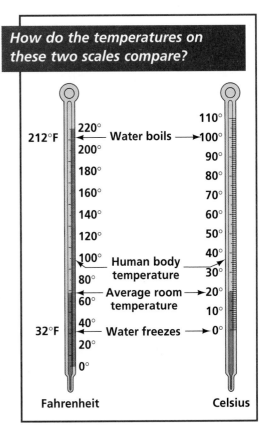

How do the temperatures on these two scales compare?

212°F

220° ← Water boils → 100°
110°
200°
90°
180°
80°
160°
70°
140°
60°
120°
50°
100° — Human body temperature — 40°
80° — 30°
← Average room → 20°
60° temperature
10°
40°
32°F ← Water freezes → 0°
20°
0°

Fahrenheit   Celsius

Temperature Conversion Table			
°C	°F	°C	°F
100	212	45	113
95	203	40	104
90	194	35	95
85	185	30	86
80	176	25	77
75	167	20	68
70	158	15	59
65	149	10	50
60	140	5	41
55	131	0	32
50	122		

If you know the temperature of a substance on one scale, you can convert to an equal temperature on the other scale. The table shows how temperatures convert from one scale to the other.

Freezing Point

What happens when you place a container of water in the freezer? The water gradually changes to ice. Suppose you recorded the temperature of the water every five minutes. You would notice that as time passed, the temperature would decrease. As the temperature of the water decreases, the water loses heat. Eventually the liquid water becomes solid.

Freezing point

The temperature at which a liquid changes to a solid.

The temperature at which a liquid changes to a solid is called its **freezing point.** The figure below shows the freezing point of water. On the Celsius scale, the temperature at which water freezes is 0°. On the Fahrenheit scale, the temperature at which water freezes is 32°.

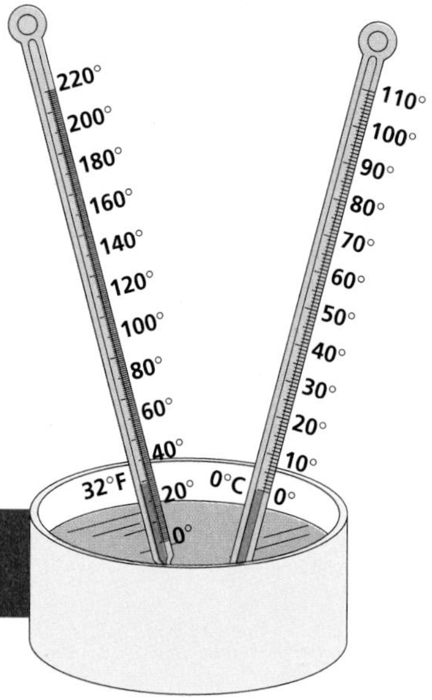

How do these two scales differ in how they measure the freezing point of water?

Melting point
The temperature at which a solid changes to a liquid.

Boiling point
The temperature at which a liquid changes to a gas.

Melting Point

The temperature at which a solid changes to a liquid is called its **melting point.** The melting point of a substance is the same as its freezing point. The term *melting point* is used when a substance is being heated. When ice is heated, it changes to a liquid at a temperature of 0°C. Therefore, the melting point of ice is 0°C.

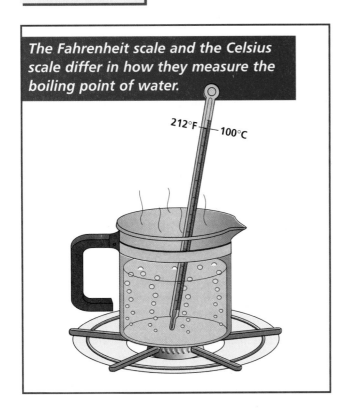

The Fahrenheit scale and the Celsius scale differ in how they measure the boiling point of water.

212°F — 100°C

Boiling Point

The **boiling point** of a substance is the temperature at which it changes from a liquid to a gas. You can see in the figure that the temperature at which water boils is 100° on the Celsius scale. On the Fahrenheit scale, the boiling point is read as 212°.

Every substance has its own freezing and boiling points. Scientists use the freezing and boiling points of substances to help identify unknown substances. You can see the freezing and boiling points of a few substances in the table.

Substance	Freezing/Melting Point		Boiling Point	
	°F	°C	°F	°C
water	32	0	212	100
aluminum	1,220	660	4,473	2,467
iron	1,762	961	4,014	2,212
alcohol	−202	−130	173	78

Changing Freezing Point and Boiling Point

You can change the freezing point and the boiling point of a substance by mixing substances together. For example, if you add alcohol to water, the freezing point of the mixture will be lower than the freezing point of water alone. Antifreeze contains alcohol. Adding antifreeze to an automobile radiator lowers the freezing point of the water in the radiator. This keeps the water from freezing and prevents engine damage. The antifreeze also has a higher boiling point than water. Antifreeze boils more slowly than water in hot weather.

Certain compounds of sodium and calcium are used on icy roads and walkways in winter. These compounds lower the freezing point of water and change the ice back to a liquid.

Self-Check

1. How does the motion of molecules affect temperature?
2. Explain how a liquid thermometer works.
3. Write the following temperatures:
   a. thirty-four degrees Fahrenheit
   b. sixty-six degrees Celsius
   c. four degrees below zero on the Fahrenheit scale
   d. one hundred ten degrees on the Celsius scale
4. What is meant by the freezing point and the melting point of a substance?
5. What is meant by the boiling point of a substance?
6. How can the freezing point of a substance be changed?

Objectives

After reading this lesson, you should be able to

▶ explain how temperature and heat differ.

▶ explain how heat is measured.

▶ calculate heat gain and loss.

Suppose you fill a tub with warm water. Then you fill a cup with water from the tub. The temperature of the water in each container would be the same. However, the water in the tub would give off more heat than the water in the cup. The amount of heat given off depends on the mass of the water, as well as on the surface area and the temperature of the air.

Temperature and Heat

Temperature and heat are different. Temperature is a measure of how fast the molecules in a substance are moving. Heat depends on the temperature of a substance and the amount of matter, or mass, the substance has.

As the temperature of an object increases, the amount of heat in the object also increases. If two objects of different mass are at the same temperature, the object with the greater mass will give off more heat. The temperature of the lighted candle in the picture is the same as the temperature of the bonfire. The bonfire contains more mass than the candle. Therefore, the bonfire gives off more heat.

The bonfire gives off more heat than the candle.

Measuring Heat

You know that temperature is measured in units called degrees. Scientists measure heat in units of energy called **calories.** A calorie is the amount of heat needed to raise the temperature of 1 gram of water by 1 degree Celsius.

Calorie

Unit of heat; the amount of heat needed to raise the temperature of 1 g of water by 1°C.

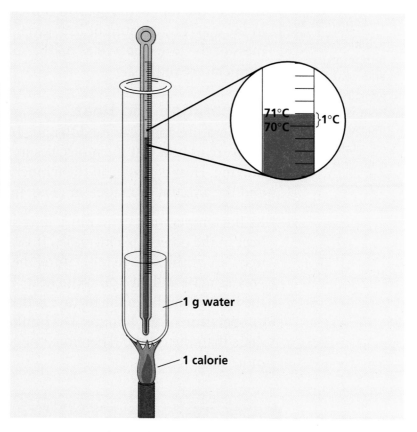

71°C
70°C }1°C

1 g water

1 calorie

You can use a formula to find out the amount of heat (calories) you would need to change the temperature of a substance.

Heat (calories) = change in temperature (°C) × mass (grams)

How many calories of heat are needed to raise the temperature of 1 gram of water by 3 degrees C?

Heat = change in temperature × mass
Heat = 3°C × 1 g
Heat = 3 calories

You can also calculate a problem such as the following.

How many calories of heat are needed to raise the temperature of 6 grams of water from 5°C to 15°C?

First, calculate the temperature change.
        Change in temperature = 15°C – 5°C
        Change in temperature = 10°C

Then calculate the heat.
        Heat = change in temperature × mass
        Heat = 10°C × 6 g
        Heat = 60 calories

Self-Check

1. If two objects of the same temperature have a different mass, which object gives off the most heat?

2. Suppose 25 grams of water are heated to 5°C. How many calories are needed?

3. Suppose 15 grams of water are heated from 12°C to 22°C. How many calories are needed?

4. If 20 grams of water are heated 1°C, how much heat is added?

Cooling

Heat can also be lost or given off by a substance when it is cooling. To indicate that the water is being cooled, a minus sign (−) is placed in front of the answer.

Suppose 20 grams of water are cooled from 20°C to 8°C. How much heat is given off?

First, calculate the change in temperature.
Change in temperature = 20°C − 8°C
Change in temperature = 12°C

Then, calculate the calories.
Heat = change in temperature × mass
Heat = 12°C × 20 g
Heat = 240 calories

The answer is expressed as −240 calories to show that heat is given off.

Write the answers to the following questions. Show your work.

1. Suppose 35 grams of water are cooled from 15°C to 10°C. How much heat is given off?

2. Suppose 88 grams of water are cooled from 22°C to 16°C. How much heat is given off?

3. Suppose 16 grams of water are cooled from 13°C to 1°C. How much heat is given off?

INVESTIGATION

Measuring the Rate of Heat Loss

Materials

✓ large jar
✓ hot tap water
✓ small jar
✓ 2 Celsius thermometers
✓ clock or watch

Purpose

To measure the cooling rates of different volumes of water

Procedure

1. Copy the data table below on your paper. Continue the table down to 15 minutes.

Time	Temperature (°C)	
	Large jar	Small jar
0 minutes		
1 minute		
2 minutes		

2. Fill the large jar with hot tap water. *Safety Alert: Do not use water hot enough to cause a burn.*

3. Fill the small jar about halfway with hot tap water.

4. Place the jars next to each other on a flat surface.

5. Place a thermometer in each jar, as shown in the picture on the following page. Immediately read the temperature on each thermometer. Record the temperatures in the section of your data table marked *0 minutes*.

6. Leave the thermometers in the jars. Use the clock or watch to keep track of the time. Record the temperature of each water sample every minute for 15 minutes.

Questions

1. What was the temperature of the water in each jar the first time you measured it? After 8 minutes? After 15 minutes?

2. How did the amount of water in the jar affect how fast the temperature of the water dropped?

3. What happened to the heat from the water as the water cooled?

Explore Further

Repeat the activity, using a jar of ice water.

1. How does the temperature of the water change after 8 minutes? After 15 minutes?

2. Explain the change of temperature that occurred in the ice water.

Objectives

After reading this lesson, you should be able to

- ▶ explain how matter is heated by radiation.
- ▶ explain how matter is heated by conduction.
- ▶ explain how matter is heated by convection.

Vacuum

Space that contains no matter.

Radiation

The movement of energy through a vacuum.

Think about different ways you can travel from one place to another. You might walk or run. You might ride a bicycle. You might travel in cars, buses, trains, boats, or airplanes. Energy also has different ways of moving from warm matter to cool matter.

Radiation

The sun is a very long distance from Earth—150 million kilometers, in fact. Yet the sun heats Earth. How does the sun's energy travel the long distance from its surface to Earth? It must travel through a **vacuum.** A vacuum is a space that has no matter. Energy from the sun reaches us by **radiation.** Radiation can carry energy across space where there is no matter. The energy can heat matter.

Heat from sources other than the sun can also travel by radiation. You can see an example in the diagram. Heat energy from the fire moves into the room by radiation and then heats the air.

Conduction

You probably know that if you held a strip of metal in a flame it would get hot. Why does this happen? The metal gets hot because of **conduction.** Heat travels by conduction when molecules bump into each other.

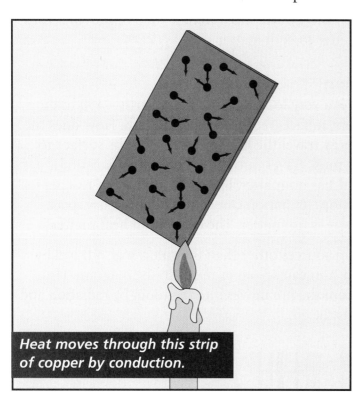

Heat moves through this strip of copper by conduction.

Look at the strip of copper in the diagram. Heat from the flame makes the copper particles near the flame move faster. As the particles move faster, they hit other particles. These particles then bump into the particles farther up on the strip of copper. They transfer energy. As a result, the slower particles move faster. Eventually, all the molecules in the copper are moving fast. In other words, the entire piece of copper becomes hot.

Energy moves easily through some kinds of matter. A substance that allows heat energy to flow through it easily is called a **conductor.** Most metals, such as copper, silver, gold, aluminum, and tin, are good conductors.

A material that does not conduct heat well is called an **insulator.** Insulators are used in the walls of homes to keep heat out in summer and cold out in winter. Some good insulators are glass, wood, sand, soil, Styrofoam, and air.

Convection

Convection is a method of heat movement that happens when the particles of a gas or a liquid rise. As they rise, they carry heat.

Find the heater in the diagram. First, conduction heats the air touching the heater. Then the warm air rises. Cool air moves in to take its place. The heater warms the cool air and it rises. The warm air cools as it moves through the room. Then it flows back to the heater and is warmed again. The arrows show how heat energy flows up and around the room. Convection keeps the air moving.

Convection also happens in liquids. Suppose a pot of cold water is placed on the stove. Heat is conducted from the hot burner to the pot and then to the water at the very bottom of the pot. Then convection heats the rest of the water. The warm water rises and the cooler water sinks.

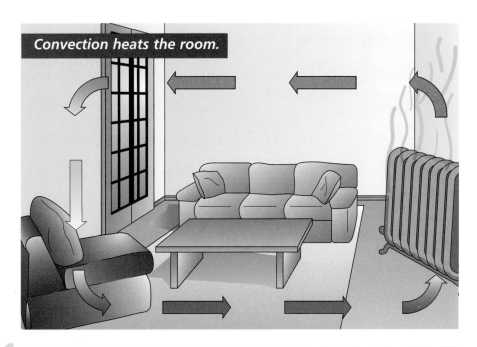

Convection heats the room.

1. How does the sun's heat travel to the earth?
2. How does heat move by conduction?
3. Explain how convection heats a room.

How do different heating systems work?

How can you control the temperature of your home? The chart describes some types of heating systems that people use to keep their homes at a comfortable temperature.

Heating Systems

Type of System	Description	Special Features
Hot water	A furnace heats the water. A pump circulates the water through pipes to a radiator in each room.	Convection and radiation circulate heat throughout the room.
Steam	A boiler sends steam to pipes. Steam forces the heat through the pipes to radiators in each room.	Radiation and convection circulate heat throughout the room.
Forced air	Air is heated by a furnace. It is then pumped into rooms through vents at the floor of each room.	Forced convection circulates heat throughout the room.
Passive solar	The sun's rays pass through a large door or window. They heat up a large tile or rock wall. Heat radiates into the room from the wall and sets up convectioncurrents.	Radiation and convection distribute heat.
Radiant electric	Electric current heats up wires in baseboards, walls, and/or ceilings.	Heat radiates from these specific places.

1. Which heating systems heat a home by convection?

2. Which heating systems provide radiant heat?

3. Which type of heating system would be more efficient in a hot, sunny climate than in a cold climate? Why?

- Heat is a form of energy. It results from the motion of the particles in matter. Heat energy flows from a warmer object to a cooler object.

- Mechanical, solar, electrical, chemical, and nuclear energy are sources of heat.

- Heat can cause matter to change from one state to another.

- Heat causes matter to expand; loss of heat causes matter to contract.

- Temperature measures the motion of molecules.

- The Fahrenheit and Celsius scales are used to measure temperature.

- The freezing point, the melting point, and the boiling point are important temperatures for all substances.

- Heat is measured in calories.

- Heat depends on the temperature and the mass of an object.

- The number of calories gained or lost by water equals the change in Celsius temperature multiplied by the mass.

- Heat travels by radiation, conduction, and convection.

Science Words

boiling point, 223	Fahrenheit scale, 221
calorie, 226	freezing point, 222
Celsius scale, 221	heat, 212
conduction, 232	heat source, 213
conductor, 232	insulator, 232
contract, 216	melting point, 223
convection, 233	radiation, 231
degree, 221	temperature, 219
evaporate, 215	thermometer, 220
expand, 216	vacuum, 231

Vocabulary Review

Number your paper from 1 to 12. Then choose a word or words from the Word Bank that best complete each sentence. Write the answer on your paper.

WORD BANK

calorie
Celsius scale
conductors
contracts
convection
degree
expands
freezing point
heat
insulators
melting point
thermometer
vacuum

1. _____ are materials that carry heat easily.
2. A device used to measure temperature is a(n) _____.
3. A _____ is a unit of heat.
4. The temperature at which water changes to ice is the _____ of water.
5. Scientists use the _____ to measure temperature.
6. The _____ of a substance is the same as its freezing point.
7. The flow of energy that occurs when a warm gas rises is _____.
8. A _____ is a unit of measurement on a temperature scale.
9. Matter usually fills up more space when it _____.
10. _____ is the flow of energy from a warmer object to a cooler object.
11. The sun's heat travels through a(n) _____.
12. When matter _____, it usually takes up less space.
13. Glass, wood, and air are examples of _____.

Concept Review

Number your paper from 1 to 10. Then choose the word or words that best complete each sentence. Write the letter of the answer on your paper.

1. The flow of heat energy from one molecule to the next is _____.
   a. convection   b. conduction   c. radiation
2. The earth's most important heat source is _____.
   a. heating systems   b. heating oil   c. the sun

3. When water changes from a liquid to a gas, it _____.
   a. evaporates   b. radiates   c. conducts
4. The temperature scale commonly used in the United States is the _____.
   a. Fahrenheit scale b. calorie scale c. Celsius scale
5. A vacuum is a space that has no _____.
   a. heat   b. radiation   c. matter
6. A material that does not carry heat well is a(n) _____.
   a. conductor   b. insulator   c. vacuum
7. _____ calories of heat are needed to raise the temperature of 1 gram of water by 6°C.
   a. 12   b. 6   c. 3
8. The faster an object's particles move, the _____ its temperature is.
   a. higher   b. less accurate c. lower
9. The motion of particles of matter produces _____.
   a. vacuums   b. radiation   c. heat energy
10. Alcohol _____ the freezing point of water.
    a. raises   b. lowers   c. does not change

Critical Thinking

Write the answer to each of the following questions.

1. The objects shown in the picture to the left have the same temperatures. Do they give off the same amount of heat? Explain your answer.

2. Look at the picture to the right. Explain how the water in the pot is being heated.

Test Taking Tip When you read over your written answer, imagine that you are someone reading it for the first time. Ask yourself if the information makes sense. Revise your answer to make it as clear as you can.

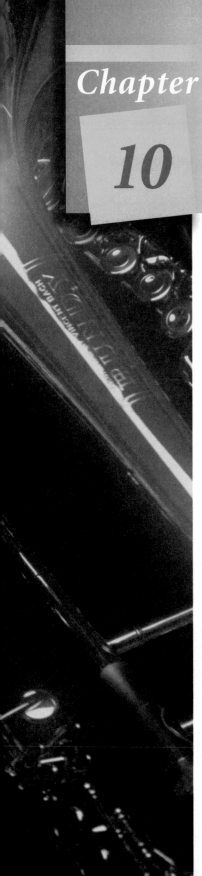

Chapter

10

Sound and Light

Perhaps you have heard your favorite music being played on one or more of the instruments in the photo. Musical instruments usually make pleasing sounds. In this chapter, you will learn about different sounds and how they are produced. You will learn how sounds travel from one place to another. You also will find out that sound and light are alike in some ways.

ORGANIZE YOUR THOUGHTS

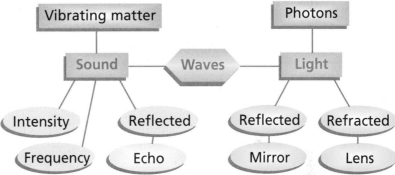

Vibrating matter

Photons

Sound — Waves — Light

Intensity

Frequency

Reflected

Echo

Reflected

Mirror

Refracted

Lens

Goals for Learning

▶ To explain how sounds are produced

▶ To explain how sound travels

▶ To describe reflected sound

▶ To describe the nature of light

▶ To describe the visible spectrum

▶ To explain reflection and refraction of light

▶ To explain how mirrors and lenses affect light rays

Objectives

After reading this lesson, you should be able to

▶ explain what sound is.

▶ explain how sound is produced.

▶ explain how sound energy moves in waves.

Vibrate

To move rapidly back and forth.

You hear many kinds of sounds every minute of every day. But do you know what sound is? Sound is a form of energy. Scientists who study sound also study human hearing and the effect of sound on different objects.

How Sound Is Produced

All the sounds you hear are made when matter **vibrates.** To vibrate means to move quickly back and forth. Look at the bell on this page. When the clapper hits the bell, energy from the clapper causes the bell to vibrate. When the bell vibrates, it moves back and forth. The bell pushes the air around it. You can see in the diagram that as the bell vibrates to the right, it pushes together the air particles to the right of the bell. When it vibrates back to the left, the air particles to the right of the bell move apart. Those particles to the left of the bell are squeezed together. As the bell continues to vibrate, the air particles on each side are squeezed together and spread apart many times.

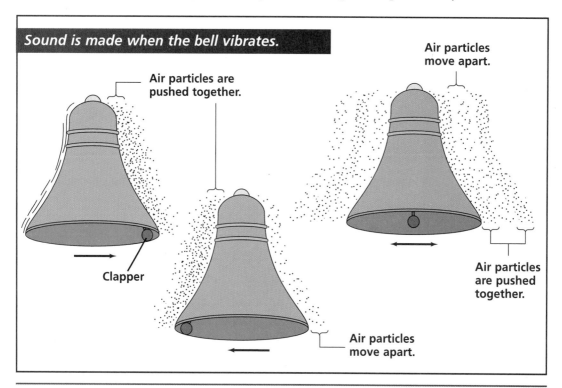

Sound is made when the bell vibrates.

Air particles are pushed together.

Clapper

Air particles move apart.

Air particles move apart.

Air particles are pushed together.

How Sound Travels

The movement of the air molecules around a vibrating object is a **sound wave.** You cannot see a sound wave. Sound waves move out from the object in all directions. As the sound waves travel farther from the object, they become weaker. The figures of the wire spring show how sound energy travels in waves.

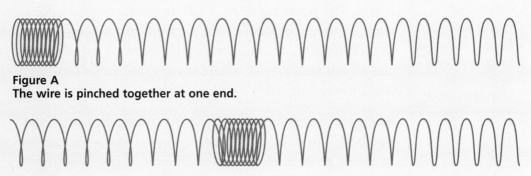

Figure A
The wire is pinched together at one end.

Figure B
The "wave" moves across the spring.

Some things make sounds even though you cannot see them vibrate. For example, if you strike a tuning fork, you will not see it vibrate. But you will hear the sound it makes. You can see evidence of sound waves by placing the end of a tuning fork that has been struck into a small container filled with water. You will notice water splashing out of the container. The vibrations of the tuning fork cause the water to move about.

A tuning fork vibrates, producing sound waves, when it is struck.

Self-Check

1. How is sound produced?
2. How does sound travel?

Intensity

The strength of a sound.

Decibel

A unit that measures the intensity of sound.

How would you describe the sounds around you? You might point out that some sounds are loud or soft. You might also describe some sounds as high or low.

Loud and Soft Sounds

You might barely be able to hear the sounds of rustling leaves. The noise made by a jet, however, might make you want to cover your ears. The strength of a sound is known as its **intensity.** A sound wave that carries a lot of energy has a high intensity. A sound wave that carries less energy has a lower intensity.

Scientists measure the intensity of sounds in units called **decibels.** The sounds of rustling leaves would be measured at about 20 decibels. The roar of a jet engine would be approximately 135 decibels. You can see the decibel levels of some common sounds below.

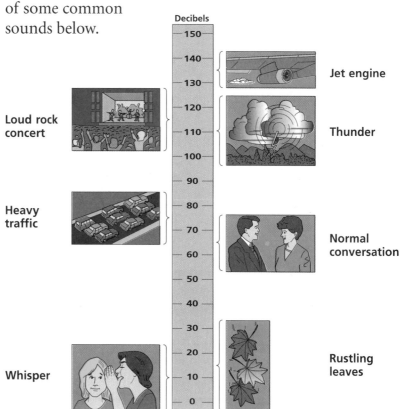

Decibels

- 150
- 140 — Jet engine
- 130
- 120
- Loud rock concert
- 110 — Thunder
- 100
- 90
- Heavy traffic
- 80
- 70 — Normal conversation
- 60
- 50
- 40
- 30
- 20 — Rustling leaves
- Whisper
- 10
- 0

Your hearing interprets the intensity of a sound as loud or soft. The loudness or softness of a sound is the **volume** of the sound. The more intense a sound, the higher its volume seems.

In some cases, loud sounds can help keep you safe. For example, the siren on a fire truck is loud enough to be heard above other sounds.

Loud sounds can also be harmful. Listening to loud music or other loud sounds for a long period of time can damage your hearing. Sounds above 90 decibels can cause pain to your ears. Sounds above 130 decibels can damage your ears.

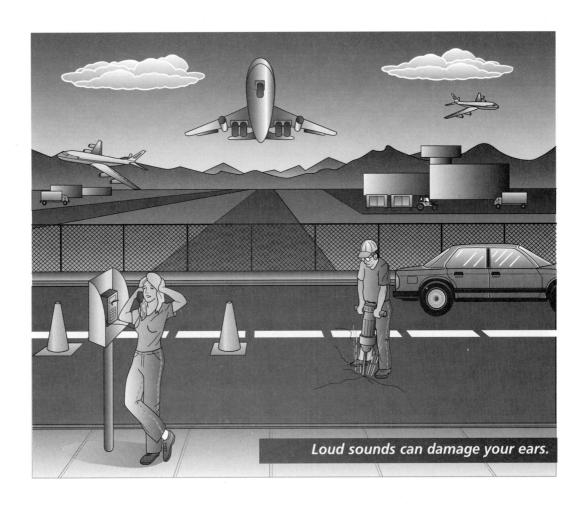

Loud sounds can damage your ears.

High and Low Sounds

How does the sound of a flute differ from the sound of a tuba? The flute has a high sound. The tuba has a low sound. We say that the flute has a higher **pitch** than the tuba. Pitch is how high or low a sound seems. Look at the sound waves in the figure below. You can see that the sound waves made by the flute are closer together than those made by the tuba. The flute produces more sound waves per second than the tuba.

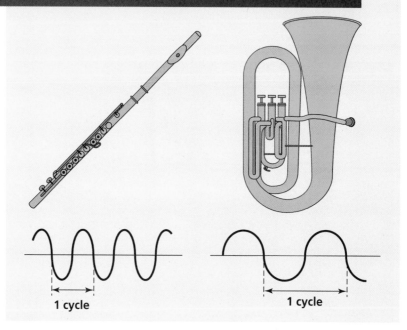

The flute has a higher pitch than the tuba. The flute produces more sound waves per second.

1 cycle 1 cycle

Cycle
The complete back-and-forth motion of a vibration.

Frequency
The number of vibrations per second of a sound wave.

Hertz
The unit used to measure frequency of a sound. One Hertz equals one cycle per second.

Pitch
How high or low a sound is.

The **frequency** of a sound wave describes the number of sound waves in one second. If an object vibrates 5 times in each second, the resulting sound wave would have a frequency of 5 cycles per second. A **cycle** is one complete back-and-forth motion.

Frequency is measured in units called **Hertz.** One Hertz equals one cycle per second. For example, an object that has a frequency of 10 Hertz, has 10 back-and-forth motions in one second. The abbreviation for Hertz is *Hz.*

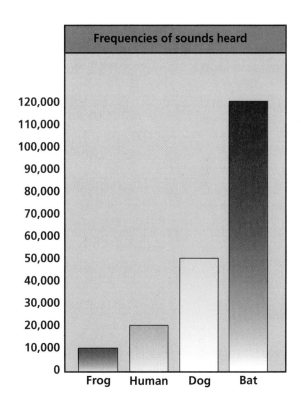

D

Although objects can vibrate at many different rates, the human ear can hear only a certain range of frequencies. Generally, the human ear can detect sounds with frequencies ranging from 20 Hz to 20,000 Hz. The range can vary somewhat depending on a person's hearing ability.

The graph compares the frequencies of sounds that can be heard by a human with those that can be heard by some other animals.

Frequencies of sounds heard	
	Frequencies
Frog	50 to 10,000 Hz
Human	20 to 20,000 Hz
Dog	15 to 50,000 Hz
Bat	1,000 to 120,000 Hz

Self-Check

1. Describe the intensity of a sound wave that carries a lot of energy.
2. How does volume relate to intensity?
3. How does the frequency of a sound wave affect pitch?

Objectives

After reading this lesson, you should be able to

▶ explain how sound travels through matter.

▶ compare the speed of sound in solids, liquids, and gases.

▶ explain how sound can be reflected.

▶ explain how sound waves are used to measure distances under water.

Suppose you wake up to the roar of a jet plane. It is high in the air. How does the noise from the jet reach you in your home?

Sound Moves Through Matter

Heat energy can move through empty space. In outer space, there are no molecules of matter. Sound energy cannot travel through empty space. You can only hear sound when it travels through matter. Therefore, no sounds can travel through outer space. Sound, however, can travel through air.

Sound travels through all matter in a similar way. Sound waves travel through matter by causing the particles in matter to vibrate. When a particle begins to vibrate, it bumps into another particle. Then that particle bumps into another particle, and so on.

The dominoes in the picture help illustrate how sound travels through matter. As each domino falls, it strikes the next domino, causing it to fall over. Each of the dominoes travels only a short distance. But the effect of one domino's motion can travel a large distance.

The Speed of Sound

If you put the dominoes closer together, they fall down in less time. In the same way, sound waves travel more quickly through substances with molecules that are closer together.

Chapter 3 described molecules in solids, liquids, and gases. Molecules of matter in solids are closest together. For this reason, sound moves fastest through solids.

Molecules in liquids are farther apart than those in solids. Sound travels more slowly through liquids. Molecules of gases are the farthest apart. Gases carry sound more slowly than either solids or liquids.

The speed of sound in air depends on the temperature of the air. In higher temperatures, molecules of air move farther apart. As a result, sound travels more slowly. The speed of sound through air is about 346 meters per second (or 700 miles per hour) at a temperature of 25 degrees Celsius. The graph below lists the speed of sound through some different materials.

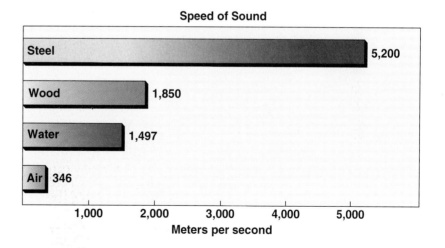

Speed of Sound

Steel — 5,200
Wood — 1,850
Water — 1,497
Air — 346

Meters per second

Sound travels quickly, but light travels even faster. Because light travels faster than sound, you will see a flash of lightning before you hear the thunder. You can use the speeds of sound and light to figure out how far away a storm is. To calculate the distance of a storm, use this procedure.

1. When you see a flash of lightning, count the number of seconds until you hear the thunder.

2. Divide the number of seconds by 3 seconds per kilometer. The answer tells you how many kilometers away the storm is. (If it takes 3 seconds for you to hear the thunder, the flash of lightning was about 1 kilometer away.)

Sound travels more slowly than light.

Suppose you see a flash of lightning. You find that it takes 6 seconds until you hear the thunder. How far away is the storm?

$$\text{distance of storm} = \frac{6 \text{ sec}}{3 \text{ sec/km}}$$

distance of storm = 2 kilometers

Self-Check

1. How do sound waves move from place to place?
2. Does sound move most quickly through solids, liquids, or gases? Explain your answer.
3. How does air temperature affect the speed of sound?

How Sound Bounces

Suppose a radio is playing in the next room. You may hear music from the radio because some of the sound travels through the solid wall. However, some of the sound might not travel through the wall. The matter in the wall might absorb, or trap, some of the sound. For this reason, the sound of the music might seem softer to you than to a person standing next to the radio.

Reflect

To bounce back.

Echo

A sound that is reflected to its source.

Other sound waves from the radio might be **reflected.** That is, the sound might bounce back from the wall. The picture of the ball bouncing against the wall illustrates how sound can be reflected. Sound that bounces back from an object is an **echo.** Echoes can be heard best when sound bounces from hard, smooth surfaces.

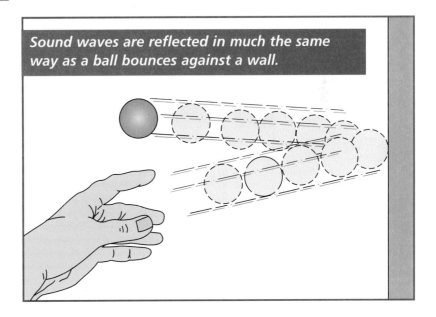

Sound waves are reflected in much the same way as a ball bounces against a wall.

You have probably heard echoes at one time or another. Did you ever call out someone's name in a large, empty room? If so, you might have heard an echo of your voice even after you stopped speaking.

Sonar

A method of using sound to measure distances under water.

Did You Know?

A cane developed for sightless people sends out sound waves. The sound waves reflect off obstacles and return to a sensor that the person wears. The sensor gives off sounds to indicate the distances to obstacles.

Measuring Distances with Sound Waves

Scientists can use echoes to find objects below the surface of water. This method is called **sonar.** People can use sonar to locate schools of fish, to explore shipwrecks, and to find other underwater objects.

Scientists can use sonar to find out exactly how deep water is at a particular location. The figure illustrates how sonar works. Instruments on the ship send out sound waves. The sound waves are reflected by the ocean bottom back to the surface of the water. Scientists can measure the time it takes for the sound to reach the bottom of the ocean and return to the surface. Because scientists know how fast sound travels through water, they can tell how far the sound travels. Scientists can use sonar to measure very deep parts of the ocean. They can also use sonar to map the ocean floor.

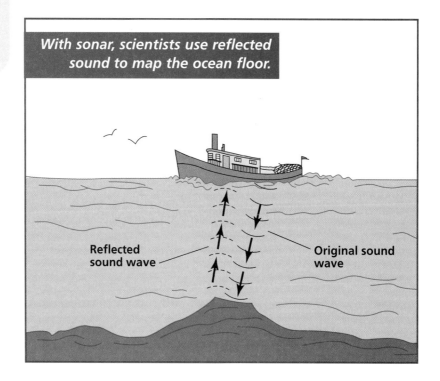

With sonar, scientists use reflected sound to map the ocean floor.

Reflected sound wave

Original sound wave

Ultrasound

A technique that uses sound waves to study organs inside the human body.

"Seeing" Inside the Body With Sound

Scientists also use sound waves, called **ultrasound,** to "see" inside the human body. Ultrasound waves are sound waves that humans cannot hear. When these waves are beamed into the body, some are reflected back. Each part of the body reflects the waves a little differently. Ultrasound equipment picks up these reflected waves and makes a picture. By looking at the picture, doctors can tell if an organ is an unusual size or shape. Doctors can also use the picture to find tumors.

One use of ultrasound is to study the development of an unborn baby. Ultrasound waves are directed into the mother's body. These waves echo off the unborn baby. The picture below shows an image made by an ultrasound screen. Ultrasound waves do not hurt the mother or the baby.

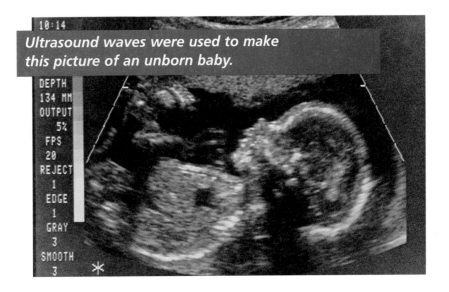

Ultrasound waves were used to make this picture of an unborn baby.

Self-Check

1. What is an echo?
2. Explain how sonar can be used to measure distances in the ocean.
3. List two ways that echoes can be used for medical purposes.

INVESTIGATION

Inferring How Sound Waves Travel

Materials

- ✓ safety goggles
- ✓ pencil with sharpened point
- ✓ large plastic-foam cup
- ✓ 2 rubber bands (one cut)
- ✓ plastic food wrap
- ✓ salt

Purpose

To demonstrate that sound waves are vibrations that travel through matter

Procedure

1. Copy the data table below on your paper.

How the rubber band was plucked	Observations

2. Put on your safety goggles.

3. Use the point of the pencil to punch a small hole in the bottom of the cup.

4. Push one end of the cut rubber band through the hole in the cup. Tie a knot in the end of the rubber band so that it cannot be pulled through the hole. The knot should be inside the cup.

5. Stretch a piece of plastic wrap tightly over the top of the cup. Use the other rubber band to hold the plastic wrap in place, as shown in the figure on the next page.

6. Hold the cup with the plastic wrap facing up. Sprinkle a few grains of salt on the plastic wrap.

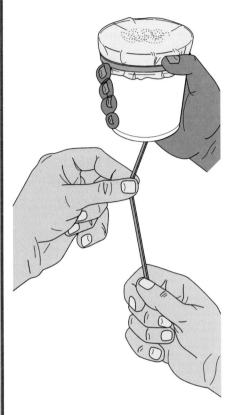

7. Hold the cup while your partner slowly stretches the rubber band. Gently pluck the stretched rubber band and observe what happens to the salt. Record your observations in the data table.

8. Vary the force used to pluck the rubber band. Notice the difference in sound the rubber band makes as you vary the force.

Questions

1. In Step 7, what happened to the salt when you plucked the rubber band?

2. What do you think caused the salt to move? Explain.

3. In Step 8, how did the force you used to pluck the rubber band affect the sound it made?

4. In Step 8, how did the force you used to pluck the rubber band affect the salt on the plastic wrap?

Explore Further

1. Use a tuning fork and a plastic beaker half-filled with water. Gently tap the tuning fork against the heel of your hand and place the tips of the fork into the beaker of water. What happens to the water?

2. Vary the force used to tap the tuning fork. Notice what happens to the water as you vary the force.

Light

A form of energy that can be seen.

Photons

Small bundles of energy that make up light.

You see **light** everywhere. You see objects because light is reflected from them. But what is light? Light is a form of energy that you can sometimes see. Visible light is produced by objects that are at high temperatures. The sun is the major source of light on Earth.

Light as a Particle

Scientists have done experiments to gather information about light. Some scientific experiments suggest that light acts like a particle. Evidence tells scientists that light is made up of bundles of energy called **photons.** Photons are like small particles. A single photon is too small to be seen.

Look at the light coming from the flashlight. Streams of photons make up each beam of light. Each photon carries a certain amount of energy.

Streams of photons make up a beam of light.

Light as a Wave

Other scientific evidence suggests that, like sound, light travels in waves. As a result of their findings, most scientists agree that light seems to have properties of both particles and waves. Scientists agree that light travels as waves in a straight line. Most properties of light can be explained in terms of its wave nature.

Light waves move like waves in water.

Light waves move like waves in water. However, light waves travel fastest through empty space. Light waves move more slowly as they pass through matter. In fact, light waves cannot pass through some matter at all.

Light waves travel more quickly than sound waves. Light waves travel about 300,000 kilometers per second. This is the fastest possible speed anything can travel.

Colors in White Light

The light you see from the sun is white light. Did you know that white light is actually made of many colors of light? If you have ever seen a rainbow, you have actually seen the colors that make up white light. The rainbow below shows the colors that make up the white light you see.

A rainbow contains all the colors of the visible spectrum.

The band of colors you see in a rainbow is known as the **visible spectrum.** The colors of the visible spectrum always appear in the following order: red, orange, yellow, green, blue, indigo, and violet.

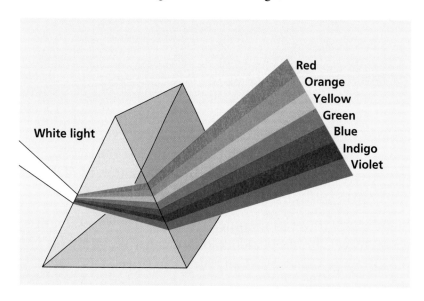

White light

Red
Orange
Yellow
Green
Blue
Indigo
Violet

You can use a **prism** like the one in the picture to see the colors in white light. A prism is a piece of glass or plastic shaped like a triangle. A prism can separate white light into the colors of the visible spectrum.

Self-Check

1. What makes up a beam of light?
2. How does light travel?
3. Would light travel faster through space or through a window? Explain.
4. What colors make up white light?

SCIENCE IN YOUR LIFE

How are lasers used?

A laser is a device that produces a powerful beam of light. Ordinary light travels in all directions from its source, like the waves made when a stone is thrown into a puddle of water. Laser light travels in only one direction. As a result, laser beams can be brighter and narrower than ordinary light beams. In fact, laser beams can be so bright that they can seriously damage your eyes if you look directly into them or even into their reflection. The table shows some of the many uses for lasers.

Some Uses of Lasers	
Communication	■ transmission of telephone signals ■ production of compact discs ■ transmission of television signals
Business	■ bar code identification on products for inventory and sales transactions
Medicine	■ detection of medical problems, diseases, and disorders ■ surgery, such as removing cataracts from eyes, removing cancerous cells, clearing blocked arteries, removing tonsils ■ treatment of skin conditions including removal of birthmarks
Environment	■ detection of pollutants in air ■ detection of natural gas leaks
Scientific research	■ collection of data from the moon ■ studies of the atom ■ studies of chemical reactions

After reading this lesson, you should be able to

▶ describe how plane mirrors reflect light.

▶ describe how concave and convex mirrors reflect light.

What happens when you look into a mirror? Why can you see yourself? These questions can be answered by understanding how light waves act.

Light Bounces

When you throw a ball to the floor, it bounces back. Light also bounces back when it hits an object. When light bounces off a surface, we say that the light is reflected. Reflection is the bouncing back of a light wave. Few objects give off their own light. We see most objects only because of the light they reflect.

The figure illustrates how light is reflected. Notice that light waves bounce off a surface at the same angle that they hit the surface.

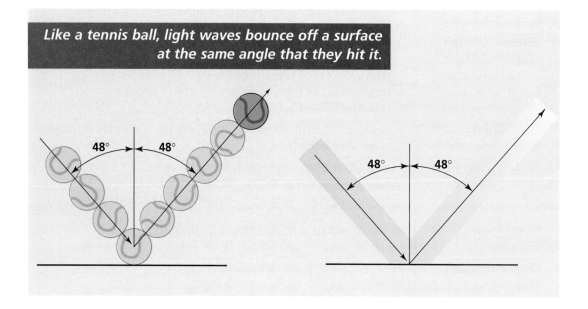

Like a tennis ball, light waves bounce off a surface at the same angle that they hit it.

Image

A copy or likeness.

Plane mirror

A flat, smooth mirror.

You can see an **image,** or likeness, in a mirror because light waves are reflected. As you can see in the diagram, light from the cup hits the mirror and is reflected toward your eye. Then your eye forms an image. But the cup looks as if it is behind the mirror. The image is the same size as the original cup, but it is reversed. The handle of the cup appears on the opposite side when you see it in the mirror. The angles at which the light reflects back causes this reversal. Follow the lines of light in the diagram to see how this happens.

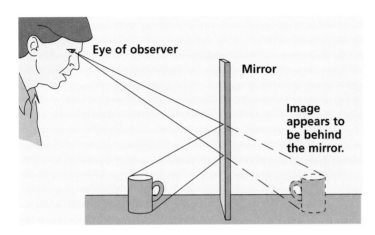

Eye of observer

Mirror

Image appears to be behind the mirror.

Plane Mirrors

A mirror with a flat, smooth surface is called a **plane mirror.** The flatter the surface of the mirror, the clearer the image. Few surfaces are completely flat, including surfaces of plane mirrors. You can see below how light reflected from a completely flat surface differs from light that is reflected from a surface that is not flat. The small bumps in the surface on the right cause the reflected light to return at many different angles. The result is that the image you see is not as clear.

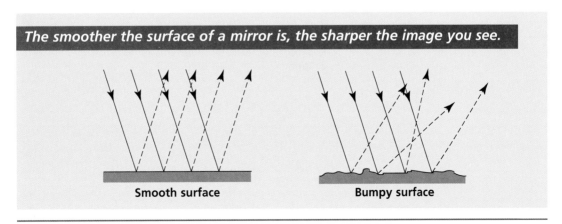

The smoother the surface of a mirror is, the sharper the image you see.

Smooth surface

Bumpy surface

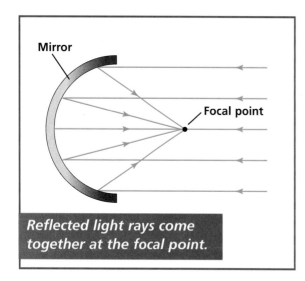

Mirror

Focal point

Reflected light rays come together at the focal point.

Concave Mirrors

Many mirrors have curved surfaces rather than flat surfaces. Look at the curved mirror in the diagram. This kind of mirror is called a **concave mirror.** A concave mirror has a reflecting surface that curves inward, like the inside of a spoon. The diagram shows how a concave mirror reflects parallel light rays. Notice that the light rays come together at one point, the **focal point.**

Concave mirror

A mirror that curves in at the middle.

Focal point

The point where reflected light rays from a concave mirror come together in front of the mirror.

Now look at the diagram below. The tree is behind the focal point of the mirror. Find the focal point of the mirror in the diagram. Rays of light from the tree hit the mirror's surface and are reflected back. Notice how the reflected rays pass through the focal point. If you put a piece of paper at Point A, you could see an image on it. The image would be upside down and larger.

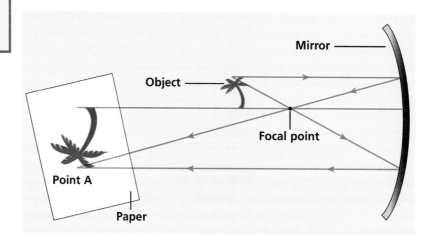

Object

Mirror

Focal point

Point A

Paper

What would happen if the tree were between the concave mirror and the focal point? Look at the diagram on the next page. If you follow the rays, you can see that the image of the tree would appear larger, right-side-up, and behind the mirror. When you use a magnifying mirror to shave or apply makeup, you hold the mirror so that your face is between the focal point and the mirror.

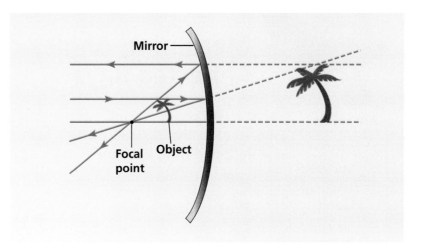

Convex Mirrors

The reflecting surface of some mirrors curves outward like the outside of a spoon. These kinds of mirrors are called **convex mirrors.** A convex mirror creates an image that looks smaller than the real object. However, you can see much more area in a convex mirror. For this reason, rear-view and side-view mirrors on cars often have convex lenses.

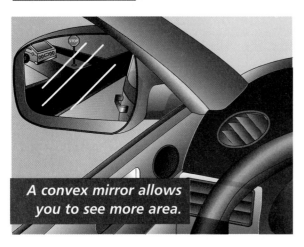

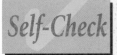
A convex mirror allows you to see more area.

Self-Check

1. Why are images reflected from a rough surface not as clear as those reflected from a smooth surface?
2. How do a concave mirror and a convex mirror differ?

INVESTIGATION

Measuring Angles of Reflected Rays

Materials

- ✓ mirror
- ✓ textbook
- ✓ masking tape
- ✓ unlined white paper
- ✓ pencil
- ✓ flashlight
- ✓ comb
- ✓ protractor
- ✓ ruler

Purpose

To measure angles at which a light ray hits and is reflected from a mirror

Procedure

1. Copy the data table below on your paper.

Trial	Angle A	Angle B
1		
2		
3		

2. Using masking tape, tape the mirror to the book, as shown below.

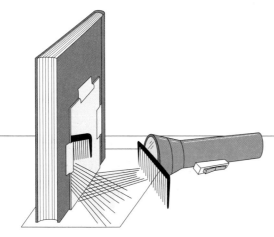

3. Place the book on its edge on a sheet of paper. Draw a line along the bottom of the mirror.

4. Turn on the flashlight. Hold the comb in front of the flashlight. Shine the flashlight on the mirror. Move the light around until you see a pattern of light rays and reflected rays like those shown in the drawing.

5. Find a single light ray. Then find the reflected ray for that light ray. Trace both lines on the paper. The point where the two rays meet should be on the mirror line that you drew.

6. Remove the flashlight and turn it off. Move the book and the mirror. Lay the protractor along the mirror line. Place the center of the bottom of the protractor on the point where the rays meet. Draw a line at a right angle to the mirror line, as shown below.

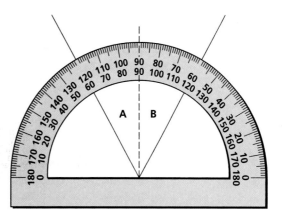

7. Use the protractor to measure angles A and B. Record the measurements.

8. Repeat steps 3 to 7 two more times. Each time, draw rays with different angles.

Questions

1. Which angle—A or B—shows the angle at which the light traveled to the mirror?

2. Which angle shows the angle at which the light was reflected from the mirror?

3. How do angles A and B compare?

Refraction

The bending of a wave as it moves from one material to another.

Lens

A curved piece of clear material that refracts light waves.

Concave lens

A lens that is thin in the middle and thick at the edges.

When light moves from one kind of matter to another, the light waves change speed. As a result, the direction of the light changes. The bending of a light wave as it moves from one material to another is called **refraction.**

Notice that the pencil in the picture appears to be bent. Light travels more slowly in water than it does in air. When light passes from the water to the air, the light waves change speed and change direction. As a result, the pencil seems to bend.

Refraction causes the pencil to look bent.

Lenses

A **lens** bends light by acting like the water in the container. A lens is a curved piece of glass or other clear material that refracts light waves that pass through it. Lenses are used in eyeglasses, cameras, magnifying glasses, microscopes, and telescopes. What you see through a lens depends on the kind of lens you use.

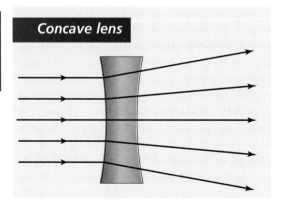

Concave lens

A **concave lens** is curved inward. The lens is thin in the middle and thick at the edges. Light rays that pass through a concave lens are spread apart.

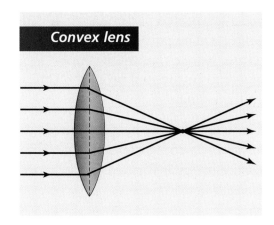

Convex lens

A **convex lens** is curved outward. The lens is thick in the middle and thin at the edges. Light rays that pass through a convex lens are refracted inward. You can see that a convex lens focuses light.

If you hold a convex lens close to your eye, the lens will magnify an image. If you hold a convex lens far from your eye and observe an object at a distance, you see an upside-down image.

Convex lens

A lens that is thick in the middle and thin at the edges.

Nearsighted

Able to see clearly only things that are close up.

Lenses in Eyeglasses

The human eye has a convex lens. The lens forms an image on the retina, or the back wall of the eye. Figure A shows a normal eye. You can see that the image formed is an upside-down image. Your brain interprets the image as right-side-up.

Figure B shows the eye of a **nearsighted** person. People who are nearsighted can form clear images of close objects but not of distant objects. Notice that the image is formed in front of the retina instead of on it.

Concave lenses are used in eyeglasses for people who are nearsighted. Figure C shows how a concave lens refracts, or bends, light before it enters the eye. As a result, a proper image is formed on the retina.

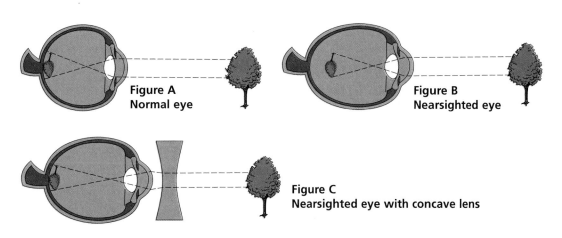

Figure A
Normal eye

Figure B
Nearsighted eye

Figure C
Nearsighted eye with concave lens

Figure A shows the eye of a **farsighted** person. A farsighted person can see distant objects. The person has difficulty seeing objects that are close. Notice that there is not enough room for the image to be focused properly. The image is focused behind the retina.

Convex lenses are used in eyeglasses for people who are farsighted. Figure B shows how a convex lens changes the focus of the light so that the image is formed properly on the retina.

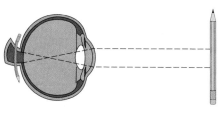

**Figure A
Farsighted eye**

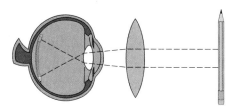

**Figure B
Farsighted eye
with convex lens**

Self-Check

1. How do a concave lens and a convex lens refract light in different ways?

2. How do concave lenses correct the vision of a nearsighted person?

3. How do convex lenses correct the vision of a farsighted person?

- Sound is caused by vibrations.
- Sound travels in waves.
- The intensity of sound is measured in decibels.
- A person's hearing interprets intensity as volume.
- Frequency of sound waves determines pitch.
- Sound travels at different speeds through different kinds of matter.
- An echo is a reflected sound.
- Scientists use sonar to measure distances under water.
- People see objects because light is reflected from them.
- Light is made up of bundles of energy called photons.

- Light has properties of both particles and waves.
- Light waves travel fastest through empty space.
- White light can be broken into the colors of the visible spectrum.
- Refraction is the bending of a light wave.
- A mirror is an object that reflects light.
- Three types of mirrors are plane, concave, and convex.
- Concave and convex lenses refract light and can correct vision.

Science Words		
concave lens, 264	light, 254
concave mirror, 260	nearsighted, 265
convex lens, 265	photons, 254
convex mirror, 261	pitch, 244
cycle, 244	plane mirror, 259
decibel, 242	prism, 256
echo, 249	reflect, 249
farsighted, 266	refraction, 264
focal point, 260	sonar, 250
frequency, 244	sound wave, 241
Hertz, 244	ultrasound, 251
image, 259	vibrate, 240
intensity, 242	visible spectrum, 256
lens, 264	volume, 243

Vocabulary Review

Number your paper from 1 to 12. Then choose a word or words from the Word Bank that best complete each sentence. Write the answer on your paper.

1. A glass _____ breaks light into bands of colors.

2. A(n) _____ lens is thick in the middle.

3. Sound is produced when matter _____.

4. Sound that bounces back from an object is a(n) _____.

5. The complete movement of a vibration is a(n) _____.

6. The reflecting surface of a _____ mirror curves inward.

7. The high sound of a flute is called a high _____.

8. A(n) _____ reflects light rays.

9. The strength of a sound is its _____.

10. _____ measures distances under water.

11. The bending of a light wave is called _____.

12. A sound's intensity is measured in _____.

Concept Review

Number your paper from 1 to 6. Then choose the answer that best completes each sentence. Write the letter of the answer on your paper.

1. _____ lenses are used for a person who is nearsighted.
   a. Convex   **b.** Magnifying   **c.** Concave

2. Sound can travel through _____.
   a. empty space   **b.** matter   **c.** optics

3. Frequency measures _____ of a sound wave.
   a. vibrations per second
   b. intensity
   c. volume

4. A concave lens _____ light waves.
   a. reflects   b. reverses   c. refracts

5. Sound travels fastest through_____.
   a. gases   b. liquids   c. solids

6. Particles of light are called _____.
   a. protons   b. photons   c. electrons

Critical Thinking

Write the answer to each of the following questions.

1. Copy the drawings of the lenses below. Draw lines to show how the light waves are refracted as they pass through the lens. Write a sentence to explain what you drew for each lens.

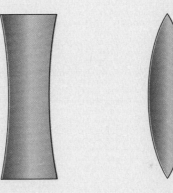

2. How far away is an object whose echo takes 9 seconds to return?

| Test Taking Tip | Drawing pictures or diagrams is one way to help you understand and solve problems. |

Chapter 11

Electricity

E lectricity! It flows, on demand, from outlets in the wall. It flashes across the sky during summer storms. It is useful in many ways. Yet it can be dangerous. How can something so familiar also seem so mysterious? Electricity is not hard to understand, once you know a few basics. By reading this chapter, you can unlock electricity's secrets.

ORGANIZE YOUR THOUGHTS

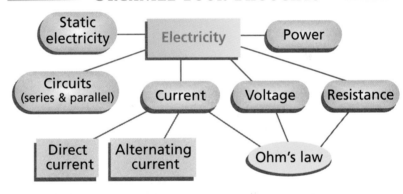

Goals for Learning

▶ To explain how electric current flows through a circuit

▶ To compare insulators and conductors

▶ To explain how resistance is useful

▶ To describe how batteries produce current

▶ To explain direct current and alternating current

▶ To apply Ohm's law

▶ To compare series and parallel circuits

▶ To describe how electricity is measured

How Does Electricity Flow Through a Circuit?

Electricity

Flow of electrons.

Static electricity

Buildup of electrical charges.

In Chapter 3, you read about atoms and the particles that make them. Electrons are negatively charged particles. Under the right conditions, electrons can escape from one atom and move to another one. The atom that loses the electron becomes positively charged. The atom that has picked up the electron becomes negatively charged. In turn, this negatively charged atom can pass the electron on again. This movement of electrons is the basis of **electricity.**

Static Electricity

Have you ever gotten a shock when you touched metal after walking across a carpet? The shock was caused by a buildup of charge, called **static electricity.** Walking across the carpet caused electrons to leave the carpet and enter your body. When you touched the metal, the extra electrons jumped from your finger to the metal.

When electrons move from one place to another, energy is transferred. Lightning is a discharge of static electricity between clouds or between a cloud and Earth.

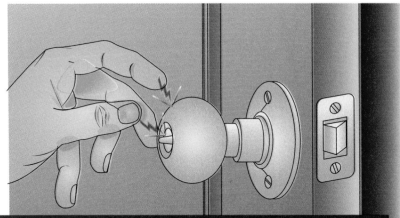

The spark you sometimes see when you touch metal is a discharge of static electricity. So is a lightning bolt.

Closed Circuits

The movement of electrons from one place to another is called **electric current.** The rate at which electrons move from one place to another can vary. Electric current is measured in **amperes.** An ampere tells how much current is moving past a point in a circuit in one second. One ampere is the flow of about 6 billion billion electrons per second! An ampere is often called an amp.

Currents from static electricity are not easy to control. But an electric current produced by a power source can be controlled and is easy to use.

When electrons travel in an electric current, they follow a path. This path is called a **circuit.** Follow the path of current in the figure below. The circuit begins at the power source. It travels through the wire to the light bulb. It lights up the bulb, and then returns to the power source.

Electrons can only follow a complete, unbroken path. You can see that the path in this circuit is unbroken. This path is called a **closed circuit.** As long as the current continues to flow in the circuit, the light will remain lit.

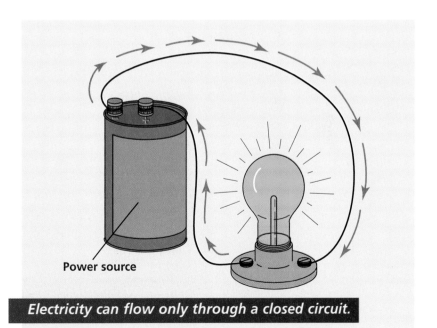

Power source

Electricity can flow only through a closed circuit.

Open Circuits

Suppose you have a light turned on in your room. You decide you want to turn off the light. What do you do? Most likely you turn off a switch. To turn on the light again, you turn the switch on.

How does a switch work? Look at Figure A below. You can see that the wires of the circuit are connected to a switch. When the switch is closed, the electrons can flow in an unbroken path. The light stays lit.

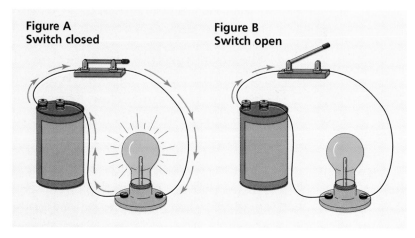

**Figure A
Switch closed**

**Figure B
Switch open**

A doorbell switch

A lamp switch

A wall switch

In Figure B, the switch is open. The current can't pass through it. The bulb doesn't light. This is an incomplete path. It is called an **open circuit.**

The switches you see in the diagram above are called knife switches. The switches that you use in your home are different from a knife switch, but they work the same way. They break the flow of electrons when the switch is turned off. The pictures show some of the switches you might find in your home.

How many of these common switches can you find in your home?

Schematic Diagrams

Scientists often use drawings of circuits. To make this job easier, they have developed symbols to show different parts of a circuit. Wires, switches, bulbs, and power sources are each represented by a different symbol. You can see some of these symbols below.

A diagram of a circuit that uses such symbols is called a **schematic diagram.** The schematic diagram below shows a battery in a circuit with a closed switch, wiring, and a bulb.

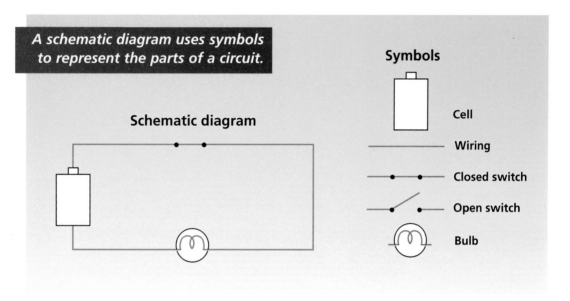

A schematic diagram uses symbols to represent the parts of a circuit.

Schematic diagram

Symbols

Cell

Wiring

Closed switch

Open switch

Bulb

Self-Check

1. Explain what happens when you get a shock from a metal doorknob after walking across a carpet.

2. Look at the following schematic diagrams, A and B. Which of the circuits is a closed circuit? Which is an open circuit?

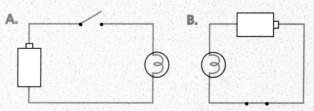

A.

B.

3. In which of the schematic diagrams above would current flow? Explain.

After reading this lesson, you should be able to

- explain the difference between a conductor and an insulator.
- give examples of conductors and insulators.
- explain what resistance is.
- list three things that affect the resistance of a material.
- explain how resistance is useful.

Conductor

Material through which electricity passes easily.

Insulator

Material through which electricity does not pass easily.

Look at the electrical cords that carry electric current in your home. You will notice that the metal wire that carries the electricity is covered with a material. This material is often plastic. Why do you think electrical cords have this covering?

Conductors and Insulators

Look at the cross section of the electrical cord. The wire in the center of the electrical cord is a **conductor.** A conductor is a material through which electrons can flow easily. The wire carries electricity from a power source to the lamp.

Metals, such as copper, gold, aluminum, and silver, are good conductors. Silver is a very good conductor of the metals. But it is too expensive to use in most wires. Most lamps use copper wire to conduct electricity.

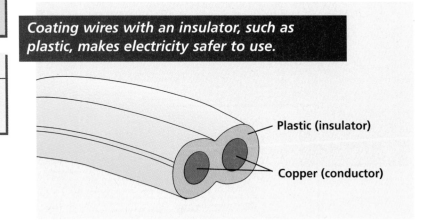

Coating wires with an insulator, such as plastic, makes electricity safer to use.

Plastic (insulator)

Copper (conductor)

The outer covering of the electrical cord is an **insulator.** An insulator doesn't conduct electricity well. The electrons in an insulator are not as free to move as the electrons in a conductor. Examples of good electrical insulators are glass, rubber, wood, and plastic.

The insulator that covers the electrical cord keeps the electricity flowing in the wire. The covering prevents the current from flowing to places where it might cause fires or electrical shock. For example, if you touch a wire that is carrying an electric current, the electrons are free to travel to your body. You will get a shock. But if the wire is covered with an insulator like the one in the picture on page 276, the electricity can't flow to your body.

When using electrical cords, be sure to check for worn insulation. If the bare wire is exposed, the cord is dangerous. The cord should be replaced or repaired. Electrical tapes that are good insulators can be used to repair the area where the wire is exposed.

Resistance

Not all conductors allow electricity to pass through them in the same way. Likewise, not all insulators slow down electricity equally well.

Resistance

Measure of how easily electric current will flow through a material.

Ohm

The unit used to measure resistance.

Resistance is a measure of how easy or hard it is for electric current to move through a material. Resistance is measured in **ohms.** To understand resistance, think about two water hoses. They are the same in every way, except one has a larger hole running down the middle than the other. A pump pushes water through the two hoses equally. Through which of the hoses will more water pass in one minute?

If you answered that more water would pass through the hose with the larger opening, you are correct. The hose with the larger opening offers less resistance to the water flow than the hose with the smaller opening. In a similar way, more current flows through a substance with less resistance than through a substance with more resistance. Insulators have high resistance. Conductors have low resistance.

The resistance of a wire depends on three things.

- **The material the wire is made of.** Some materials have more resistance than others. For example, tungsten has a greater resistance than copper. Tungsten wire is used in light bulbs.

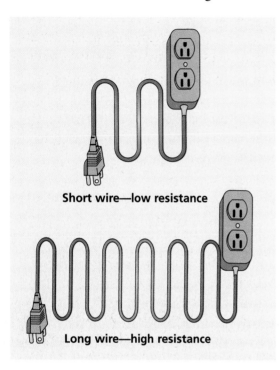

Short wire—low resistance

Long wire—high resistance

- **The length of the wire.** The longer a wire is, the greater its resistance. Look at the two wires to the left. One wire is longer than the other. The longer wire has greater resistance. If you use a long extension cord to plug in a lamp, less electric current will go through the wire to the lamp.

- **The thickness of the wire.** The thinner the wire, the greater its resistance. You can see wires of two thicknesses below. The thinner wire has greater resistance than the thicker wire. For this reason, power lines that run along roads are made of thick wires.

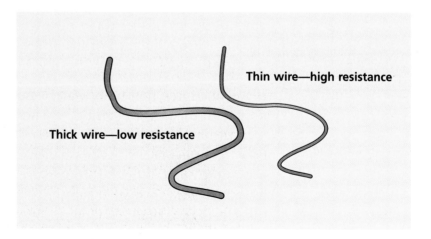

Thin wire—high resistance

Thick wire—low resistance

Resistance causes electrical energy to change into heat and light energy. Without resistance, many appliances in your home would not work.

Nichrome is a metal with a high resistance. When electricity is passed through a nichrome wire, it gets hot. The wire coils in a toaster are made of nichrome. When electricity passes through the toaster, the wires get hot and toast your bread. Other appliances that use materials with high resistance include curling irons, hair dryers, and irons.

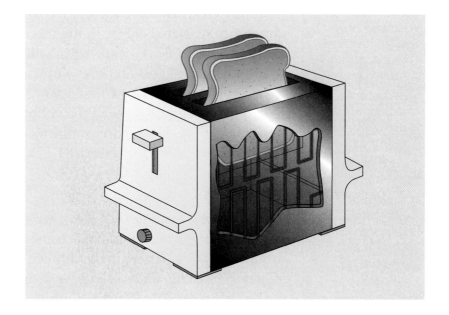

Self-Check

1. What is the difference between a conductor and an insulator?
2. Give two examples of conductors and two examples of insulators.
3. Sometimes the insulation on an electrical cord gets destroyed. Why would it be dangerous to use such a cord?
4. What are three things that affect the resistance of a wire?
5. How is resistance useful?
6. List the appliances you used in the last 24 hours. Put a check behind those that use materials with high resistance to produce heat and light.

What Are Some Sources of Electric Current?

Objectives

After reading this lesson, you should be able to

▶ explain what electromotive force is.

▶ explain how voltage relates to electromotive force.

▶ describe the structure and use of dry cell batteries.

▶ describe wet cell batteries.

▶ explain the difference between direct current and alternating current.

In order for current to move through a circuit, something has to "push" it. You might compare the flow of current to the flow of water through a hose. Something has to push the water through the hose. A water pump provides this push.

The push that keeps the current flowing in a circuit is called the **electromotive force.** Electromotive force is sometimes written as EMF. In the metric system, electromotive force is measured in **volts.** A volt tells the amount of push. It also tells how much energy the electrons have. The energy that a power source gives to electrons in a circuit is called the **voltage.** When voltage is high, electrons have more energy available to do work.

Dry Cell Batteries

Batteries are a common source of voltage. All batteries change chemical energy into electrical energy. One common type of battery is the **dry cell battery.** This type of battery is called a dry cell because the materials inside the battery are somewhat dry or pastelike. Dry cells are used in flashlights, radios, and other small appliances. These batteries come in many sizes and shapes. D-size dry cell batteries are used in flashlights and large radios. Smaller dry cell batteries are used with devices that do not require much power.

Battery	Dry cell battery	Electromotive force	Volt	Voltage
A source of voltage that changes chemical energy into electrical energy.	Electric power source with a dry or pastelike center.	The push that keeps electrons moving in an electric circuit.	Metric unit used to measure electromotive force.	The energy that a power source gives to electrons in a circuit.

Negative terminal — − + — Positive terminal

Cardboard casing — — Zinc can

Carbon rod — — Paper liner

— Manganese dioxide paste

Most dry cell batteries are constructed similar to the one above. Dry cell batteries are not completely dry. They are made of a zinc container filled with black, moist manganese dioxide powder. In the center of the cell is a long rod made of carbon.

Terminal

Points where electrons leave or enter a battery.

Each dry cell battery has two **terminals,** or points where electrons leave or enter the cell. Wires can be attached to the terminals to connect the cell to an electrical device. Larger batteries have both terminals on top. The center terminal is the positive terminal. It is attached to the carbon rod. The positive terminal is marked with a plus sign (+). The other terminal is the negative terminal. It is connected to the zinc container. The negative terminal is labeled with a minus sign (−). This terminal is negative because it has an excess of electrons. The "pressure" at the negative terminal "pumps" the electrons along the circuit to the positive terminal.

A smaller dry cell battery, such as the kind you use in an ordinary flashlight, has only one terminal on top. This is the positive terminal. The negative terminal is located on the bottom of the battery.

Wet Cell Batteries

The lead storage battery that you find in most cars is an example of another kind of battery—a **wet cell battery.** Wet cell batteries are different from dry cells because they are filled with a liquid, rather than a fairly dry chemical. Most wet cell batteries have a hard rubber case filled with a solution of sulfuric acid. Plates are placed inside the sulfuric acid. Often, these plates are made of lead or lead dioxide.

A chemical reaction between the acid and the plates causes a series of reactions. As the reactions happen, electrons flow from one plate to another. This produces an electric current.

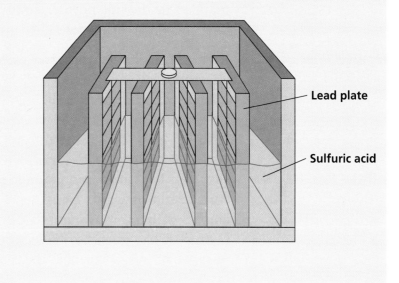

A wet cell battery has a liquid center.

Lead plate

Sulfuric acid

Did You Know?

The bite of the South American bushmaster snake is sometimes treated with electric shock. A series of short shocks is given at about 20,000 volts. At times, car or outboard motors are used to deliver the voltage.

Direct and Indirect Current

The current in a wet cell battery and a dry cell battery flow in one direction. This type of current is called **direct current.** It sometimes is referred to as DC. Direct current is not the most common kind of current.

The electricity in your home probably is **alternating current.** Alternating current is also called AC. In alternating current, the flow of electrons changes direction regularly. Alternating current is produced by machines called generators. The generators that produce electricity for your home change the direction of the current about 60 times per second.

Alternating current is used to supply electricity to homes because it can travel through wires over long distances. Direct current dies out when it travels through wire over long distances.

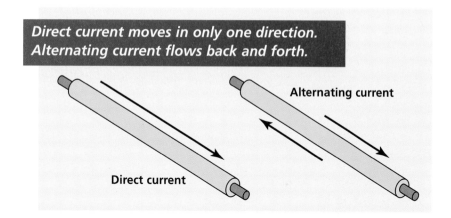

Direct current moves in only one direction. Alternating current flows back and forth.

Alternating current

Direct current

Self-Check

1. What is electromotive force?
2. How is a battery like a water pump?
3. Explain how a dry cell battery works.
4. How does a wet cell battery differ from a dry cell battery?
5. What is the difference between direct current and alternating current?
6. What type of current—direct or alternating—is used in your home? Why?

Objectives

After reading this lesson, you should be able to

▶ explain how current, voltage, and resistance are related.

▶ use Ohm's law to calculate current.

Ohm's law

Current equals voltage divided by resistance.

In the early 1800s, Georg Ohm, a German schoolteacher, was the first person to discover that volts, amps, and ohms in an electrical circuit are all related to one another. To understand Ohm's idea, remember these things that you already have learned about electricity:

■ Power sources, such as batteries, provide the push (voltage) to the current in a circuit.

■ The rate at which the current flows can be measured in amperes.

■ The flow of current can be slowed down by the resistance of the material through which the current flows. Resistance is measured in ohms.

Ohm put these relationships into a formula. This formula is known as **Ohm's law.**

$$\text{current (amperes)} = \frac{\text{electromotive force (volts)}}{\text{resistance (ohms)}}$$

This formula is more commonly written as:

$$I = \frac{V}{R}$$

Notice in the equation that the letter *I* is the symbol for current. The symbol for resistance is *R*. The law shows that as resistance increases, current tends to decrease. Using this equation, you can find the current of a circuit if you know the voltage and resistance.

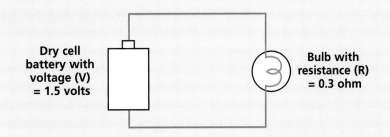

The diagram above shows an electric circuit. It has a 1.5-volt dry cell battery and a lamp, or bulb. A lamp is a resistor. How much current is in the circuit?

$$\text{current} = \frac{\text{voltage}}{\text{resistance}}$$

$$\text{current} = \frac{1.5 \text{ volts}}{0.3 \text{ ohms}}$$

$$\text{current} = 5 \text{ amperes}$$

Notice that dividing volts by ohms produces an answer in amperes.

Self-Check

Find the current in amperes for each circuit in the table. The first one is done for you.

Voltage (volts)	Resistance (ohms)	Current (amperes) $\frac{V}{R}$
10	5	10 volts/5 ohms = 2 amperes
15	5	
50	5	
35	10	

Objectives

After reading this lesson, you should be able to

▶ describe a series circuit.

▶ explain how adding electrical devices or batteries to a series circuit affects the voltage of the circuit.

▶ explain the advantage of using fuses and circuit breakers.

Have you ever had a string of decorative lights? You might know that with some strings of lights, if one light burns out, all the remaining lights stay lit. But in other strings, all the lights will go out if one burns out. Then you have to change each bulb on the string until you find the one that's burned out. Why do these strings of lights act differently? The answer is in the way the circuit is made.

Devices in Series Circuits

Look at the circuit below. It includes a source of energy, such as a battery, and wire to carry the current. It also has different electrical devices attached to it. This kind of circuit is called a **series circuit.**

Series circuit

Circuit in which all current flows through a single path.

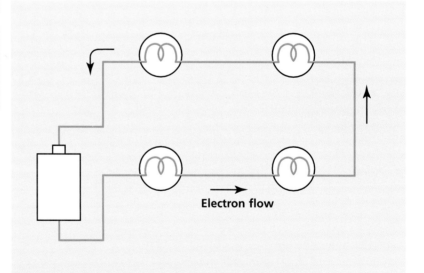

Electron flow

In a series circuit, all electrons must pass through each electrical device.

In a series circuit, electrons can flow through only one path around the circuit. You can see in the circuit on page 286 that all the electrons must pass through each electrical device. In the example of the decorative lights, each light is a separate device. The electrons must pass through each light bulb.

Series circuits have a disadvantage. If one light is unscrewed or burns out, all of the other lights will go out. That is because the circuit becomes open, and electrons cannot flow.

When electrical devices are connected in series, the current is the same throughout the circuit. However, adding electrical devices lowers the voltage through each device. Notice in the diagram below that if only one bulb is connected to a dry cell, the bulb may shine brightly. If another bulb is added in series, each of the bulbs will be dimmer than the single bulb was.

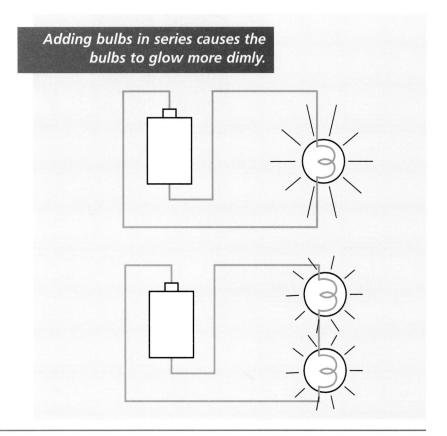

Adding bulbs in series causes the bulbs to glow more dimly.

Batteries in Series Circuits

Batteries in a circuit can be connected in series, too. Batteries in series increase the voltage of the circuit. To find the total voltage, add the voltages of the cells together.

In the circuit shown below, the batteries are in series. A wire connects a positive terminal to a negative terminal. A second wire connects the lamp and switch to the batteries. When batteries are connected in series, they can deliver more energy in the same amount of time. Bulbs in this kind of circuit burn brighter because the voltage is higher.

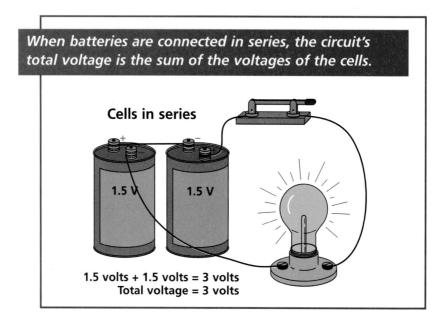

When batteries are connected in series, the circuit's total voltage is the sum of the voltages of the cells.

Cells in series

1.5 V   1.5 V

1.5 volts + 1.5 volts = 3 volts
Total voltage = 3 volts

In a flashlight, dry cell batteries are usually connected in series. You can see in the diagram to the left how the positive terminal of one battery touches the negative terminal (the bottom metal plate) of the next battery.

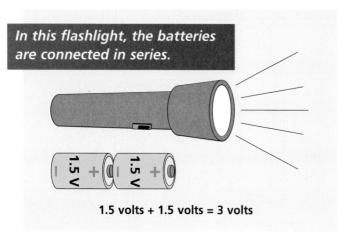

In this flashlight, the batteries are connected in series.

1.5 V   +   1.5 V   +

1.5 volts + 1.5 volts = 3 volts

Fuses and Circuit Breakers

Connecting electrical devices in series can be inconvenient. But there are practical uses for series circuits, too. For example, your home is probably protected by fuses or circuit breakers. Fuses and circuit breakers help prevent fires.

Look at the fuse in the drawing. Notice the piece of metal on the top of the fuse. It is designed to melt at a certain temperature. When the wires get too hot, the fuse will melt and break the circuit. When a fuse melts, it must be replaced. A circuit breaker, on the other hand, is a switchlike device that can be reset after the circuit has been repaired.

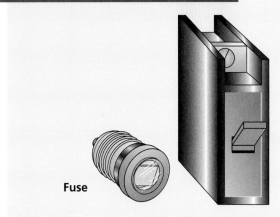

Fuses and circuit breakers are designed to prevent fires.

Fuse

Circuit breaker

Self-Check

1. What is a series circuit?
2. What is one advantage of a series circuit?
3. What happens to the brightness of a bulb when more bulbs are added to the same series circuit?
4. When two cells with the same voltage are connected in series, what happens to the voltage?
5. Compare a fuse and a circuit breaker.

Constructing Series Circuits

Materials

✓ two 1.5-volt dry cell batteries

✓ 2 holders for batteries

✓ 2 flashlight bulbs

✓ 2 bulb sockets

✓ 1.5 m-long piece of common bell wire, cut into various lengths

✓ switch

Purpose

To construct and study a series circuit

Procedure

1. Copy the data table below on your paper.

Circuit	Schematic diagram	Prediction	Observations
A			
B			
C			

2. Copy each of the schematic diagrams A–D shown below onto the correct space in the data table. Label each item in the diagrams.

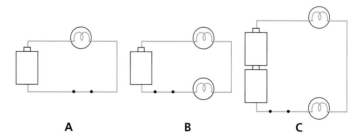

A   B   C

3. Use the materials to construct circuit A. What do you think will happen to the bulb when you close the switch? Write your prediction in the data table. Close the switch. Record how brightly the bulb shines.

4. Take apart circuit A. Construct circuit B. Predict how brightly the bulbs will shine compared to the single bulb in circuit A. Record your prediction. Close the switch. Record your observations.

5. Unscrew one of the bulbs and record what you observe.

6. Construct circuit C. Predict how brightly the bulbs will shine compared to the bulbs in circuit B. Close the switch. Record your observations.

Questions

1. What items make up circuit A? What kind of circuit is it?

2. What items make up circuit B? What kind of circuit is it?

3. How brightly did the bulbs in circuit B shine compared to the bulb in circuit A? Explain.

4. What happened in circuit B when one of the bulbs was unscrewed? Why did that happen?

5. How brightly did the bulbs in circuit C shine compared to the bulbs in circuit B? Explain.

Explore Further

What do you think would happen if you added more bulbs or more batteries to your circuit? Construct a circuit and find out.

Lesson 6 What Is a Parallel Circuit?

Objectives

After reading this lesson, you should be able to

- describe a parallel circuit.
- explain what happens to the brightness of bulbs in a parallel circuit when more bulbs are included.
- explain what happens to voltage when two batteries with the same voltage are connected in parallel.

Parallel circuit

Circuit in which there is more than one path for current.

The lights and appliances in your home are not wired in a series circuit. If they were, every time a bulb burned out, none of the other lights and appliances would work! Instead, most circuits in houses are **parallel circuits.** In a parallel circuit, there is more than one path for the current to follow.

Devices in Parallel Circuits

Look at the following diagram of two lamps connected in parallel. As you can see, there are two paths around this circuit. If one bulb burned out, the other bulb would stay lit. The reason is because there is more than one path for the electrons.

In a parallel circuit, there is more than one path for current.

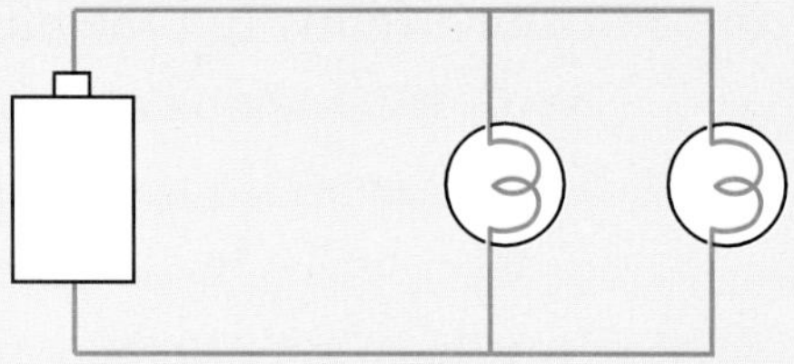

Parallel circuit

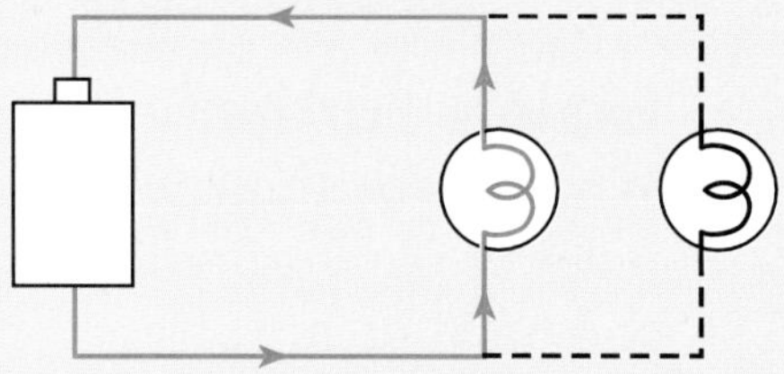

First path in circuit

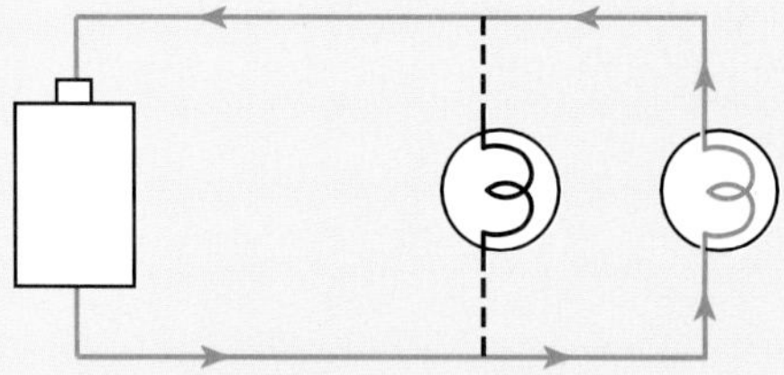

Second path in circuit

When several bulbs are connected in parallel, all the bulbs will remain as bright as just one bulb alone would. However, more current must be drawn from the battery to power the extra bulbs. Therefore, the battery will not last as long as in a series circuit.

When more electrical devices are added to the same circuit, more current runs through the circuit. As current in a circuit increases, wires begin to heat up. If they get too hot, the wires can start a fire in the walls. The fuses you read about in Lesson 5 help prevent this problem.

Batteries in Parallel Circuits

Batteries can be connected in parallel. A parallel connection between batteries allows them to keep providing energy longer. A parallel connection does not increase the voltage.

Look at the diagrams below. Figure A shows a circuit with only one 1.5-volt battery. The circuit in Figure B has two 1.5-volt batteries connected in parallel. The bulb in the circuit will stay lit longer. However, it will not burn brighter than the other bulb. The total voltage is still only 1.5 volts.

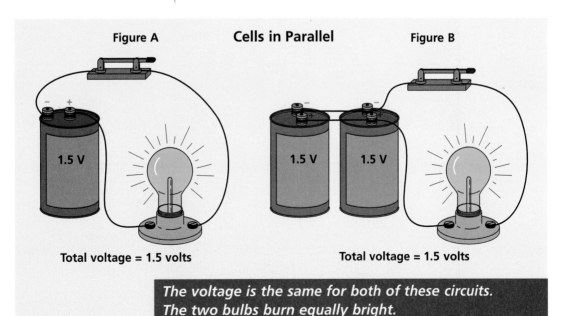

Figure A **Cells in Parallel** **Figure B**

1.5 V

Total voltage = 1.5 volts

1.5 V   1.5 V

Total voltage = 1.5 volts

The voltage is the same for both of these circuits. The two bulbs burn equally bright.

1. How can you recognize a parallel circuit?

2. What happens to the bulbs in a parallel circuit when one bulb burns out?

3. Determine the number of paths in each of the following parallel circuits.

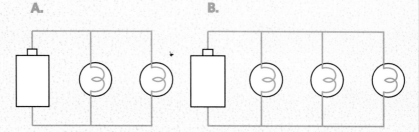

A.   B.

4. What happens to the brightness of bulbs in a parallel circuit when more bulbs are added?

5. When two batteries with the same voltage are connected in parallel, what happens to the voltage?

6. Identify each of the following circuits as parallel or series circuits.

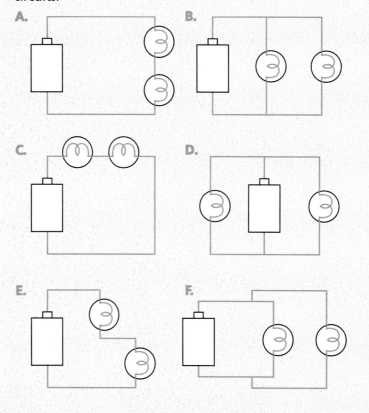

Constructing Parallel Circuits

Purpose

To construct and study parallel circuits

Procedure

1. Copy the data table below on your paper.

Circuit	Schematic diagram	Prediction	Observations
A			
B			
C			
D			
E			

2. Copy each of the schematic diagrams A–E shown below onto the correct space in your data table. Label each item in the diagram.

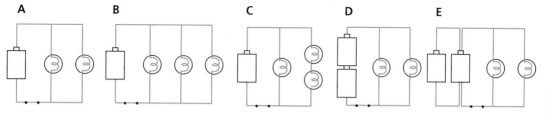

A   B   C   D   E

3. Use the materials to construct circuit A. How brightly do you think the bulb will shine when you close the switch? Record your prediction in your data table. Close the switch and note what happens. Notice how brightly the bulbs shine.

Materials

- ✓ two 1.5-volt dry cell batteries
- ✓ 2 holders for batteries
- ✓ 3 flashlight bulbs
- ✓ 3 bulb sockets
- ✓ 1.5 m-long piece of common bell wire, cut into various lengths
- ✓ switch

4. Unscrew one of the bulbs and observe what happens. Record your observations. Then tighten the bulb again and unscrew the other one. Record your observations.

5. Take apart circuit A. Construct circuit B. Predict how brightly the bulbs will shine compared to the bulbs in circuit A. Close the switch. Record your observations.

6. Unscrew different combinations of bulbs. Record your observations.

7. Construct circuit C, and close the switch. Try loosening various combinations of bulbs. Record your observations.

8. Construct circuit D. Predict how brightly the bulbs will shine compared to the bulbs in circuit A. Close the switch. Record your observations.

9. Construct circuit E. Predict how brightly the bulbs will shine compared to the bulbs in circuit D. Close the switch. Record your observations.

Questions

1. What items make up circuit C? What kind of circuit is it?

2. Are the cells in circuit D connected in series or in parallel?

3. Are the cells in circuit E connected in series or in parallel?

4. What happened in circuit A when one of the bulbs was unscrewed? Why?

5. How brightly did the bulbs in circuit B shine compared to the bulbs in circuit A? Why?

6. What happened in circuit B when various bulbs were unscrewed? Why?

7. What happened in circuit C when various bulbs were unscrewed? Why?

8. How brightly did the bulbs in circuit D shine compared to the bulbs in circuit A? Why?

9. How brightly did the bulbs in circuit E shine compared to the bulbs in circuit D? Why?

Your home has many electrical devices. Every time you turn one of them on, you use electricity. How can you measure how much electricity you use?

Electric Power

Look at the light bulb below. Notice that the top of the bulb has *100 W* stamped on it. The *W* stands for **watt.** It was named for James Watt, one of the inventors of the steam engine. The watt is the unit used to measure **electric power.** Electric power is the amount of electrical energy used in a certain amount of time. This light bulb uses 100 watts. It uses four times as much energy each second as a 25-watt bulb.

The W on this light bulb tells how much power the bulb uses.

Objectives

After reading this lesson, you should be able to
- ▶ explain what electric power is.
- ▶ explain how electric power is measured.

Watt

The unit used to measure electric power.

Electric power

The amount of electrical energy used in a given time.

Kilowatt-hour

A unit to measure how much electric energy is used.

Using Electricity

When you pay your electric bill, you are paying for the amount of electricity you use. The electric company measures the amount of electricity you use in **kilowatt-hours.** A kilowatt-hour is 1,000 watts used in one hour. A meter measures the number of kilowatt-hours you use.

1. A light bulb has *25 W* stamped on it. What does this mean?

2. Which would use more energy, a 50-watt bulb or a 75-watt bulb of the same kind?

3. What is a kilowatt-hour? How is it used?

SCIENCE IN YOUR LIFE

How can you do a home electrical inventory?

Your home has many devices that use or control electricity. Draw a floor plan of your home, like the one pictured below. Go through each room and note on the plan where all the outlets and wall switches are. Also note where major appliances are plugged in.

Locate your circuit breaker box. Note how the breakers are used and reset. If you have a fuse box, note that fact, but do not loosen or remove any fuses. In either case, note the current rating, in amperes, for each circuit. If there is a labeled chart next to the box showing which areas of your home are controlled by each circuit breaker or fuse, copy the chart down.

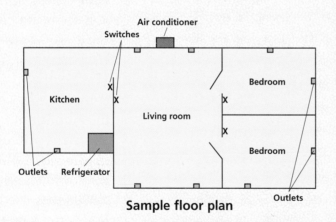

Sample floor plan

1. How many electrical outlets are there in your home?

2 How many circuit breakers are there?

3. Do all the circuits have the same current rating?

4. How does the current rating relate to the kinds of appliances in the circuit?

- Electricity is the flow of electrons.
- Static electricity is a buildup of electric charge.
- Current, the rate of flow of electricity, is measured in amperes.
- A closed circuit is a complete, unbroken path for current. An open circuit is an incomplete or broken path for current.
- A schematic diagram uses symbols to show the parts of a circuit.
- A conductor is a material through which a current can easily pass. An insulator is a material through which a current cannot easily pass.
- Resistance is a measure of how easily electric current will flow through a material. It is measured in ohms.
- Fuses and circuit breakers protect against overly high currents.

- Electromotive force is the force that keeps current flowing. It is measured in volts.
- Batteries are a common source of voltage. Two types of batteries are dry cells and wet cells.
- Two types of current are direct current and alternating current. Direct current flows in one direction. Alternating current changes direction regularly.
- According to Ohm's law, current equals voltage divided by resistance.
- In a series circuit, all current flows through a single path. In a parallel circuit, current flows in more than one path.
- Power is the rate at which work is done. It is measured in watts.

Science Words		
alternating current, 283	ohm, 277	
ampere, 273	Ohm's law, 284	
battery, 280	open circuit, 274	
circuit, 273	parallel circuit, 292	
closed circuit, 273	resistance, 277	
conductor, 276	schematic diagram, 275	
direct current, 283	series circuit, 286	
dry cell battery, 280	static electricity, 272	
electric current, 273	terminal, 281	
electric power, 297	volt, 280	
electricity, 272	voltage, 280	
electromotive force, 280	watt, 297	
insulator, 277	wet cell battery, 282	
kilowatt-hour, 297		

Vocabulary Review

Number your paper from 1 to 12. Then choose a word or words from the Word Bank that best complete each sentence. Write the answer on your paper.

1. The metric unit for power is the _____.
2. A path for current to flow is a(n) _____.
3. The amount of electrical energy used in a certain amount of time is _____.
4. Electric "pressure" is _____.
5. In a(n) _____, all current flows through a single path.
6. An electron path that is incomplete or broken is called a(n) _____.
7. When there is _____, electrons can flow in both directions.
8. The _____ is the unit of resistance.
9. In a(n) _____, current can flow through more than one path.
10. The _____ is the unit of current.
11. A complete, unbroken path for current is called a(n) _____.
12. _____ is a buildup of electrical charges.

Concept Review

Number your paper from 1 to 5. Then choose the answer that best completes each sentence. Write the letter of the answer on your paper.

1. A material through which electricity passes easily is called a(n) _____.

    a. conductor   b. insulator   c. resistor

2. When cells are in _____, the voltage is the sum of the voltages of the cells.

   a. parallel   b. series   c. an open circuit

3. A good conductor of electricity is _____.

   a. glass   b. copper   c. rubber

4. The formula for Ohm's law is _____.

   a. $I = \dfrac{V}{R}$ b. $V = \dfrac{I}{R}$ c. $I = \dfrac{R}{V}$

5. Electricity used in a home is measured in _____.

   a. amperes   b. kilowatt-hours   c. volts

Critical Thinking

Write the answer to each of the following questions.

1. Based on the following schematic diagram, calculate the current.

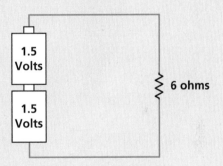

2. Explain what circuit breakers are and why they are important.

3. How much power, in kilowatts, is used by a device if the voltage is 220 volts and the current is 12 amperes?

| Test Taking Tip | When you study for chapter tests, practice the step-by-step formulas and procedures. |

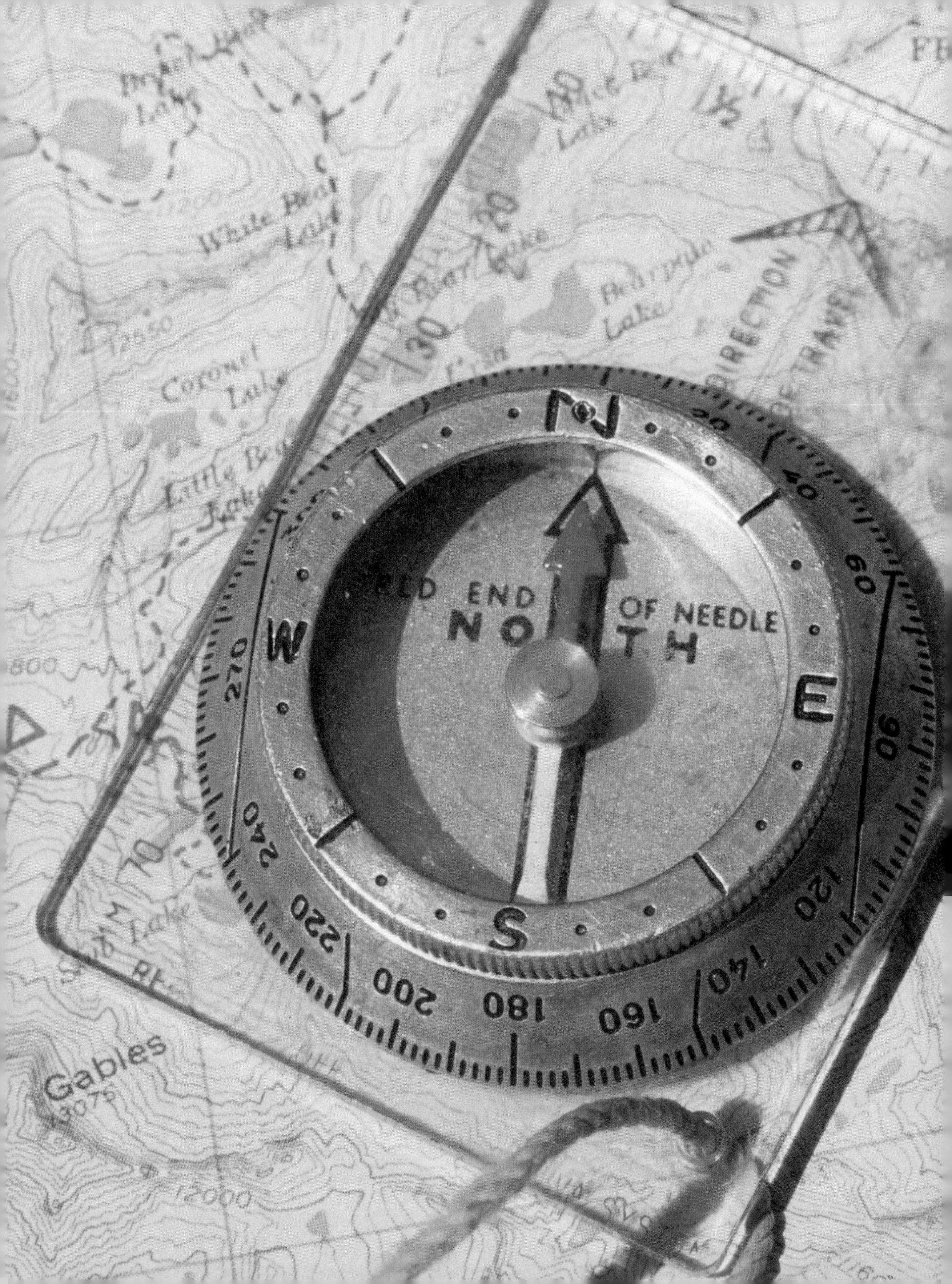

OF NEEDLE
DIRECTION
White Bear Lake
Coronet Lake
Gables

Chapter

12

Magnets and Electromagnetism

Have you ever gone for a long walk in the woods and gotten lost? If so, you know how frightening that can be. However, if you have a compass along with you, it is much easier to know what to do. Like magic, its needle tells you which way is north. A compass works because of a property called magnetism. In this chapter, you will learn about what magnets are and how they work.

ORGANIZE YOUR THOUGHTS

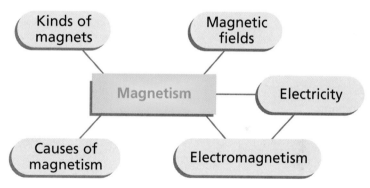

Kinds of magnets

Magnetic fields

Magnetism

Electricity

Causes of magnetism

Electromagnetism

Goals for Learning

▶ To describe various kinds of magnets
▶ To explain what a magnetic field is
▶ To explain what causes magnetism
▶ To describe electromagnetism and its uses

After reading this lesson, you should be able to

▶ describe several kinds of magnets.

▶ explain what magnetic poles are.

▶ describe how magnetic poles behave.

You probably are familiar with **magnets.** If you have ever used them, you know that they can pick up certain objects, such as paper clips and other things made from iron. Most of the magnets you have seen are made by people. But did you know that there are naturally occurring magnets? Lodestone is one such magnetic material. It is made of iron oxide. It is found naturally in the earth and comes in many sizes and shapes.

Most magnets that are made by people come in one of several common shapes. These shapes include the horseshoe, bar, cylinder, and doughnut shapes. You can see some of these magnets in the figure below.

Magnet

An object that attracts certain kinds of metals, such as iron.

Did You Know?

The ancient Greeks knew about the magnetic properties of lodestone, also called magnetite. The word *magnet* comes from the name Magnesia, the Greek province where the mineral was mined.

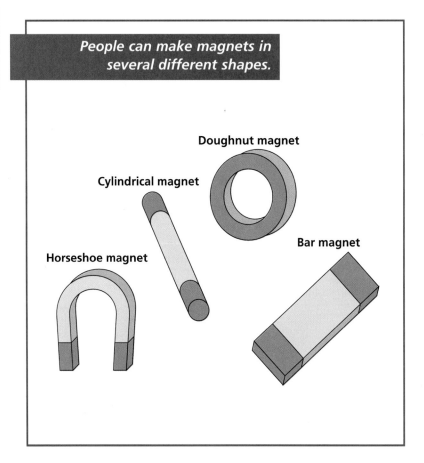

People can make magnets in several different shapes.

Doughnut magnet

Cylindrical magnet

Bar magnet

Horseshoe magnet

Magnetic Poles

Look at the magnets shown on this page. The ends of the magnet are called its **magnetic poles.** Whatever the shape, all magnets have two opposite magnetic poles. The magnetic forces are greatest at the poles. You know this because the ends of the magnet will pick up more paper clips than the center of the magnet.

The poles on a magnet are called the north pole and the south pole. On a marked magnet, the north pole is shown by an *N*. The south pole is marked with an *S*.

You can't tell whether the end of an unmarked magnet is a north pole or a south pole simply by looking at it. But you can find out by placing the magnet close to another magnet whose poles are marked. Observe whether the poles **attract** (pull together) or **repel** (push away). To figure out the poles of the unmarked magnet, use the following rules.

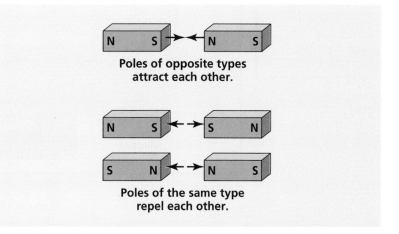

Poles of opposite types
attract each other.

Poles of the same type
repel each other.

Self-Check

1. How can you determine the poles of an unmarked magnet?
2. If two south poles are placed close together, what will happen?
3. If a north and a south pole are placed close together, what will happen?

Objectives

After reading this lesson, you should be able to

▶ explain what a magnetic field is.

▶ describe Earth as a magnet.

▶ explain how a magnet works.

Magnetic field

Area around a magnet in which magnetic forces can act.

Lines of force

Lines that show a magnetic field.

Surrounding all magnets is a **magnetic field.** A magnetic field is an area in which magnetic forces can attract or repel other magnets.

Although you cannot see magnetic fields, you can easily see their effects. All you need to do is place a bar magnet under a sheet of paper. Then sprinkle iron filings on top of the paper. The filings will line up in a pattern of curving lines like those shown in the figure. These lines are called **lines of force.** They are caused by the magnetic field. The lines of force reach around the magnet from one pole to another. The lines are closest together near the poles. That is where the field is strongest and the forces are greatest.

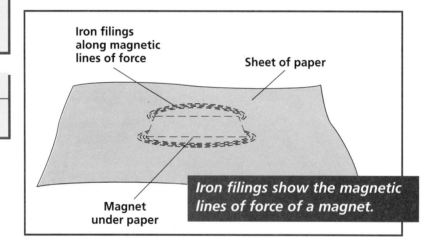

Iron filings along magnetic lines of force

Sheet of paper

Iron filings show the magnetic lines of force of a magnet.

Magnet under paper

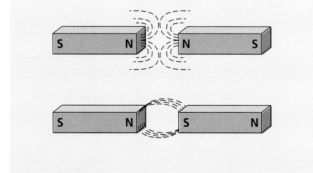

You can see in the figure to the left how the lines of force of two magnets affect each other. Notice how they cause the poles of magnets to attract or repel each other.

The Earth as a Magnet

You may be surprised to learn that Earth itself is a giant bar magnet. Like other magnets, Earth has magnetic poles. These magnetic poles are located near the geographic north and south poles.

Earth's natural magnetism allows compasses to work. The needle of a compass is a magnet, too. It has a north pole and a south pole. They are located at opposite ends of the needle.

Like magnetic poles repel each other. However, you can see in the figure that the north magnetic pole of Earth attracts the north pole of a compass. This happens because Earth's north magnetic pole is actually like the south pole of a magnet. But it is called the north magnetic pole because it is located near the geographic North Pole. Earth's south magnetic pole is really like the north pole of a magnet.

Earth's magnetic field attracts and lines up the compass needle. The north pole of the magnet in a compass is attracted to the Earth's magnetic pole. As a result, it points north.

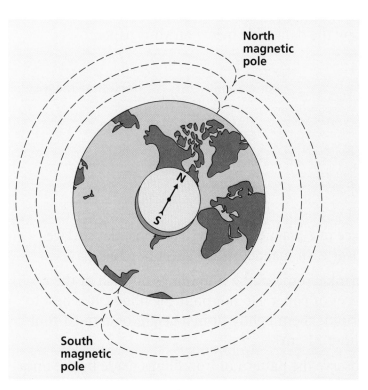

North magnetic pole

South magnetic pole

Self-Check

1. What is a magnetic field?
2. What pattern is made by magnetic lines of force around a bar magnet?
3. How does a compass work?

Observing Magnetic Lines of Force

Materials

✓ 2 horseshoe magnets

✓ 2 bar magnets

✓ 2 sheets of paper

✓ cup of iron filings

Purpose

To observe the lines of force around magnets

Procedure

Part A

1. Copy the data table below on your paper.

	Bar magnet	Horseshoe magnet
Part A		
Part B		
Part C		

2. Place one magnet of each shape on a flat surface. Cover each magnet with a sheet of paper.

3. Sprinkle some of the iron filings on each of the pieces of paper. Do not pour the filings. It is best to sprinkle them lightly from a height of about 1 foot (about 31 cm).

4. Observe the pattern of iron filings made by the lines of force. Record your observations on your data table.

5. Carefully pour the iron filings from each paper back into the cup.

Part B

6. Place the bar magnets end to end with like poles close together.

7. Place a sheet of paper over the magnets and sprinkle with iron filings.

8. Record your observations.

9. Carefully pour the iron filings from the paper back into the cup.

Part C

10. Reverse the poles of one of the bar magnets so that opposite poles are close together. Cover with a sheet of paper.

11. Sprinkle the paper with iron filings. Record your observations.

12. Repeat Part B and Part C with the horseshoe magnets. Record your observations.

Questions

1. Describe the pattern made by the lines of force of the single bar magnet.

2. In Part B, did the poles of the bar magnets attract or repel each other? How did the lines of force show this?

3. In Part C, did the poles of the bar magnets attract or repel each other? How do you know?

4. How were the patterns on the bar magnet similar to those on the horseshoe magnet?

What Causes Magnetism?

Objectives

After reading this lesson, you should be able to

▶ explain what causes magnetism.

▶ describe how to make a magnet.

▶ describe how magnetism is destroyed.

▶ list materials that are attracted by magnets.

Scientists have observed that some atoms have north and south magnetic poles. In most substances, the atoms point in all different directions. As a result, the atoms cancel out each other's magnetism. The substance is not magnetic. Materials that are not magnetic include wood, copper, plastic, rubber, gold, and glass. These materials are not attracted by magnets either.

In some substances, atoms can be made to line up so that most of them are aligned in the same direction. This arrangement causes the substance to act like a magnet. Only a few materials can be made into magnets. They include iron, nickel, and cobalt. These materials are also attracted by magnets.

In a nonmagnetized material, the magnetic fields of atoms do not line up.

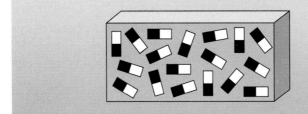

In a magnetized material, the magnetic fields of atoms line up.

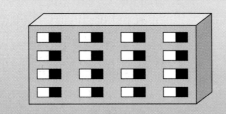

How to Make a Magnet

One of the simplest ways to make a magnet is to take an iron wire and stroke it with a magnet. Hold one of the poles of the magnet at one end of the wire. Slowly stroke the magnet down the length of the wire. After four or five strokes, the wire will become a magnet.

What do you think will happen if you break the wire into two pieces? Each of the two pieces will become magnets. You can see in the figure below that each piece still contains atoms that are lined up in the same direction.

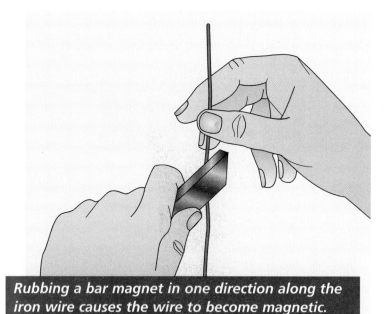

Rubbing a bar magnet in one direction along the iron wire causes the wire to become magnetic.

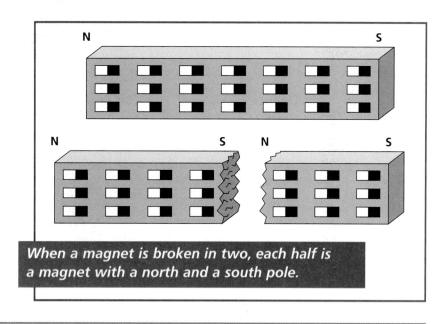

When a magnet is broken in two, each half is a magnet with a north and a south pole.

How to Destroy Magnetism

Breaking a magnet into two parts does not destroy the magnetism. But it is possible to destroy magnetism.

Two common ways to demagnetize a magnet are by heating it or by striking it with a hard blow. Both of these actions can cause atoms to rearrange themselves so that they are no longer facing the same direction.

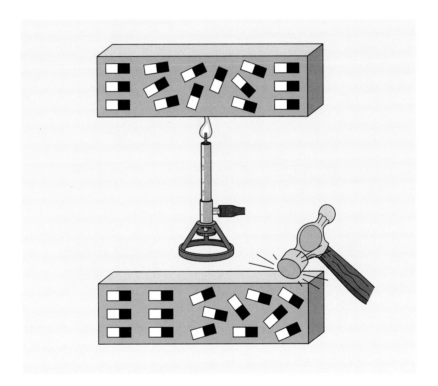

Self-Check

1. What causes magnetism?
2. What happens when you break a magnet into two pieces?
3. How can you destroy magnetism?
4. Name some materials that can be made into magnets.
5. Name some materials that are not magnetic.

How Are Magnetism and Electricity Related?

Objectives

After reading this lesson, you should be able to

▶ explain how magnetism and electricity are related.

▶ describe electromagnetism.

▶ list devices that use electromagnetism.

▶ explain how magnetism can be produced from electricity.

Electromagnetism

Relationship between magnetism and electricity.

Electromagnet

Temporary magnet made by passing a current through a wire wrapped around an iron core.

Magnets are not the only things that can produce a magnetic field. Electricity can also produce a magnetic field. You can see this for yourself if you place a compass near a wire that is carrying electricity. The compass needle will turn until it is at right angles to the wire. The current produces a magnetic field around the wire.

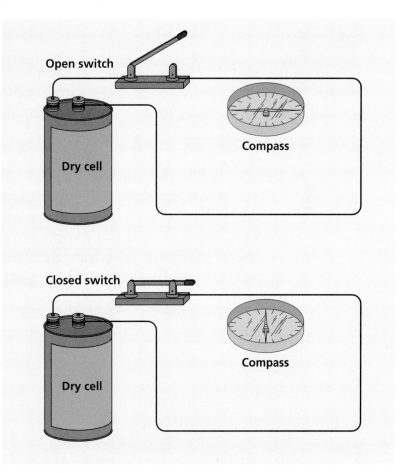

The relationship between magnetism and electricity is called **electromagnetism.** Electricity can be used to make a type of magnet called an **electromagnet.** An electromagnet is an object that is magnetic as long as an electric current is flowing.

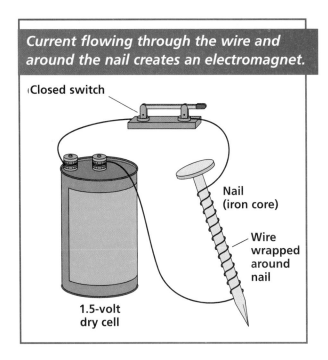

Current flowing through the wire and around the nail creates an electromagnet.

Closed switch

Nail (iron core)

Wire wrapped around nail

1.5-volt dry cell

An electromagnet, like the one on this page, can be made with a large nail, some common bell wire, and a 1.5-volt dry cell. The nail serves as the iron core. The flow of current through the wire surrounding the core creates a magnetic field.

The strength of an electromagnet depends on a number of factors. Power sources with higher voltages make more powerful electromagnets. More turns of wire around the core will also increase the strength of a magnet.

Using Electromagnets

The magnetism produced by electromagnets is the same as the magnetism produced by a magnet. An electromagnet has a magnetic field and a north and south pole. Unlike a regular magnet, an electromagnet can be switched off and on. This quality makes electromagnets very useful. For

When the current is turned on, the electromagnet attracts pieces of metal.

example, the crane in the photo uses an electromagnet. When the current is turned on, the electromagnet picks up pieces of metal from piles of scrap. When the current is turned off, the electromagnet loses it magnetism. The metal pieces fall to the ground.

You may not be aware that you use electromagnets every day. Many appliances use electromagnets. Speakers, earphones, and telephones use electromagnets to change electric currents into sound waves.

Find the electromagnet in the diagram below. Notice the device that provides electric current to the electromagnet. The level of electric current passing to the electromagnet from this device changes. These changes cause the strength of the electromagnet to change, too. As the strength of the electromagnet changes, the plate located in front of the electromagnet vibrates back and forth. The vibration of the plate creates sound waves.

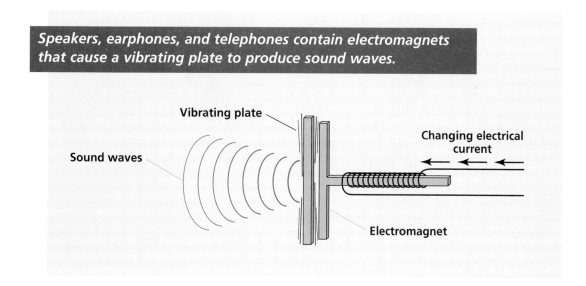

Speakers, earphones, and telephones contain electromagnets that cause a vibrating plate to produce sound waves.

Vibrating plate

Sound waves

Changing electrical current

Electromagnet

Motors

Motors also make use of electromagnetism. A motor changes electrical energy to mechanical energy, which is used to do work. Follow the diagrams to understand how a motor works.

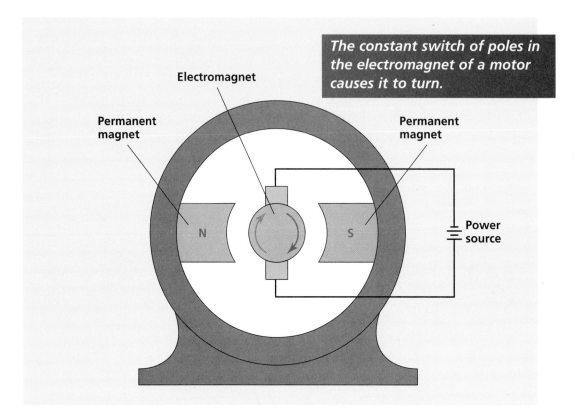

The constant switch of poles in the electromagnet of a motor causes it to turn.

Electromagnet

Permanent magnet

Permanent magnet

N

S

Power source

A motor has three basic parts. One part is a permanent magnet that cannot move. A second part is an electromagnet that is free to turn between the opposite poles of the permanent magnet. A third part is a device that supplies alternating electric current to magnetize the electromagnet. As you learned in Chapter 11, alternating current changes direction at a regular rate.

When current is supplied to the electromagnet, each pole of the electromagnet is attracted to the opposite pole of the permanent magnet. This attraction causes the electromagnet to turn so that its poles line up with the opposite poles of the permanent magnet.

As the direction of current changes, the poles of the electromagnet are reversed. As a result, the lined-up poles repel each other. And the electromagnet continues to turn. The current in the electromagnet continues to reverse direction after every half turn, causing the electromagnet to continue to turn.

The spinning motion of the electromagnet in a motor can be used to do work or operate other devices. Motors are used to operate cars, refrigerators, electric toys, hair dryers, air conditioners, and many kitchen appliances.

Motors are used to operate these devices.

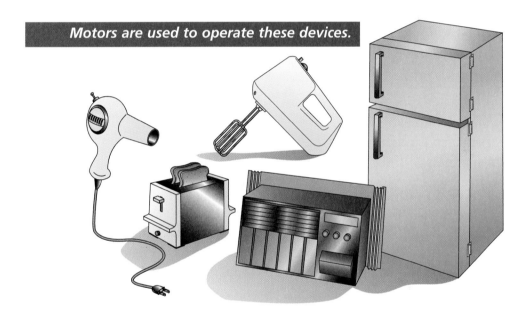

Self-Check

1. What is electromagnetism?
2. Explain how an electromagnet works.
3. Name two devices that use electromagnets.
4. Explain how a motor works.

How can magnetism be used to move a train?

Imagine riding a train that moves on a cushion of air instead of rolling along tracks. In Germany and Japan, scientists are experimenting with trains that have been designed to move in this way.

Such trains use electromagnetism to travel at very fast speeds. These vehicles are called maglev trains—short for "magnetic levitation." Electromagnetism is used to levitate, or lift up, the train, to move it forward, and to guide it. There is no friction with the track to slow down the train. These maglev trains actually float about 10 centimeters above the tracks!

The maglev train starts out by rolling on rubber wheels. Once the train reaches a faster speed, current is sent through the metal coils on the sides of the train. This current causes the coils to become magnetized. The track also is magnetized. The coils on the train are repelled by the electromagnets in the track. This causes the train to lift off the tracks.

The train moves forward because poles in the magnets in the tracks can be changed. The magnets in the track in front of the train have poles that are opposite to those of the train. The attraction between the train and the track ahead moves the train forward. The repulsion between the train and the track below it keeps the train levitated. By controlling the current to the tracks, a magnetic wave is created that keeps the train moving forward.

Scientists are still testing maglev trains. Perhaps in the future, maglev trains will be a common form of transportation.

Electromagnetism moves maglev trains.

Materials

- ✓ copper wire, 0.5 m long
- ✓ large nail
- ✓ metric ruler
- ✓ electrical tape
- ✓ 1.5 volt D-cell battery
- ✓ paper clips

Constructing an Electromagnet

Purpose
To demonstrate how to increase the magnetic properties of an electromagnet

Procedure
1. Copy the data table below on your paper.

Number of turns of wire coil	Number of paper clips
5	
10	
15	
25	

2. Make a small loop in both ends of the copper wire.

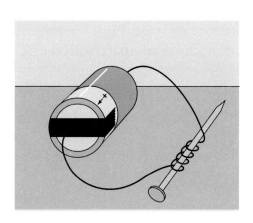

3. Start 10 cm from one end of the wire. Wrap the wire around the nail 5 times, as shown to the left.

4. Using electrical tape, tape one end of the wire to one end of the battery. Tape the other end of the wire to the other end of the battery.

5. Hold the nail near the paper clips. Observe what happens. Record your observations in your data table.

6. Remove one end of the wire from the battery. Wrap the wire around the nail 5 more times. You should now have a total of 10 coils. Tape the end of the wire to the battery again.

7. Hold the nail near the paper clips. Record your observations.

8. Repeat steps 6 and 7, making the coil with 15 turns of the wire.

9. Repeat steps 6 and 7, making the coil with 25 turns of the wire.

Questions

1. In step 6, what happened to the paper clips when you removed one end of the wire from the battery?

2. How did the number of coils in the wire affect the electromagnet?

Explore Further

1. Sprinkle iron filings on a sheet of paper. Hold the paper over the wire when the coil has 25 turns of the wire. Describe the pattern made by the iron filings.

2. Hold the paper with the iron filings over the wire coil when it has 10 turns of the wire. How does the pattern made by the iron filings compare with the pattern you saw in step 1?

3. How does the number of turns in the wire coil affect the magnetic force around the wire?

- Magnets can attract materials such as iron. Magnets may be natural, such as lodestone, or made by people.

- A magnet has a north pole and a south pole. Unlike poles attract. Like poles repel.

- A magnetic field surrounds a magnet. Magnetic lines of force extend from pole to pole.

- The earth is a magnet. It has a north magnetic pole and a south magnetic pole.

- Materials that can be magnetized and that are attracted to magnets include iron, nickel, and cobalt.

- Magnets can be made by stroking an iron wire with a magnet. Magnets can be destroyed by heat or by hard blows.

- Electromagnetism is the relationship between magnetism and electricity.

- Speakers, earphones, and telephones are devices that use electromagnets.

- Motors make use of electromagnets and permanent magnets to turn electrical energy into mechanical energy.

Science Words		
attract, 305	magnetic field, 306	
electromagnet, 313	magnetic poles, 305	
electromagnetism, 313	motor, 316	
lines of force, 306	repel, 305	
magnet, 304		

Vocabulary Review

Number your paper from 1 to 6. Then choose a word or words from the Word Bank that best complete each sentence. Write the answer on your paper.

1. A(n) _____ is the area around a magnet in which magnetic forces can act.

2. A device that converts electrical energy into mechanical energy is a(n) _____.

3. A(n) _____ may be either north or south.

4. The relationship between magnetism and electricity is called _____.

5. A(n) _____ is a temporary magnet formed by passing current through a wire wrapped around an iron core.

6. Any object that can attract materials such as iron is called a(n) _____.

Concept Review

Number your paper from 1 to 6. Then choose the answer that best completes each sentence. Write the letter of the answer on your paper.

1. A device that converts mechanical energy to electrical energy is a _____.
   a. magnet   b. telegraph   c. motor

2. When a magnet is broken in half, _____ result.
   a. two magnets
   b. two electromagnets
   c. no magnets

3. An example of a material that is not attracted to magnets is _____.
   a. glass   b. cobalt   c. nickel

4. A north pole of one bar magnet is _____ by the north pole of another bar magnet.
    a. not affected   b. attracted   c. repelled

5. Magnetic lines of force of a magnet are closest together _____.
    a. midway between the poles
    b. near both poles
    c. near the north pole only

6. In a nonmagnetized piece of iron, the magnetic fields of individual atoms _____.
    a. do not line up
    b. line up

Critical Thinking

1. Suppose a bar magnet like the one shown to the right was cut into three pieces. What would happen to the magnet's poles?

2. How could you find the poles of the magnet shown here?

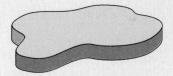

3. What do you think would happen if the amount of current supplied to a motor were reduced?

Test Taking Tip Prepare for a test by making a set of flash cards. Write a word on the front of each card. Write the definition on the back. Use the flash cards in a game to test your knowledge.

Glossary

Glossary

A

Acceleration—rate of change of velocity (p. 166)

Acid—a compound that reacts with metals to produce hydrogen (p. 121)

Alloy—a mixture of two or more metals (p. 93)

Alternating current—current that changes direction regularly (p. 283)

Ampere—unit used to describe how much electric current flows through a wire (p. 273)

Area—amount of space the surface of an object takes up (p. 14)

Atom—the building block of matter (p. 53)

Atomic mass—the average mass of all the isotopes of a particular element (p. 89)

Atomic number—number equal to the number of protons in the nucleus of an atom (p. 70)

Attract—to pull together (p. 305)

B

Balance—an instrument used to measure mass (p. 34)

Balance—to keep the number of atoms the same on both sides of the equation (p. 138)

Base—a compound that contains the hydroxyl (OH) radical (p. 123)

Battery—a source of voltage that changes chemical energy into electrical energy (p. 280)

Boiling point—the temperature at which a liquid changes to a gas (p. 223)

C

Calorie—unit of heat; the amount of heat needed to raise the temperature of 1 g of water by 1° C (p. 226)

Celsius scale—the temperature scale used by scientists and by people in most countries, in which water freezes at 0° and boils at 100° (p. 221)

Chemical bond—the attractive force that holds atoms together (p. 113)

Chemical change—a change that produces one or more substances that differ from the original substances (p. 104)

Chemical equation—a statement that uses symbols, formulas, and numbers to stand for a chemical reaction (p. 136)

Chemical formula—a way to write the kinds and numbers of atoms in a compound (p. 114)

Chemical reaction—chemical change in which elements are combined or rearranged (p. 132)

Chemistry—the study of matter and how it changes (p. 5)

Circuit—path for electric current (p. 273)

Closed circuit—complete, unbroken path for electric current (p. 273)

Coefficient—a number placed before a formula in a chemical equation (p. 138)

Compound—a substance formed when atoms of two or more elements join together (p. 60)

Concave lens—a lens that is thin in the middle and thick at the edges (p. 264)

Concave mirror—a mirror that curves in at the middle (p. 260)

Conduction—the movement of heat energy from one molecule to the next (p. 232)

Conductor (electrical)—material through which electricity passes easily (p. 276)

Conductor (heat)—material through which heat travels easily (p. 232)

Constant speed—speed that does not change (p. 159)

Contract—to become smaller in size (p. 216)

Convection—flow of energy that occurs when a warm liquid or gas rises (p. 233)

Convex lens—a lens that is thick in the middle and thin at the edges (p. 265)

Convex mirror—a mirror that curves outward at the middle (p. 261)

Cycle—the complete back-and-forth motion of a vibration (p. 244)

D

Deceleration—rate of slowdown (p. 167)

Decibel—a unit that measures the intensity of sound (p. 242)

Decomposition reaction—a reaction in which a compound breaks down into two or more simple substances (p. 142)

Degree—a unit of measurement on a temperature scale (p. 221)

Density—a measure of how tightly the matter of a substance is packed into a given volume (p. 42)

Deuterium—an isotope of hydrogen that has one proton and one neutron (p. 88)

Direct current—current that flows in only one direction (p. 283)

Displacement of water—method of measuring the volume of irregularly-shaped objects (p. 40)

Dissolve—break apart (p. 133)

Distance—the length of the path between two points (p. 155)

Double-replacement reaction—a reaction in which the elements in two compounds are exchanged (p. 144)

Dry cell battery—electric power source with a dry or pastelike center (p. 280)

E

Echo—a sound that is reflected to its source (p. 249)

Efficiency—how well a machine performs (p. 196)

Effort arm—distance between the fulcrum and effort force of a lever (p. 199)

Effort force—force applied to a machine by the user (p. 192)

Elapsed time—length of time that passes from one event to another (p. 154)

Electric current—movement of electrons from one place to another (p. 273)

Electric power—the amount of electrical energy used in a given time (p. 297)

Electricity—flow of electrons (p. 272)

Electromagnet—temporary magnet made by passing a current through a wire wrapped around an iron core (p. 313)

Electromagnetism—relationship between magnetism and electricity (p. 313)

Electromotive force—the push that keeps electrons moving in an electric circuit (p. 280)

Electron—a tiny particle of an atom that moves around the nucleus (p. 65)

Element—matter that has only one kind of atom (p. 56)

Energy—the ability to do work (p. 185)

Energy level—one of the spaces around the nucleus of an atom in which an electron moves (p. 108)

English system—system of measurement that uses inches, feet, and yards (p. 8)

Evaporate—to change from a liquid to a gas (p. 215)

Expand—to become larger in size (p. 216)

F

Fahrenheit scale—the temperature scale commonly used in the United States, in which water freezes at 32° and boils at 212° (p. 221)

Family—group of elements with similar properties, arranged together in a column of the periodic table (p. 90)

Farsighted—able to see clearly only things that are at a distance (p. 266)

Focal point—the point where reflected light rays from a concave mirror come together in front of the mirror (p. 260)

Force—a push or a pull (p. 170)

Freezing point—the temperature at which a liquid changes to a solid (p. 222)

Frequency—the number of vibrations per second of a sound wave (p. 244)

Friction—force that opposes motion and that occurs when things slide or roll over each other (p. 170)

Fulcrum—fixed point around which a lever rotates (p. 192)

G

Gas—a form of matter that has no definite shape or volume (p. 55)

Generator—a device used to convert mechanical energy to electrical energy (p. 187)

Graduated cylinder—a round glass or plastic cylinder used to measure the volume of liquids (p. 37)

Gram—basic unit of mass in the metric system (p. 21)

Gravity—force of attraction between any two objects that have mass (p. 173)

H

Heat—a form of energy resulting from the motion of particles in matter; heat energy flows from a warmer object to a cooler object (p. 212)

Heat source—a place from which heat energy comes (p. 213)

Hertz—the unit used to measure frequency of a sound; one Hertz equals one cycle per second (p. 244)

I

Image—a copy or likeness (p. 259)

Inclined plane—simple machine made up of a ramp, used to lift an object (p. 204)

Indicator—a substance that changes color when in an acid or a base (p. 123)

Inert—a description of an element whose atoms do not react in nature with atoms of other elements (p. 96)

Inertia—tendency of an object to resist changes in its motion (p. 171)

Insulator (electrical)—material through which electricity does not pass easily (p. 276)

Insulator (heat)—a material that does not conduct heat well (p. 232)

Intensity—the strength of a sound (p. 242)

Ion—an atom that has either a positive or a negative charge (p. 113)

Isotope—one of a group of atoms of an element with the same number of protons but different numbers of neutrons (p. 88)

J

Joule—metric unit of work (p. 182)

K

Kilowatt-hour—a unit to measure how much electric energy is used (p. 297)

Kinetic energy—energy of motion (p. 185)

L

Law of conservation of energy—energy cannot be created or destroyed (p. 188)

Law of conservation of matter—matter cannot be created or destroyed in any chemical change (p. 137)

Law of universal gravitation—gravitational force depends on the masses of the two objects involved and on the distance between them (p. 173)

Lens—a curved piece of clear material that refracts light waves (p. 264)

Lever—simple machine containing a bar that can turn around a fixed point (p. 192)

Light—a form of energy that can be seen (p. 254)

Lines of force—lines that show a magnetic field (p. 306)

Liquid—a form of matter that has a definite volume but no definite shape (p. 54)

Liter—basic unit of volume in the metric system (p. 19)

M

Magnet—an object that attracts certain kinds of metals, such as iron (p. 304)

Magnetic field—area around a magnet in which magnetic forces can act (p. 306)

Magnetic poles—opposite points or ends of a magnet, where magnetic forces are greatest (p. 305)

Mass—the amount of material an object has (p. 71)

Mass number—a number equal to the sum of the numbers of protons and neutrons in an atom of an element (p. 4)

Matter—anything that has mass and takes up space (p. 4)

Mechanical advantage—factor by which a machine multiplies the effort force (p. 198)

Melting point—the temperature at which a solid changes to a liquid (p. 223)

Meniscus—the curved surface of a liquid (p. 37)

Metal—one of a group of elements that is usually solid at room temperature, often shiny, and carries heat and electricity well (p. 92)

Meter—the basic unit of length in the metric system (about 39 inches) (p. 9)

Meter stick—a common tool for measuring length in the metric system (p. 10)

Metric system—system of measurement used by scientists (p. 8)

Mixture—a combination of substances in which no reaction takes place (p. 132)

Model—a picture, an idea, or an object that is built to explain how something else looks or works (p. 64)

Molecule—the smallest particle of a substance that has the same properties as the substance (p. 52)

Motion—a change in position (p. 154)

Motor—device that converts electrical energy to mechanical energy (p. 316)

N

Natural element—an element that is found in nature (p. 57)

Nearsighted—able to see clearly only things that are close up (p. 265)

Neutron—a tiny particle in the nucleus of an atom that is similar in size to a proton (p. 66)

Noble gas—one of a group of elements made up of gases that do not combine with other materials under ordinary conditions (p. 96)

Nonmetal—one of a group of elements with properties opposite to those of metals (p. 94)

Nucleus—the central part of an atom (p. 65)

O

Ohm—unit used to measure resistance (p. 277)

Ohm's law—current equals voltage divided by resistance (p. 284)

Open circuit—incomplete or broken path for electric current (p. 274)

P

Parallel circuit—circuit in which there is more than one path for current (p. 292)

Periodic table—an arrangement of elements by increasing atomic number (p. 84)

pH—a number that tells whether a substance is an acid or a base (p. 124)

Photons—small bundles of energy that make up light (p. 254)

Physical change—a change in which the appearance of a substance changes but the properties stay the same (p. 105)

Physical science—the study of the things around you (p. 4)

Physics—the study of how energy acts with matter (p. 5)

Pitch—how high or low a sound is (p. 244)

Plane mirror—a flat, smooth mirror (p. 259)

Plasma—a very hot gas made of particles that have an electric charge (p. 55)

Potential energy—stored energy (p. 185)

Prism—a piece of glass or plastic that is shaped like a triangle and can be used to separate white light (p. 256)

Product—a substance that is formed in a chemical reaction (p. 137)

Property—a characteristic that helps identify an object (p. 28)

Proton—a tiny particle in the nucleus of an atom (p. 65)

Precipitate—a solid that is formed and usually sinks to the bottom of a solution (p. 144)

Pulley—simple machine made up of a rope, chain, or belt wrapped around a wheel (p. 202)

R

Radiation—the movement of energy through a vacuum (p. 231)

Radical—a group of two or more atoms that acts like one element (p. 116)

Reactant—a substance that is changed to form a product in a chemical reaction (p. 137)

Reflect—to bounce back (p. 249)

Refraction—the bending of a wave as it moves from one material to another (p. 264)

Repel—to push apart (p. 305)

Resistance—measure of how easily electric current will flow through a material (p. 277)

Resistance arm—distance between the fulcrum and resistance force of a lever (p. 199)

Resistance force—force applied to a machine by the object to be moved (p. 193)

S

Schematic diagram—diagram that uses symbols to show the parts of a circuit (p. 275)

Screw—simple machine made up of an inclined plane wrapped around a straight piece of metal (p. 205)

Series circuit—circuit in which all current flows through a single path (p. 286)

Simple machine—tool with few parts that makes it easier or possible to do work (p. 192)

Single-replacement reaction— a reaction in which one element replaces another in a compound (p. 143)

Solid—a form of matter that has a definite shape and volume (p. 54)

Solute—the substance that is dissolved in a solution (p. 133)

Solution—a mixture in which one substance is dissolved in another (p. 133)

Solvent—the substance in which the dissolving occurs in a solution (p. 133)

Sonar—a method of using sound to measure distances under water (p. 250)

Sound wave—a wave produced by vibrations (p. 241)

Speed—rate at which the position of an object changes (p. 155)

Standard mass—a small object that is used with a balance to determine mass (p. 34)

State of matter—the form that matter has—solid, liquid, or gas (p. 55)

Static electricity—buildup of electrical charges (p. 272)

Subscript—a number in a chemical formula that tells the number of atoms of an element in a compound (p. 115)

Symbol—one or two letters that represent the name of an element (p. 80)

Synthesis reaction—a reaction in which elements combine to form a compound (p. 140)

T

Temperature—a measure of how fast an object's particles are moving (p. 219)

Terminal—points where electrons leave or enter a battery (p. 281)

Thermometer—a device that measures temperature (p. 220)

Tritium—an isotope of hydrogen that has one proton and two neutrons (p. 88)

U

Ultrasound—a technique that uses sound waves to study organs inside the human body (p. 251)

Unit—a known amount used for measuring (p. 7)

V

Vacuum—space that contains no matter (p. 231)

Velocity—the speed and direction in which an object is moving (p. 162)

Vibrate—to move rapidly back and forth (p. 240)

Visible spectrum—the band of colors that make up white light (p. 256)

Volt—metric unit used to measure electromotive force (p. 280)

Voltage—the energy that a power source gives to electrons in a circuit (p. 280)

Volume—the amount of space an object takes up (p. 18)

Volume—the loudness or softness of a sound (p. 243)

W

Watt—the unit used to measure electric power (p. 297)

Wedge—simple machine made up of an inclined plane or pair of inclined planes that are moved (p. 205)

Weight—the measure of how hard gravity pulls on an object (p. 32)

Wet cell battery—electric power source with a liquid center (p. 282)

Wheel and axle—simple machine made up of a wheel attached to a shaft (p. 206)

Work—what happens when something moves due to a force being applied (p. 182)

Work input—work put into a machine by its user (p. 195)

Work output—work done by a machine against the resistance (p. 195)

Index

Index

Circuit breakers, 289

Citric acid, 121

Closed circuit, 273

Cobalt, 80

Coefficients, 138

Colors in white light, 256

Compass, 305, 309

Compounds, 60–61, 103–24
    characteristics of, 104–05
    common, 61
    formation of, 108–13
    formulas for, 114–15
    naming, 118–20
    radicals in, 116–17

Concave lenses, 264, 265

Concave mirrors, 260–61

Conduction, 232

Conductor, 232, 276

Conservation of matter, 137

Constant speed, 159

Contract, 216

Convection, 233

Convex lenses, 265, 266

Convex mirrors, 261

Cooling, 228

Copper, 57, 81, 92, 232

Cubic centimeter, 18–19

Cubit, 8

Current, finding, 284–85

Cycle, 244

measuring with sound waves, 250
    predicting, 161

Double-replacement reaction, 145

Dry cell battery, 280

Magnets, 303–05
    definition of, 304
    earth as, 307
    making, 311
Manganese, 81
Mars, gravity of, 33
Mass, 4
    differences between weight and, 32–33
    of element, 71–74
    measuring liquid, 35–36
    measuring solid, 34
    using metric system to find, 21–22
Mass equivalents, 21–22
Mass number, 71–72
Matter
    changes in, 131–46
    definition of, 4
    effect of heat on, 215–16
    expanding and contracting, 216
    law of conservation of, 137
    movement of sound waves through, 246
    properties of, 27–46
    states of, 54–56
    structure of, 51–74
Measurement, 6–7
    of heat, 225–28
    systems of, 8
    units of, 7–8
Mechanical advantage (MA), 198, 203
Mechanical energy, 186, 213, 318
Melting point, 223
Mendeleev, 84
Meniscus, 37
Mercuric oxide, 142
Mercury, 57, 81, 92
Mercury, gravity of, 33
Metals, 92–93
    as conductors, 232, 276–77
Meters, 9
Meter stick, 10
Methyl chloride, 137
Methyl fluoride, 137
Metric system, 3–22
    prefixes in, 11
    using to find area, 14–15
    using to find length, 9–10
    using to find mass, 21–22

    using to find volume, 18–20
Milligram, 22
Milliliter, 20
Millimeter, 10, 11
Mirrors
    concave, 260–61
    convex, 261
    plane, 259
Mixture, 132
Models, 64
    of atoms, 65–67
Molecules, 52–53
    definition of, 52
    describing, 52–53
    size of, 52
    of water, 60, 105
Money system, 9
Motion, 153–74
    definition of, 154
    laws of, 170–72
    using graph to describe, 159–63
Motors, 318–19

N

Natural elements, 57
Nearsighted person, 265
Negative charge, 112
Neon, 57, 67, 70, 72, 80, 91, 96
Neutrons, 66, 71
Newton, Sir Isaac, 170, 173
    first law of motion, 170
    second law of motion, 171
    third law of motion, 172
Newton-meters, 183
Nitrogen, 57, 67, 70, 72, 80, 94, 95
Noble gases, 96
Noise, damage from loud, 243
Nonmetals, 94–95
Nuclear energy, 186, 214
Nucleus, 65

O

Ohm, Georg, 284
Ohm's law, 284–85
Open circuit, 274
Oxygen, 67, 70, 72, 80, 94, 95